Mia & Woody
Love and Betrayal

Mia & Woody

Love and Betrayal

Kristi Groteke
THE NANNY
with Marjorie Rosen

Carroll & Graf Publishers, Inc.
New York

Copyright © 1994 by Kristi Groteke and Marjorie Rosen

First Carroll & Graf edition May 1994

Carroll & Graf Publishers, Inc.
260 Fifth Avenue
New York, NY 10001

Library of Congress Cataloging-in-Publication Data

Groteke, Kristi.
    Mia & Woody : love and betrayal / Kristi Groteke with Marjorie Rosen.—1st
Carroll & Graf ed.
      p. cm.
    ISBN 0-7867-0066-1 : $21.00
    1. Allen, Woody. 2. Farrow, Mia, 1945-   . I. Rosen, Marjorie.
II. Title.   III. Title: Mia and Woody.
PN2287.A53G76   1994
791.43'092'273—dc20
[B]   94-7139
                                                                    CIP

Manufactured in the United States of America

For Mom, Dad, and Kelly
Kristi Groteke

For Jenny, Ben, Jeremy, and Marcus, with all my love
Marjorie Rosen

Acknowledgments

I owe many thanks: to David Fishof, my friend and agent, who gave me my start; to Jane Dystel, who believed in this book and sold it; to Marjorie Rosen for sharing her gifted writing, her dedication and her friendship; to William and Susan for their much appreciated advice; to Kent Carroll and the people at Carroll & Graf for their efforts; to my cousin Trisha Kelleher who shares my gypsy soul; to my dear friends Matt Tagley and Pam Riley for always being there; to Mia Farrow for showing me the deepest capacity to love, and who shared the most precious gift with me, her family; to Dan Guadagnoli for his endless love and support; to my grandparents James and Evelyn Kelleher, Clair Hoffman and godmother Terry Desiderio for spoiling me incessantly; to the Guadagnoli family, for their warmth and kindness; to Casey, Lorrie and Leslie for sharing their thoughts; to my mother, father and sister for their love; and finally, to the late John "Hopper" McGrath who taught me life's greatest lesson.

—Kristi Groteke

I would like to extend my sincere thanks to Joy Gould Boyum, Bonnie Dry, Mary Huzinec, and Mary Shaunessy for their thoughtful insights and generous contributions to this project.

—Marjorie Rosen

Contents

Author's Note

In the summer of 1991, when I first came to work for Mia Farrow as her nanny, I hardly suspected that the next two years would emerge as the most nightmarish of her life. Nor could I imagine that we would become friends and confidantes, drawn closer, no doubt, by the tragedy that would envelop her family.

One year later, in the heat of the summer of 1992, photographers and reporters camped out on Mia's doorstep daily, trying to scoop the Woody–Soon-Yi affair or uncover a crumb or two about Mia and Woody's private world. During this media crisis we could not walk outside our door without being bombarded by flashbulbs and questions. I myself was turning down offer after offer from tell-all tabloids and TV shows. At the time Mia said to me, almost as an invitation, "Someday, Kristi, you can write your own book about all this." And so I have.

What follows is not intended as an objective account of what happened. Nor did I want to tell tales out of school or write a bit of publicity fluff. I wanted instead to explain how the events of 1992, combined with the storm of intimate and embarrassing details aired in public, conspired to ravage one woman's confidence and test a family's bond. I also wanted to recount my observations of how the Farrow family struggled to survive the devastation of Woody's betrayal. I was in the midst of it all, and even for me, a bystander, the toll was terrible.

11

I hope that the small details and anecdotes of this book, the retelling of the bits and pieces that make up a family's life, help readers to understand the tapestry of the Farrow family's unique world. Perhaps, too, it will restore Mia and her children from their inevitable diminishment by cartoonlike tabloid headlines. In the end, it was my best intention to make real their pain and their noble effort to get beyond it.

Cast of Characters

PARENTS

Mia Farrow, actress and mother
Woody Allen, actor, director, writer, father
Andre Previn, composer, symphony conductor,
                 Mia's ex-husband, and father
                 to six of her children

CHILDREN OF MIA FARROW AND ANDRE PREVIN

Matthew Previn, 23	biological twins
Sascha Previn, 23	
Fletcher Previn, 19	biological son
Daisy Previn, 19	
Lark Previn, 22	adopted daughters
Soon-Yi Previn, 21	

CHILDREN OF MIA FARROW AND WOODY ALLEN

Satchel Farrow, 6	biological son
Dylan Farrow, 8	adopted daughter (contested)
Moses Farrow, 15	adopted son (contested)

MIA'S SOLO ADOPTIONS

Tam Farrow, 13
Isaiah Farrow, 2

EMPLOYEES

Mavis Smith	Mia's long-time housekeeper
Monica Thompson	Children's former nanny
Sophie Bergé	French tutor
Don Harris	Woody's driver

OTHERS

Priscilla Gilman	Matthew's girlfriend
Carrie Englander	Sascha's girlfriend
Jesse Spongeon	Lark's ex-beau
James McDonald	Daisy's boyfriend
Casey Pascal	Mia's close friend since childhood
Chris Rush	Security expert
Eleanor Alter	Mia's attorney
Elkan Abramowitz	Woody's attorney
John McGrath	Kristi's late boyfriend
Alison Stickland	Casey Pascal's babysitter

Time Line

1935	Woody, a.k.a. Allen Stewart Konigsberg, is born
1945	Mia, a.k.a. Maria Villiers Farrow, is born
1956	Woody weds Harlene Rosen (five years)
1966	Woody weds Louise Lasser (three years)
1966	Mia weds Frank Sinatra (two years)
1969	Woody Allen starts seeing Diane Keaton (three years)
1970	Mia marries and makes home with Andre Previn (eight years)
1979	Mia and Woody meet
1980	Mia adopts Moses
	Mia and Woody start going together
1982	Woody and Mia make *A Midsummer Night's Sex Comedy*
1983	Woody and Mia make *Zelig*
1984	Woody and Mia make *Broadway Danny Rose*
1985	Mia adopts Dylan
	Woody and Mia make *The Purple Rose of Cairo*
1986	Woody and Mia make *Hannah and Her Sisters*
1987	Woody and Mia film *Another Woman*
	Mia gives birth to Satchel
	Woody and Mia make *Radio Days* and *September*
1989	Woody and Mia make *Oedipus Wrecks* (in *New York Stories*)
	Woody and Mia make *Crimes and Misdemeanors*

	Woody and Mia film *Alice*
	Woody makes *Scenes from a Mall*
1991	Woody and Mia make *Shadows and Fog*
	Woody and Mia shoot *Husbands and Wives*
December 18, 1991	Adoptions of Dylan and Moses are legalized
January 13, 1992	Mia discovers nude photos of Soon-Yi
August 4, 1992	Alleged molestation of Dylan takes place
August 13, 1992	Woody sues for custody of Dylan and Moses
August 18, 1992	Opening of *Husbands and Wives*
Fall, 1992	Woody shoots *Manhattan Murder Mystery* without Mia
March 17, 1993	The Yale report is published, clearing Woody of child molestation charges
March 18, 1993	Custody hearings for Dylan and Moses begin
June 7, 1993	Judge's verdict in custody hearings

MIA & WOODY

"But Miles, don't you see, meaningful relationships between men and women don't last. That was proven by science. You see, there's a chemical on our bodies that makes it so that we all get on each other's nerves sooner or later."

Luna Schlosser (Diane Keaton)
to Miles Monroe (Woody Allen)
in *Sleeper*

ONE

Taking the Stand

April 10, 1993: My day in court.

I felt as I had when I was about to run in the 1990 Millrose Games. The Games were the greatest collegiate track event of the year, and I knew my butt was on the line. That is, my entire full-tuition scholarship to Manhattan College in Riverdale, N.Y., depended on how fast I ran.

Although my specialty was the half-mile, that day I was the leadoff leg in the 4 x 400 relay, and even before I headed onto the track in my little green bloomers and white tank top, I was overcome by nerves. As I stepped onto the turf, I could see Madison Square Garden, packed with families and fans. Immediately I picked out my parents, my mother in her white fur coat, waving her arms like crazy, yelling, "Come on, Kristi." But their presence did nothing to soothe me. My hands were so cold and clammy that I was afraid I would drop the metal baton as I handed it over. My mouth was dry. My stomach had so many butterflies, I could have started a collection.

That same feeling of frozen fear was now rolling over me. The beads of perspiration. The icy hands. But this was no race, it was April 10, 1993, my day to testify in the custody battle known in the vast legal bureaucracy as WOODY ALLEN, Petitioner, against MARIA VILLIERS FARROW, a.k.a. MIA FARROW, Respondent. I was here because I had been Mia Farrow's baby-

21

sitter and nanny on and off for the past two years, and her friend and confidante during the last eight months. I had seen the trail of tears, the sea of flashbulbs, the ocean of damning headlines that Mia and her family had endured. I knew about the parade of shrinks trying to help them all survive.

Yet at that moment I felt less like the lean half-miler who could sometimes pull out a victory than the big, scared, clumsy Catholic girl from Bridgewater, Connecticut. As I walked across the holding room in Manhattan Surrogate Court down at 31 Chambers Street, I was nervous. I saw Mia sifting through her mammoth straw pocketbook, finally picking out the heavy wooden rosary beads with the silver cross, beads that had once belonged to her father. "Here, Kristi, do you want these while you testify?" she asked, holding them out to me. I took them gratefully, hoping they would lend me a serenity I didn't really feel.

I should have been more confident. I had been in witness preparation for about two weeks before I testified. Marty Jubileer, an associate of Mia's attorney, Eleanor Alter, would sit me down and cross-examine me mercilessly, letting me know that this was how Woody's lawyers would treat me *if* I was lucky. The first morning he had spent three hours bombarding me with questions. When I left for lunch I dissolved into tears. I was terrified that I couldn't do it and would let Mia down. But after another three hours that afternoon, and what seemed like endless hours throughout the spring of 1993, I felt toughened and secure, with a stronger sense of myself. I was ready to burst out of the starting block. I promised myself that I would not drop the baton.

But an hour before I was supposed to testify, as I sat between Mia's friend Casey Pascal, and her children's French tutor Sophie Bergé, who were also about to take the stand, my composure evaporated. After all, I was about to recount the events of August 4, 1992, the summer afternoon when, under my lapsed vigilance, Woody spent between ten and twenty minutes alone with his adopted daughter Dylan and during that time allegedly sexually molested her. And, to tell the truth, in my heart I hadn't the foggiest notion of whether or not that molestation ever took place.

My fears, as I approached the courtroom, were threefold. I feared that I might trip things up for Mia, and I didn't want to. I feared that I would incriminate Woody without ever really being certain of what he had done. (I didn't want to do that either). And last, I feared that Woody's attorneys would find some embarrassing bits and pieces of my life that they could twist around and throw to the newspapers to discredit me. I already envisioned tabloid headlines the next day, perhaps accompanied by a hideously unflattering photograph of me stumbling home from a club, a little more than slightly buzzed. Or there would be a surprise witness—some old schoolmate—swearing under oath that I once cheated on an eighth-grade Spanish exam. Or some vengeful ex-boyfriend, testifying about what a bitch I had been to him.

But as I was led into the courtroom, nothing made me more fearful than the sight of Woody himself, bespectacled and poker-faced, wearing what appeared to be the same tweed jacket he had worn throughout the trial. Slumped down in his seat not more than seven feet away, he stared at me unblinkingly as I stepped into the witness box. It was a stony, unforgiving face, but it held my gaze as the clerk swore me in. I tried to look elsewhere, first to Mia in her black pleated skirt and navy blue blazer, sitting tense and straight, like a parochial-school student. I saw her give me a small, encouraging smile, then I glanced over to the sketch artists and tried to concentrate on them as they moved their pencils swiftly along their pads. I knew those in Mia's camp would make me look glamorous; those in Woody's, grotesque. Beyond them sat Woody's sister, Letty Aronson, staring down at me with disdainful eyes. I matched her, glance for glance, trying to cloak my misgivings with bravado. Yet in all honesty, the whole scene completely unnerved me. Suddenly, my head began to bob up and down, back and forth, uncontrollably. I couldn't stop it. I was afraid that my voice would shake, too, when I tried to summon it.

Get a grip, I told myself. I thought of all the races I had managed to pump myself up for—and win. I thought of all the exams I had taken—and passed. I heard my mom screaming, "Let's go, Kristi. Come on." Lifting the rosaries out of my pocket and clasping my sweaty hands around the beads, I slid them about, feeling them clanking against one another in a soothing rhythm. Everyone was looking at me. And as I had so many times in the past months, I began to wonder, *How had it come to this?* Who had thrown the grenade into this modern fairy tale? How could Woody and Mia, two highly unconventional but psychologically enlightened people, have allowed their love to erode into such an all-consuming public display?

At once the images in my brain raced back to another happier time a mere two years before.

"My heart says one thing. My head says something else. It's very difficult to get your heart and head together in life. In my case, they're not too friendly."

Cliff (Woody) in
Crimes and Misdemeanors

TWO

Summer with Mia

I remember the day I met Mia Farrow and Woody Allen. The summer of 1991 was cruel and sweltering. I was living at Manhattan College in Riverdale, New York, and that June, with only one semester left before graduation, I was frantically searching for a summer job. Although I interviewed for a few internships in physical therapy, my efforts came up with zip. After all, this was the depth of the recession, and most companies were cutting back drastically, especially when it came to summer work for college students.

My grand plan had originally been to head for Ireland during July and August to work for my boyfriend, John McGrath, who was doing marketing for the Coca-Cola Company in Dublin. I had met John, who was one of the best milers in Ireland, on our college track team, and immediately fell for his easy charm and his great, wide dimpled smile. We had fallen in love and talked seriously about marriage.

But distance had come between us. I started seeing other men. John had become jealous and was pressuring me to marry him immediately. My response was simply to withdraw. So now, although we adored each other, we weren't getting along so well, and I had decided to remain in New York until we sorted out our battered relationship.

For three weeks I looked for a job. I tossed around the idea

27

of going to acting school. I thought about working as a physical fitness trainer for extra cash, but I had done that, and it had bored me. Then my mother heard of a prospect right in our hometown of Bridgewater that, she guaranteed, would be appealing enough for me to eagerly leave my city dreams behind and return home for the summer. In two words: Mia Farrow.

Bridgewater is a small town. I had lived there most of my life, and I knew practically everyone who had been there for any length of time. With its picture-book colonial and Victorian dwellings dating back to the 1800s, its stone library, and village green which is home to a one-hundred-foot-high evergreen that has been festooned with hundreds of multicolored lights every Christmas since I can remember, Bridgewater resembles a movie set designer's dream of Americana. It exudes so much picturesque Norman Rockwellian charm that every weekend, in fact, there's an influx of urban types trying to relax in what they call "the country." You can pick them out almost immediately; they drive their Range Rovers through Main Street on Friday nights, looking smart in their L. L. Bean khakis and Top-Siders. Among the New Yorkers who have retreats there are such celebrities as actor Dustin Hoffman, director Mike Nichols, and composer/lyricist Stephen Sondheim.

It was mere coincidence that Mia Farrow, who lives about a mile and a half down the road from us, is a neighbor of the Grabels. In high school I had been good friends with their son Deron, and they have been friends of our family for the past fifteen years. They knew that Mia was looking for a reliable baby-sitter that summer, and that I was desperate for a job. Connections, isn't that how life often works? And although I had really wanted to stay in Manhattan that summer, the possibility of working for a genuine movie star was intriguing enough to lure me back home. It could be, I thought, an unexpected summer adventure.

A few afternoons later I was in my mother's sunny white kitchen when I noticed my answering machine flashing a green light indicating that I had a message. When I pushed the play button, I heard Mia's thin, wispy voice, which I recognized right away from all her movies that I had seen. "Hello, this is Mia

Farrow calling for Kristi," she said. "I'm a friend of Wendy Grabel's"—just in case I didn't know who she was!—"and I heard you were interested in working for me." Then she left her phone number. I listened to the message three or four times. Then when my sister Kelly came home, I made *her* listen to it several times. Finally, I was ready to call Mia back. I had never talked to a genuine celebrity before, and I was excited. She was very direct and asked me to come down the next day, Sunday, to her home, Frog Hollow, to meet her. I had all I could do to refrain from racing down there instantly.

Of course, I was nervous all the next morning. How do you prepare yourself to meet a movie star? As I turned my car into Mia's gravel-and-dirt driveway at the top of a hill, I tried to calm down by telling myself that she wasn't just a movie star who had been desired by Frank Sinatra and Woody Allen. She was a normal, down-to-earth suburban mother of nine children (Isaiah and Tam had not yet become part of her family). I also thought of all the times I'd driven past her driveway, wondering what her house looked like. Or what she was doing. Or if Woody, whose movies my whole family adored, was there. Sometimes I wondered if Mia was really Mother Teresa. Now I was about to find out.

When I pulled onto the road of her sixty-acre property, it was like driving through a tunnel because the trees and shrubs grow into a verdant archway that extends for maybe 250 yards. When you turn the last corner before the house becomes visible, you see a jagged white sign hanging on a tree that says CAREFUL—CHILDREN PLAYING handwritten in black paint. Then you go down the last little hill, and to the left is Mia's cheery white wooden two-story colonial home. Straight ahead there is a big pond, with two rustic log cabins sitting on its far shore. I parked the car not far from a wooden rose trellis and a gate, and walked through it, passing a garage that housed Mia's red Suburban—Big Red, she calls it—and her white Volkswagen Jetta. Not exactly the vehicle of choice for most of Hollywood, I couldn't help thinking.

I couldn't see anyone yet, but I could hear the sound of people talking, which I followed up a stone walkway lined with pachysandra. Immediately to the right, sitting on a patch of dirt and grass, was a barn-red swinging love seat which was covered in cobwebs that glistened in the sun. Just beyond it was a stone patio and a lawn littered with toys. A toy car sat in the thick milkweed and, not far away, an old-fashioned hippity-hop horse lay on its side. As I walked on a little farther, I glimpsed a slim blond woman, a much younger, very pretty, dark-haired woman with Asian features, and two blond children—Mia, Lark, Satchel, and Dylan, as it turned out. Walking over to them, I extended my hand to Mia Farrow. "Hi, I'm Kristi," I said—brightly, I hoped. And she stood up, shook my hand, and replied, as if I didn't already know, "Hi, I'm Mia. These are my kids, Lark, Dylan, and Satchel."

The first thing I noticed was how petite and delicate Mia was. Next, how short her hair was. It was almost as extreme as the close-cropped style she popularized in the mid-sixties when she hacked off her beautiful long blond tresses. Wearing shorts, an oversize white T-shirt, and in bare feet, she looked to me more like a kid herself than a woman of forty-six. On the ground lay a toy that she was trying to put together for her children. We chatted for a few moments, and when I told her that I wanted to be a physical therapist, she said, "My son went through a lot of physical therapy for cerebral palsy when he was younger." She meant, of course, Moses, now fifteen, who is Korean-born, and who has since had astonishing success with his physical therapy. Where once he limped badly, now his walk is almost perfect.

Mia then led me on a tour of her house. We moved inside through French doors off the front foyer. I had anticipated something fancy, formal, and full of precious antiques. Not at all. This place was cozy and homey. What first attracted my attention was a series of black and white photographs hanging on the walls, studio stills, as it turned out, of her parents—her mom, actress Maureen O'Sullivan, who starred as Jane in MGM's Tarzan series during the thirties, and her father, John Farrow, who directed *The Big Clock* and *Hondo*. In fact, there were photos on every wall and in every cranny—many were hanging askew, knocked off center by her kids or the passage of time.

Mia showed me the L-shaped living room which is dominated by a huge picture window that overlooks the pond. It's a room that looks lived-in, with its worn wine-colored sofa, its fireplace whose mantel is dotted with antique toys, and its old bleached wood grandfather clock. There is also an upright piano against a wall and a small chess table in a far corner. All the walls were covered by family photos. There was even one of Mia, Frank Sinatra, and a wedding cake, obviously taken during their 1966 wedding party.

Then we headed to the spacious bedroom where Lark, Daisy, and Soon-Yi slept. It had high beamed ceilings and opened onto a large deck that looked out onto the pond. On the walls hung Asian dancing costumes and slippers that Mia had bought her Asian-born daughters so that they could identify with their heritage. From there we entered the tiny TV room which has since been made part of the dining room. Here the walls were thick with photos of Woody, Dylan, and Moses.

The kitchen was, I later discovered, a lot like Mia's kitchen in Manhattan, warm and comfortable, with a big wooden table, lots of baskets hanging from the ceiling, and a lighting fixture with a multicolored stained-glass shade. Against the far wall was a wood-burning stove. On the fireplace mantel in the kitchen were spices in bowls and framed photos of Mia and the children. (Around her mirror in her bedroom she has photos of the kids simply stuck into the frame, none with formal frames of their own.) To the side of the kitchen was a big pantry and laundry room which held framed posters from Woody's films, and a bathroom. Right off that is a guest room and the boys' room which has its own bath.

From here Mia whisked me upstairs. The door was closed, the shower water was running, and Woody was inside, although I didn't know it at the time. He may even have been working on a screenplay. "This sounds silly," he told his biographer Eric Lax in *Woody*, "but I'll be working and I'll want to get into the shower for a creative stint. I'll stand there in the steaming water for thirty or forty minutes, just plotting a story and thinking out ideas."

While he was showering, Mia brought me into the children's

room which held a daybed against the wall and two sweet, tiny bedlets that are meant to be helpful transitions between cribs and big beds. "These are so cute," I remarked.

"Yes," she replied. "Andre and I had them made for Sasha and Matthew when they were small. I'm glad I took them back from England." Conductor Andre Previn had been her second husband.

Mia then showed me her bedroom, which looked exactly as it should have. There was a rocking chair in the corner, and in the center was her extremely feminine queen-size bed with its cream-colored lace canopy and dark-patterned floral quilt on top of it. A wooden rolltop desk covered with yarn and all her knitting material completed the furnishings. Off the bedroom is a small nursery which holds a crib, a dresser, another rocking chair, baby toys, and more yarn. Mia loves needlepoint and knitting. She taught the kids how to knit this past summer, and they do it constantly. Tam—Mia's blind daughter, whom she adopted in February 1992—is a whiz at it. She is also taking piano lessons, and she's just terrific.

After our tour of the house, Mia took me outside, and we sat down on the big stone steps overlooking her lake. It looked like glass in the late afternoon light.

"Gee, this is so beautiful," I said.

She smiled and replied, "Yes. I'm lucky, aren't I?" as though she had won the Connecticut lottery.

At that point I heard something behind me. Mia gazed over my shoulder, smiled, and said simply, "Woody. Meet Kristi."

My heart jumped. I hadn't expected Woody to be there. *The* Woody. The Woody who *I* knew because he brought a bakery box full of goodies to dinner at the home of a Caribbean dictator in *Bananas*. The Woody who I loved because he cloned a nose in *Sleeper*. I turned around and there he was. In the flesh he seemed all too human and, to my twenty-two-year-old eyes, well, old. He had white bags under his eyes, red hair, and a goodly amount of freckles sprinkled across his face. He was wearing his trademark black-framed glasses, a tan fishing hat, a white button-down shirt, and khaki pants that hung on him as though he were a child playing dress-up. I would see him in this outfit, or some that were similar, countless times.

Pulling myself together, I stuck out my hand in greeting. For some reason, Woody looked at it with surprise. When he finally extended his own, I couldn't help thinking what small hands he had. Well, I'm a big girl, broad-shouldered, five feet eight and a half in stocking feet, and over five ten with running shoes on. (I was always the biggest girl on my track team.) And Woody is a small man, at five six the same size as Mia.

"Nice to meet you," I managed to croak just as my parents had taught me, and tried to sound more confident than I felt. Woody smiled at me stiffly, as though his head were in a vise. Smiling wasn't something I would see him do often. Unless he was with his kids, that is.

As Woody continued across the lawn to play with the children, I sat down again on the steps next to Mia. My legs were shaking a little, but I had met him and I hadn't passed out or said anything dumb or otherwise embarrassed myself.

Now Mia and I turned our attention to my working arrangements. We agreed that I would work three days a week, doing an assortment of jobs—spring cleaning, cooking, baby-sitting, swimming lessons, laundry, errands, shopping, in general whatever needed to be done. She also asked if I could swim and seemed pleased that I had had to take an aquatics instruction course for my physical therapy major (I am a good swimmer; I received an A). Then Mia told me that she, Woody, and the children were going off to Ireland in a few days and wouldn't return for two weeks, but that I could start straightening up the house while they were away. I mentioned to her that my boyfriend John lived in Ireland, and if she needed anyone to show them around, I would be glad to give them his phone number.

As I made this offer, I glanced across the lawn to Woody, who was pacing up and down, up and down. His nervous city-type energy was apparent even from a distance, and despite the fishing cap—a little nod, I supposed, to country life—he always seemed to me as out of place up there as Mia seemed relaxed. More than that, my mind flashed to John McGrath's family in County Carlow. And I could picture Woody sitting at a table with a group of jolly, drinking, smoking Irish folk—John, his parents, and eight brothers and sisters. And I imagined John's parents regarding him the same way Annie Hall's granny did in *Annie Hall:* With long curls falling from his temples, a rabbinical beard, and a black broad-brimmed Lubavitcher hat. Luckily, Mia declined my offer of John's services. Did I detect a sigh of relief from Woody, still pacing on that lawn?

The moment I got home, my sister Kelly and her husband Gerry were all over me with questions. During the next two weeks, all my neighbors and friends, hearing about my exotic summer job, joined in the chorus: *What did he look like? What was he wearing? Was he funny? Does she really talk in that little reedy voice? What was she wearing? Who does Satchel look like, Mia or Woody? What does the house look like?* A million questions. I was so relieved to find that they were such absolutely normal people. So down-to-earth. So real. Or so it appeared at the time.

The kids were so appealing, and the house, I pointed out to everybody, was comfortable and unpretentious. In fact, in the forty minutes or so I spent with Mia and Woody, all my worries that these two might be self-absorbed, silly movie stars who had climbed onto self-constructed pedestals had vanished.

More than that, I had a summer job. Finally. I've always been a lucky sort. Lucky things just happen to me. This, I felt certain, was one of them.

So Mia, Woody, and all their kids went to Ireland. While they toured the gorgeous emerald-green countryside, I cleaned and tidied their Bridgewater farmhouse. What was supposed to take a few days ended up being a week-long operation, a task as simple as getting a satellite into orbit. It included vacuuming up piles of mouse turds, putting away mounds of toys, removing dozens of photos and knickknacks from the tables and mantels to dust and then putting them back again, doing battle with cobwebs on ceilings and between beds, and laundering and changing the sheets and pillowcases on—let's not forget!—a dozen beds.

Then the family returned to Bridgewater. After working at Frog Hollow for two weeks, I began to realize that with a household the size of Mia's, the house couldn't be perfect. It just wasn't possible to keep so many active kids clean and neat, or to pick up toys after every playtime. And Mia didn't care if the house was spotless or the kitchen table was smeared with apple sauce either. This was not her primary concern. It was making sure the younger kids weren't running outside the gates of her property or near the water, unsupervised. Like any good mother, she wanted to know that they were playing well and eating well and were generally safe and in good humor.

Still, it was difficult to get used to this hit-or-miss style of living. My first instinct was to keep mopping up after the children. Then one day shortly after I arrived, when I was loading the dishwasher and I could hear the kids screaming for Mia to help them cut string for an arts and crafts project, she came into the room. "Kristi, don't worry so much about cleaning up," she said. "Just help me take care of the children." She was polite and good-natured. And soon enough I got the hang of things. But with a house full of kids, work is never done. Within a week, my three-day job became a five-to-six day assignment. That suited me fine.

The next time I saw Woody was shortly after he and Mia returned from Ireland. I was down at Mia's pond, giving Dylan and Satchel swimming lessons, when he pulled up in his limousine and came down to the beach to watch us. A pattern began to develop. After I was finished with the lessons, he would either sit the kids down at the kitchen table and tell them truly amazing stories, or he would take the kids' toys out and play a game with them. He especially liked crafts games.

Mia often used this time when Woody was with the children to stop in New Milford, to see her friend Casey Pascal, or even to take Moses out to lunch or buy him a pair of sneakers. When Woody came over during the day, he would usually spend the entire afternoon with Satchel and Dylan, showering them with his attention. Most of the time he ignored Moses, even though he was already in the process of trying to adopt him. Sometime in early 1991, after she had expressed interest in adopting yet another Vietnamese child, Woody and Mia had struck an agreement. Woody said he would not take "a lousy attitude toward it," if she in turn would sponsor his adoption of Dylan, and Moses as well (whom Mia later said he had thrown in "as an afterthought"). Occasionally, though, Woody would bring his son-to-be a gift—once he gave him a pocket watch which the boy received indifferently. I could see that Moses was really happy that Woody had remembered him, but bewildered that his stepfather had picked out something so useless to a budding teenager. Mostly, however, I thought Woody's lack of interest in Moses was curious and sad. Sometimes I would think, Something is wrong here. If this were *my* lover or husband, I'd *never* let him treat my son so dismissively. But that was how it went in the Farrow household. Then in the evenings Woody and Mia would see each other alone, usually when they went out to dinner.

From what I saw that summer, the pair got along well enough. At least, they rarely argued or raised their voices to each other. Yet the Mia and Woody who worked so well together in the movies were not really the Mia and Woody whom I knew. That summer of 1991 they didn't seem to have much contact with each other. They didn't talk much. They floated about and around each other, as if suspended in a huge cloud of indifference. Sometimes they reminded me of an old married couple who have been together for forty years and no longer have much interest in each other.

Recently, Mia told me that, in her view, their relationship was "completely normal back then. We were still having sex, we were still sleeping together—from time to time we would sneak off to hotels for the night. But you're right, Kristi, we were like an old married couple. We were very very comfortable with each other."

The only argument that I ever witnessed between Mia and Woody occurred one day when I arrived to give Dylan and Satchel a swimming lesson. That afternoon Dylan was being very fussy. She complained and cried that she didn't want to go in the water. Woody, outside by the pond in uniform—fishing hat, button-down shirt, and brown-on-brown saddle shoes—looked at me and said, "Well, Dylan doesn't have to go in if she doesn't want to." But he tried to coax her to change her mind. "Come on, it will be fun," he assured her. "Daddy will watch you have this lesson."

Dylan, out on the sandy area around the pond which we called "the beach," couldn't be swayed. Not even by Mia, who walked down to the lake at that moment and said with as much authority as she could muster in her sweet, light voice, "Come on, Dylan, let's go. We're going to go in the water. Mommy will go in with you." Every once in a while Mia does that; she jumps into the water with the kids, but never *ever* wearing a bathing suit. Instead, she wears shorts and a T-shirt, almost as though she's embarrassed by the idea of a scanty swimsuit. And she never submerges her head. She sits in an inner tube, kicking and floating around with them.

In fact, there's a little island in the middle of the pond, about 150 feet away from shore, and it's a tremendous treat for the kids to slip into the inner tubes and to kick out to the island, accompanied by the adults. Once Satchel, Dylan, Mia, Daisy, and I all paddled out there together. When we got to the island, we discovered that it was teeming with ants. And Satchel, who was delighted, said, "Let's have a campout here." But Dylan felt as I did. "No, it's disgusting," she frowned. "There will be ants all over us." She looked extremely distressed. So we all just swam back.

But on this day Dylan was cantankerous. Even though Mia had volunteered to jump into the water with her, she cried, she whined, and said, "I won't. I won't."

Woody sided with Dylan, saying, "She doesn't have to go in."

Mia felt otherwise. "No, she's got to understand that when somebody is here to help her learn something," she countered, "she can't simply say no and get her own way. She's got to have some discipline. If my parents had hired somebody to come here and give me swimming lessons, I could not have cried and gotten my own way."

It wasn't that Dylan was afraid of swimming, she had had plenty of lessons. She was just being bratty. Woody and Mia discussed at length whether Dylan should be allowed to skip her lesson. Then they both looked at me for my opinion. I shrugged.

I knew that it would change nothing, certainly not Dylan's mind, which was made up.

As it happened, an hour later she herself changed it. I was still there, so I gave her the lesson she had avoided earlier. After about twenty minutes of working together, I said to her, "Call Daddy and show him what you learned."

And she proudly showed Woody how she could float on her back and put her face in the water. "Oh, that's *so* wonderful, Dylan," he said in his singsong, nerdy voice. "Look at you. You look great out there." He was supportive and sweet.

While Woody was watching the kids swim, sometimes Mia would join him. They would sit on wooden chairs under the faded yellow-striped beach umbrella, and sometimes they would discuss the movie that he was either shooting or planning. Often they would talk about which actors could fill which roles, throwing about famous names in the most casual way. These conversations, which I eavesdropped on, always thrilled me. I remember Mia mentioning her friend Michael Caine, and Woody agreeing with her that Caine was so talented, he could be cast in almost any role. Another time he toyed with the idea of hiring Jane Fonda for a movie, but was concerned about what he called her "astronaut's wife's haircut." Apparently he had made inquiries about the possibility of working with Fonda if she agreed to change her hairstyle, but she had refused, and that was that for any artistic collaboration. Once in a while, after Woody would leave, Mia would even ask *me* who could play a certain part. Although I was bent on learning enough to keep up with my new boss, I didn't feel even slightly qualified to offer an opinion.

Other times Mia, who loves books, would lie in a hammock and read while Woody and I watched the kids. Sometimes, as I worked around the house, I would hear Woody making his business calls on her phone. He would always use the old rotary phone and *never* the cordless; I noticed that and wondered if he worried that on the portable, his business discussions might get intercepted on the New York State Thruway. I heard him discussing movie-deal details several times. It all sounded so glamorous to me, but I'd pick up only little snatches and would never be able to put together much in the way of significant information. Or significant gossip.

Mia saw a great deal of Casey Pascal that summer. Casey would either come over with her three kids—John, eight, and her adopted twins, Emma and Kate, five—to swim at the pond, or all of us would go over to her old white wood house to play with them. Casey and Mia knew each other as far back as the Marymount School, a private boarding high school in Kingston, England, and have been close ever since. Casey has long, pin-straight brown hair and is pretty in a simple, elegant way. Like Mia, she wears little makeup and dresses mostly in khaki pants or jeans, cotton shirts, and Top-Siders. Her husband is a successful New York banker, and they have an apartment in the Gramercy Park area of Manhattan as well as their house about fifteen minutes away from Mia's.

Casey, like Mia, is a mother with a capital M, and devotes one hundred percent of her time to her children. She is a loyal friend to Mia. What they have in common is their childhood friendship and their overwhelming sense of family. Still, on spending time with Casey, I couldn't help observing that she and Mia were like night and day. Where Casey seemed utterly practical and street smart, Mia appeared eccentric, poetic, and artistic. Mia was often overwhelmed by trying to schedule her own life and that of her nine children, but Casey could reel off a no-nonsense plan in seconds. She could also deal with the whimsical changes in Mia's own plans, so that if Mia canceled an afternoon's shopping or a lunch at the last minute, Casey accepted it serenely.

In the two years that followed, when Mia's life with Woody fell apart, and when Mia questioned who her real friends were, Casey was the single person she completely trusted, the single friend who was there for her all the time. Of course, Casey may have had her own mixed feelings about Woody. And with good reason. I noticed that whenever she visited, he would rarely greet or talk to her. He has a habit of doing that if he's not interested in somebody. It struck me as particularly rude and antisocial, but within Mia's own family structure, I had seen Woody do it with the other children, sometimes completely ignoring them for hours on end, so it was not unfamiliar behavior. But Casey took it all casually, simply attributing his eccentricity to the fact that he was an *artiste*.

Casey was the only friend who Mia saw on a regular basis. Sure, there were other celebrity pals, and Mia would occasionally talk on the phone with director Mike Nichols or composer Steven Sondheim, both of whom had homes nearby, but she rarely got together with them. These days things are a lot different. She seems much more available to people than she used to be. She became very close, for instance, with her attorney, Eleanor Alter, and they have a real bond. She is also close to Sondheim.

During the summer of 1991, whenever Woody would come up, he would spend hours with the children. He had taught Moses how to play chess, and sometimes I would walk into a room, and they would be sitting at the chessboard in a quiet corner, deep in strategic thought. Later on he and Mia would go out to dinner at Joey's, a seafood restaurant in New Milford, or to Maison Blanc, a local French restaurant. There were other excellent restaurants in the area as well, but Mia was always reluctant to venture too far from the house and the children. Also, their favorite restaurants seemed to cater to their stellar clients, either giving them a private room or inconspicuous seating. Once in a while Woody and Mia ate at home, and Woody would ask me to pick up Chinese food for everybody.

Early in the evening, around eight o'clock, Woody, and sometimes Mia with him, would take Dylan and Satchel up to their room, where he would either read to them or tell them a story. In one of the kids' favorite tall tales, Woody put sun screen all over himself and flew up to the sun; when he hit the sun, he slid right off because he had so much sun screen on. The children would listen, enrapt. When he spoke seriously, they listened seriously; the minute he cracked a joke, they got it and started to laugh. Satchel especially would double over with giggles and hold his stomach. Then the kids would elaborate on Woody's joke with great enthusiasm and kiddie humor.

While Woody spun his fables, he would turn on the stereo and play Vivaldi or Mozart. As a result, the kids adore classical music. In fact, if you turn on rock and roll, they will usually cover their ears and yell, "Turn that off." Finally, after these evening story festivals, Woody or I would get them chocolate milk or orange juice before they went to sleep.

Woody only occasionally spent the night at Frog Hollow. He was never really at home in the country. "I am two with nature," he once wrote. Up at Frog Hollow he has been known to wander down to Mia's pond wearing a beekeeper's hat and netting to protect himself from what he regards as the local wildlife (what a cruel irony that somebody who was always so cautious has actually managed to contract Lyme disease, as he has). During the summer of 1991, the first I worked for Mia, when Woody stayed over he would sleep in Mia's room, but by the next year, after Mia found her daughter Soon-Yi's nude photos and uncovered her affair with him, things were different. Then, whenever Woody came to visit, he would stay in the guest bedroom. And, of course, after Dylan's alleged molestation on August 4, 1992, he no longer came to visit at all.

Andre Previn, Mia's second husband, whom she married in 1970 and divorced in 1979, the year before she met Woody, also would come up to Bridgewater to see Mia and his six children. The twins, self-contained Matthew and delightfully silly Sasha, now twenty-four, as well as easygoing Fletcher, twenty, were his natural-born sons; and bold, warm-hearted Lark, twenty-one, mischievous Daisy, nineteen, and shy Soon-Yi, either twenty-four or twenty-two (her birth year is in dispute), were his adopted daughters. He visited maybe two or three times each summer, arriving on a Sunday and taking everyone out to brunch at the Pantry Restaurant in Washington, Connecticut, including the little kids. It would be on a weekend when at least four of his six kids were there. Or the family would have a cookout. Andre, who used to conduct the London Symphony Orchestra, now traveled all the time as a guest conductor, often performing in Germany, London, or Austria. He also plays piano in his own jazz trio. Sometimes his son Fletcher, who seemed to be the most interested in traveling with his dad, would accompany him. Once after Andre left Frog Hollow, Woody came up and put his hands on the piano, doodling a little. Instantly Dylan said to him,

"Andre can play the piano better than you can, Daddy." And Woody said sarcastically, "Thanks a lot."

Woody, of course, is musical too. He used to bring his clarinet with him, and sometimes while the kids were swimming or playing by the beach, he would stand in the sand, looking across the pond, and play sweet tunes. Other times he would go into the TV room by himself and practice. He actually sounded terrific. Sometimes it would be on a Monday morning, and he'd be warming up for his show that night at Michael's Pub on East 55th Street. Though Woody loved jazz and was extremely knowledgeable about it, in her house Mia would play only opera or classical music, never jazz.

That summer of 1991, Daisy, Mia's second-oldest daughter, who was then sixteen, was at summer session at the ritzy Taft Boarding School in Middletown, Connecticut, and Lark, her oldest girl, then eighteen, was at home in Frog Hollow with Jesse Spungeon, then seventeen, her boyfriend, and they were baby-sitting and helping Mia. (Both girls were in fact doing penance for being caught shoplifting lacy underwear from G. Fox at the Danbury Mall in June, an act which I consider a gesture of normal teen behavior.) Still, Jesse was allowed to stay in Bridgewater for the summer, but Mia's rule was that he had to share the boys' room with Moses, while Lark occupied the girls' room. Often Moses would hang around with Lark and Jesse, and they would play video games together. It was good company for Moses, who was in an odd position in the family—at fifteen, he was a little too young to hang out with the boys, yet much too old to spend time with the little kids. He was also the only kid who did not have a father. So he lapped up whatever crumbs of attention Woody allotted him. The older kids, Matthew and Sascha, both twenty-one at the time, their girlfriends Priscilla Gilman and Carrie Englander, and Soon-Yi, nineteen back then, came up most weekends too.

On the surface, everything was working well. I was thrilled because, by August, John and I had reconciled and I planned to meet him in Ireland in November. Moreover, I was slowly winning the confidence of outgoing Satchel and shy, cautious Dylan. The children appeared happy. Mia seemed radiant as she planned to adopt more children—a little Vietnamese boy who was to arrive that fall and a blind Vietnamese girl who was at the moment caught up in the usual adoption red tape. And Woody was preparing to shoot a new film—*Husbands and Wives.*

Their passion for each other may have cooled, but in 1991 Mia and Woody still talked as though they were a couple who shared dreams and a future. They contemplated, for instance, moving to Paris and buying an apartment there. Still, they didn't seem to me especially romantically engaged. Woody told me that they had different apartments in Manhattan—his was on Fifth Avenue and hers was directly across Central Park on Central Park West. (When they first began dating, they could—and actually did—wave towels at each other across the park.) It was in keeping with the rest of their arrangement that he only come up to Bridgewater two days a week, usually returning the same night.

Woody blamed it, in part, on the shower. Yes, he never wanted to stay, he said, because he couldn't take a shower. When they first started seeing each other, Mia had no shower in her Connecticut bathroom, only a big antique bathtub. This was fine with her because she loves to take baths. She washes her hair in the sink and *then* takes a leisurely soak. But Mia had the shower built *especially* for Woody. When it was finished, he looked at it and said that it wouldn't do; the drain was in the middle of the tile floor, and he wanted it on the side. Mia confided to me that he was afraid of germs and had decided that he would step on more of them with a middle drain, that they'd wash more easily down a side drain.

Fear of germs motivated much of Woody's behavior. In the Central Park apartment he would eat from paper plates only and drink from cardboard cups. He did this in part because he was so repulsed by the cats, Ewok, Lulu, and Patch, who occasionally jumped up on the kitchen counters and the various dogs who sometimes lapped water out of a family dish. He also found the gerbils, chinchillas, ferret, parakeets, canary, and goldfish disgusting. His own driver, Don Harris, used to call him "Nervous Nelly" because Woody is so neurotic.

From my point of view, Woody's neuroses defied logic. For

instance, he's a hypochondriac who is absolutely terrified of death, although that's the one absolute in all our lives. Mia told me that Woody stopped eating hot dogs and red meat because he constantly worries about having a heart attack. He's also afraid of the sun, which causes both wrinkles and melanoma (I don't know which he fears more). And, of course, there are the bugs.

And the funny thing is that his son Satchel is exactly the same. At the age of five he would come over to me and say, very gravely, like a little old man, "Kristi, I think you should take my temperature. I'm afraid I have a fever." Where most little kids fall, get a cut, and barely notice it, Satchel receives a little scratch and panics. "Oh, no, I'm bleeding," he screams. "Oh, my God, Kristi, I'm going to die, I'm going to die." I just laugh, because he's a shaving off the old block of Woody.

Of course, Woody's neuroses would have been a great deal more palatable if they didn't seem like such a wedge threatening his relationship with Mia. To me, fear of germs from a drain placed in the center of a shower seems less like an eccentric phobia than a lame, lunatic excuse to stay away. In fact, I thought, after twelve years together, what kind of a relationship is it when each partner clings unbendingly to his own home and his own schedule? And what does it say about this twosome that Woody needs to sleep in his own bed every night, almost like a kid afraid to attend a sleepover?

In all their time together, Woody had never once spent the night at Mia's Central Park West apartment. Before the arrival of Dylan in 1985, Mia would take her brood—at the time there were seven children—to Woody's Fifth Avenue duplex on week-end nights when she didn't go to the country. She and Woody set up what she called "a sort of nursery there with a lot of games, Monopoly, Chinese checkers, cards." She also had him install bunk beds so the children could sleep there, because Mia refused to be away from them overnight. So while Woody and Mia went out to dinner, the kids would watch television and play games. Then, she said, "I would say good night to him, put them to bed, and we would go upstairs to his bedroom."

Surely, it would have been easier for one man to sleep at Mia's home than for her to transport her entire army of kids to his. However, according to Mia, "[Woody] just made it clear that he had no interest in being in my apartment."

Yet in 1984 this pattern changed abruptly with Dylan's adoption. Suddenly, there was an infant to think about, and so the Farrow-Previns stopped shuttling across the park. With Satchel's birth two years later, the emotional chasm between Woody and Mia became even wider than the physical separation. By the time of my employment, I couldn't help wondering, Didn't Mia and Woody ever desire *any* romantic time together at all? Didn't they want to wake up in each other's arms? Or share toothbrushes and morning toast? What did they have against those little everyday expressions of togetherness that make up a love affair?

Woody may have whisked Mia off to the Carlyle Hotel for a high-priced evening of love, but the truth is, I never saw them kiss. Never. Not once. Nor did I ever see them hold hands affectionately or spontaneously touch. It was fortunate, I thought to myself, that Mia had all these children to hug and kiss and hold, kids who would let her love them properly. And generously.

As it turned out, Woody and Mia's physical coolness to each other just may have been a clue to the storm ahead.

" 'I falleth on the thorn of life; I bleed.' I used to think that was so romantic."

Rain (Juliette Lewis) in
Husbands and Wives

THREE

Past Lives

In their twelve years as a couple, Mia and Woody became urban icons. For young students like me, they were as much symbols of Manhattan as the Empire State Building or the Statue of Liberty. Regularly, my friends and I would see photos of them in the tabloids. Woody and Mia leaving Elaine's Upper East Side restaurant, where the literary glitterati feasted nightly. Woody and Mia walking together through Central Park, he, craggy-faced and slump-shouldered, with his fishing hat pulled down over his face and his trademark black glasses peering out from under it; she, slightly unkempt and yet still lovely in baggy jeans and sweater, usually with a baby tucked in her arms and a child or two tugging at her jacket. Always, there would be an angelic smile on her face. And we couldn't help wondering, who is this brainy little troll who has managed to captivate Beauty's heart? And what of Beauty herself? Is she an ethereal waif or frumpy mommy? An inspired do-gooder or a spoiled movie star? Who, we wanted to know, is Mia?

Over two decades ago, the press asked that same question of the delicate flower child who made headlines by marrying singer Frank Sinatra. At the time, Mia was barely twenty-one and had just begun to make a name for herself as wistful Allison MacKenzie on the ABC-TV series, "Peyton Place" (the sixties equivalent to "Beverly Hills, 90210"); Sinatra, known as Ol' Blue Eyes, was fifty-two and, as head of Hollywood's Rat Pack, the king of mainstream cool. The two had met while she was filming her series and he, the movie *Von Ryan's Express* on the 20th Century Fox lot, but the romance didn't catch fire until Mia, who then resembled a Victorian princess with golden hair tumbling down her back, appeared on the set in a negligee—her "Peyton Place" costume—and flirtatiously asked Sinatra if she might join him and some of his friends as they headed off to a Palm Springs weekend. They wed a year later, on July 19, 1966. When Sinatra's ex-wife, actress Ava Gardener, heard the news, she observed bitchily, "Ha! I always knew he'd wind up with a boy." And Johnny Carson took his own potshots at Mia and Frank, musing that the Sinatras were in for trouble whenever Mia dropped her Silly Putty in Frank's Poli-Grip.

Then in 1970, Mia, by now the ex–Mrs. Sinatra, broke up her friend Dory's marriage by absconding with Dory's husband, Andre Previn, conductor of the London Symphony Orchestra, and the press once more wanted to know the secrets of this ninety-eight-pound gamine of a temptress. *That* marriage collapsed in 1978 shortly after Mia walked into a room and, in a turn of the tables, discovered *her* best friend Heather massaging Andre's receptive foot. But there were other problems that surfaced before Heather began playing footsy with her husband. "Andre was constantly jealous," Mia explained to me last fall. "He told me that it would make him very happy if I didn't see certain people—men friends whom I loved and needed in my life, and whom I consequently didn't speak to for years."

Eventually, Andre and massage-happy Heather wed, but Mia had already created a robust family for herself—three biological sons by Previn (twins Matthew and Sascha, and Fletcher), and three adopted daughters (Daisy, Vietnamese-born Lark, and Soon-Yi, originally from Korea).

The following year Mia moved her brood to New York City and began yet another chapter in her life. She adopted a seventh child, Korean-born Moses, a toddler with cerebral palsy. She also made her Broadway debut in Bernard Slade's *Romantic Comedy*. It was in 1979, too, that she met Woody Allen. She was dining at Elaine's with her friends Michael and Shakira Caine when they casually introduced her to Woody. The following year, the Gentile goddess and the Jewish nerd would, after a leisurely lunch at the elegant French restaurant, Lutèce, begin their quirky on and off-screen relationship. It would endure for a dozen years, and in the interim Mia would adopt three more children—Dylan, now eight, Isaiah, two, and Tam, thirteen—and bear another son, Satchel, who is six. She would also collaborate with Woody as the star of thirteen of his movies.

Let's face it, few movie stars can lay claim to being parent to eleven children. But Mia, in her own offbeat way, has always had a flair for the dramatic. And why not? After all, she is, first and foremost, a daughter of Hollywood. Her father, John Farrow, an Australian-born ex-seaman, began his career during the silent movie era as an adviser on filming sea chases. Then he turned to writing and gradually became a solid director of studio movies like *The Sea Chase* and *Wake Island.* Her Irish-born mother, Maureen O'Sullivan, also earned a place in screen history as Jane, Johnny Weissmuller's vine-swinging love, in the Tarzan series. (Much later in her career, O'Sullivan was also, briefly, a hostess on NBC's "Today.")

Understandably, then, Mia and her six brothers and sisters grew up with the kind of privilege reserved for kings, queens, and movie stars. Her godfather was renowned director George Cukor. Her godmother was Louella O. Parsons, the industry's most feared and hated gossip, who had a regular column in the Hearst newspapers. And one of her closest friends was—and still is—Maria Roach, granddaughter to producer Hal Roach, whose studio made Laurel and Hardy and Our Gang comedies. There was always a sense of *noblesse oblige* about the Farrow clan. In the world into which Maria de Lourdes Villiers Farrow was born on February 9, 1945—the family called her Mia because, as a baby, that's how she pronounced Maria—anything and everything was possible.

Yet having known Mia well for almost three years now, I have come to believe that to understand her, you must consider two particular aspects of her childhood. The first is that she was brought up a devout Catholic. Just as her mother was educated at a convent near London and a Parisian finishing school, young

Mia attended the rigorous Marymount School in Kingston, England. It was there that she found her faith in the Church and was impressed by its doctrine of service. For years she fantasized about becoming another Dr. Schweitzer and helping the helpless in the tropics. Every Christmas when she would return home to Hollywood (or to wherever the family was residing that season), she would direct a play, charge the grown-ups a small sum to watch it, and then send the money she earned to the March of Dimes, an appropriate charity since as a youngster Mia herself suffered from polio. She was nine when she came down with the disease. "I was sick for about two months and spent some time in an iron lung," she has said. During that time, all her possessions were burned "because the doctor said it was contagious. They even burned my magic box, full of all the things I had that were magical to me. While I was in the hospital, I made up my own will. I left all my things to other people that I couldn't take with me if I really went away forever."

Casey Pascal remembers her this way: "She was very private and thoughtful. She was always in trouble, though." Says Casey: "Mia loved animals. She would be missing from her room or from Mass, and they would go out to look for her and find her sitting in a tree. She was very spiritual and yet was always curious and ready for adventure. And she was always very modest. I remember that she dressed in the closet."

One thing that Mia and I always had in common is that during our childhoods we both thought about becoming nuns. Mia's early recollections of them were not, however, exactly what I might have imagined. "When I saw my first nun, at the age of four and beginning convent school, I had the screaming mimis," she has said. "There was this horrible person, all bundled up like a mummy or something, like a bad dream."

Yet by the time she was ten, horror had turned to adoration; Mia had been won over by the Church. Which was, in a sense, too bad. "When I was thirteen, in England," she has recollected, "they told me they wouldn't have me. Incompatible and everything, you know. I wasn't their type."

I really don't know why. In the time I worked for Mia, I was deeply influenced by her devotion to her principles and by her virtue. She really *lived* her religion, she wanted to do the right thing. And, contrary to the public image of her, during most of the summer of 1992, after her family life crumbled about her, Mia had a passion about *not* being vengeful. She wanted to have the grace to take a slap in the face from Woody and simply walk away. She was always telling me that it was not right to strike back, that God wants us to forgive and make amends. That we are supposed to live in Christ's image and should learn to accept pain because that's what makes us stronger. "Catholicism is tattooed on your soul. You never get rid of it," she once said.

When Mia was young, she told me, she would pray with her arms fully stretched out and perpendicular to the ground, because it was more painful. (Woody later incorporated this image into a flashback of childhood recollections by Alice Tait, the trusting Catholic wife Mia plays in *Alice*.) Mia truly thought that the greater the pain, the greater the virtue. So perhaps she needs pain in her life in order to feel whole or complete.

Many years later, in December 1965, Mia petulantly snipped off her long, silky golden locks on the evening of her then-beau Sinatra's fiftieth birthday bash, to which she had *not* been invited (because he decided it was too awkward for his daughters, Nancy and Tina, who were Mia's peers). While the press reported that Mia cut her hair during a sulk over Frank, Mia later confided to a friend that she did so for another reason—because she had been too prideful about it, too vain. And vanity deserved punishment.

Mia's penchant for suffering may have been reinforced by the family dynamic she grew up in. "What can I say about my father?" Mia reflected back in 1969. "He was priest and lover, powerful and incompetent, strong and weak, a poet and a sailor." He was also an alcoholic. John Farrow, she has told me, was abusive to his wife and family. It is totally consistent that children of alcoholics "marry" their parents—that is, they choose partners who will repeat the same patterns of abuse that were heaped upon them in their formative years. In the case of Mia's relationship with Sinatra, the abuse began early—and publicly. In her book, *His Way*, Kitty Kelley reported that in November 1966, while Mia sat watching him at a ringside table, Frank, on his first Vegas appearance since marrying her four months earlier, joked, "Yeah, I sure got married . . . Well, you see, I had to. . . . I finally found a broad I can cheat on. . . ." Mia didn't laugh. Neither did the audience.

The abuse allegedly went beyond the verbal and emotional. It was also no secret that Sinatra disapproved of Mia's interest in pursuing her career, demanding a wife who was merely an ornament. Mia refused to play the part he had written for her. She may have looked docile and seemed compliant, but she can be extremely willful. Much to his surprise and annoyance, she lobbied for and won the title role as the deaf mute in an ABC-TV version of *Johnny Belinda*. Soon afterward she was hospitalized. When the show's producer, David Susskind, saw her a short time later, he observed that she had been worked over pretty badly, "with black welts all over her body . . . with mean red gashes and marks all over her arms and shoulders and throat as if she'd been badly beaten."

Still, Mia remained with Frank—and to this day denies to me that she was beaten by him. In fact, as volatile as the relationship was, she didn't end it—*he* did. When she refused to obey his orders that she walk off the set of *Rosemary's Baby* mid-picture and report to work on his film, *The Detective*, instead, Frank had had enough. He sent his attorney Mickey Rudin to visit her with divorce papers.

Today Mia maintains her fondness for Sinatra despite their stormy past. What did she see in him, I have asked her. "Everything everyone else saw," she told me. "He was handsome, a gentleman, and we still love each other. It was a bad time in our lives to start a relationship. He was nightclubbing, and I was trying to get my career going. But I respect and still love him. He was so—so—there was something very deep about our relationship. It was something very different than I had with Woody or Andre." The pair are still close today, and through the years Sinatra has been very generous to Mia. Perhaps this is because when they divorced, she refused to accept any financial settlement (she did, however, take with her a not-so-shabby array of baubles Frank had showered her with, including a rare nine-carat diamond ring, a diamond bracelet as thick as a cuff, and a mink coat).

Mia may not have wanted to give up Sinatra, her disapproving daddy-surrogate, but when she did, it was with style. The first thing she did was take off for India with her sister Prudence and the four most famous, sought-after men in the world: The Beatles. Recently, when I brought up her flower-child days to her, Mia laughed and said, "I had nothing better to do than to get deep." (The Beatles immortalized the trip by, among other things, writing a song for Prudie, inspired by the day when she refused to stop meditating and leave her room to join them. "Dear Prudence" quickly became yet another hit for them.)

Some were less captivated by Mia than others. In *Dino,* his biography of Dean Martin, author Nick Tosches describes her as "a simpering flower child." Yet her name was linked to a number of eccentric older gentlemen who were fascinated by her odd combination of emotional maturity and physical fragility: Yes, the white-bearded Maharishi Yogi, the Beatles' guru, himself was one. Another was worldly surrealist artist Salvador Dali, who, she claims, delighted her with his off-center way of looking at light, color, and the world in general. Then when Mia married Berlin-born composer Andre Previn in 1970, he was forty-one and she twenty-five. The age difference may have become more respectable, but still it was remarkable.

Woody Allen is a mere ten years older than Mia. He may not quite qualify as a daddy-surrogate by virtue of his age, but he certainly would by virtue of his job. After all, directors are the powerful, controlling, paternal center of an actress's universe. So what he lacks in traditional good looks he makes up for in creative *puissance.* His aura. His artistic vision. His gift at articulating, in comic form, the concerns of an entire generation. And his ability to organize and harmonize the various elements of the filmmaking process.

By dint of his fame and money, Woody was in control off-screen as well. It helped, too, that Mia's own father had been a director. Think how many terrific-looking movie stars, women of beauty and fame, have succumbed to the charms of filmmakers, men with ordinary appearances but extraordinary visions. Think

of Monica Vitti to Antonioni. Fanny Ardant to Truffaut. Ingrid
Bergman (and before her, Anna Magnani) to Roberto Rossellini;
Ingrid's daughter, Isabella, first to Martin Scorsese (they were
wed for four years), and then to David Lynch. Liza Minnelli also
fell for Scorsese when they were shooting *New York, New York*.
Jeanne Moreau married director William Friedkin. Steven
Spielberg teamed up with his *Indiana Jones and the Temple of
Doom* costar Kate Capshaw. The list goes on and on. Power, as
Henry Kissinger noted, "is the ultimate aphrodisiac."

As actress and director, Mia and Woody had much in common.
Yet, their work and their celebrity aside, Woody was as different
from Mia as rugelah from communion wafers. Born Allen Stew-
art Konigsberg in the Bronx on December 1, 1935, he grew up
in a lower-middle-class Jewish family in Brooklyn—quite a dis-
tance, in every sense possible, from the luxuries of Beverly Hills.
Both his parents, Nettie Cherry, a bookkeeper, and Martin
Konigsberg, who worked in the butter-and-eggs business and
later as a mail-order jeweler, bartender, cabbie, and waiter,
among other things, were born on New York City's Lower East
Side to immigrant parents—hers from Vienna, his from Russia.
Yiddish was their first language. During Woody's childhood, the
Konigsbergs moved often, and Woody and his younger sister
Letty frequently had to share small, cramped quarters in a variety
of Brooklyn neighborhoods with one set of cousins or another.

It was, for Woody, a world very much like the one he depicted
in *Radio Days*, inhabited by boisterous relatives and parents who
constantly squabbled. Alcohol wasn't an issue as it had been in
Mia's family, and neither parent ever cheated on the other. Still,
as Mia testified in court during their 1993 custody hearing, "He
was slapped a lot—primarily by his mother." Although discreet
about whatever abuse might have been heaped on him, Woody
has recalled about his parents, "Every little thing escalated into
a fight." Today, as a consequence, Woody rarely ever raises his
voice. In that sense, he and Mia are very much alike. Both are
passive and nonconfrontational.

Yet where Mia received a strict parochial school education by
Marymount nuns, Woody took advantage, in more ways than
one, of Brooklyn's public schools, choosing for himself a more

casual approach to learning. Easily bored at school and with a built-in aversion to its rules, he often scrapped homework and played hooky, taking the subway into Manhattan to partake of its wonderland of delights. Number one among them was the movies. While the Farrows were rubbing shoulders with Hollywood royalty on a day-to-day basis, Woody was spending hours in movie theaters, mesmerized by their overpowering screen images. He saw everything from *Pinocchio* to *Double Indemnity*. Afterward, with his cousin Rita Wishnick, whose family for a time lived with his, he would pore over the screen gods and goddesses featured in popular fan magazines of the day.

As for *real* girls, well, he was noticing them even back then. "I was aware of women and their potential in the earliest stages of my life," he once told critic Gene Siskel. "I don't remember having a latency period. I liked girls from kindergarten and chased them all through school."

For the most part, though, Woody was a loner, and since his parents were too busy making a living to keep their eyes on him, he was often left alone. Like many boys, he slipped into Giant games at the Polo Grounds. But he also taught himself magic (like Johnny Carson, the mark of a loner), working in his room for endless hours to perfect his tricks. And he studied the saxophone, the ukulele, and the clarinet, eventually becoming a passionate jazz buff.

Early on he discovered his gift for the one-liner. It developed in part from the years he sat in darkened movie theaters, watching comedies, and in part from seeing vaudeville comics perform (in some theaters back then, movies were shown on a double bill with live performances). At the age of sixteen, the then-junior at Midwood High School sent off some gags to famed gossip columnist Walter Winchell, carefully choosing a nom de plume so that his classmates wouldn't recognize him: Woody Allen. Winchell published them. By 1954, when he flunked out of New York University (his major was motion picture production), Allen had already established himself as a one-liner wunderkind, writing jokes for a Manhattan publicity agent. Within four years he was collaborating with some of the most brilliant comic minds in the business—Danny Simon (Neil's brother),

Mel Brooks, Larry Gelbart, and Sid Caesar—on specials like *Sid Caesar Invites You.* And by the end of the decade he was contemplating the possibility of his own stand-up career.

Woody has spoken disparagingly of his gift for comedy. "I think being funny is not anyone's first choice," he has said. "It's that life has gone sour for them in some way when they were a kid. And it may be that it didn't really go sour, but you think it did. But being funny is always a second choice." And first choice? Well, said Woody, he once yearned "to be reincarnated as Warren Beatty's fingertips."

It's striking that both Mia and Woody enjoyed early and startling success, and both entered into youthful, absurdly inappropriate marriages for themselves. In 1956, Woody, merely twenty, and by his own admission relatively inexperienced in matters of the opposite sex, wed Harlene Rosen, a Brooklyn-born seventeen-year-old who went on to study philosophy at Hunter College. As his career took flight, the pair grew apart. By 1961, they had separated, and in 1962 divorced. Soon he was head over heels in love with kooky actress-comedienne Louise Lasser. In 1966, the year he costarred with her in his second feature, *Bananas,* the couple married. It would last three years, but they would remain dear friends long after their union dissolved. In 1969 Woody would became involved with Diane Keaton, like Lasser a dazzlingly dizzy personality whom he met when they costarred on Broadway in his comedy, *Play It Again, Sam,* and another woman who would remain a loyal ally.

By the time Mia and Woody met in 1979, he was at the height of his creative powers, having already established himself as a major filmmaker. He had made a series of hilarious, sketchlike screen comedies (*Take the Money and Run, Bananas, Sleeper,* and *Love and Death*), and had then, in the mid-seventies, taken a giant creative leap, revealing himself as an astute observer of middle-class values and manners. *Annie Hall* (1977), his most popular movie to date, won the Academy Award as Best Picture, and Woody himself received Oscars as Best Director and Best Screenwriter (with Marshall Brickman). It was followed by *Interiors,* his first noncomedy, which was greeted coldly, and then

Manhattan, another stellar effort. At forty-four Woody Allen could now afford to direct his attentions to a neglected area of his life: a family.

And Mia, whom he took out for the first time in April 1980—"the day after Jean-Paul Sartre died," he would one day tell the court—came along with one ready-made. In a sense, it was a fair swap. Mia provided a rich home life for Woody. He offered her a work life of such unusual duration and breathtaking range that many a hot Hollywood star would have eagerly traded her multimillion-dollar salary and box-office status for such a chance. And it was one that Mia appreciated. Earlier in her career she had earned her share of savage reviews (*A Dandy in Aspic, The Great Gatsby*). Now, in Woody's hands, she emerged a heroine of extraordinary range and delicacy. With equal ease and enthusiasm, she could play the betrayed Catholic wife in *Alice,* the brassy babe Tina Vitale in *Broadway Danny Rose;* the yearning waitress Cecilia in *The Purple Rose of Cairo,* or the dissatisfied but dutiful wife Judy in *Husbands and Wives.* It was, Mia said, "the most ideal thing that could happen to an actress."

But there were tradeoffs: Woody refused to live with her. And Woody refused to marry her. Most of her life, Mia had been used to having her way with men, but now, for the sake of keeping the relationship alive, she agreed to almost all the unconventional conditions Woody imposed. "Yes, I always wanted to marry him," she told me in the fall of 1993. "But he said it was just a piece of paper. Besides, he wanted his own space because of his work and his writing. And he didn't want to be around the kids all the time. In other ways, however, it was a perfect partnership. We worked together, and I had guaranteed roles every year. The parts were created for me, I didn't have to audition for them. Woody was supportive of me. I had enough money. (A few years before the relationship ended, Woody made seven million dollars on a Japanese TV commercial and deposited one million in Mia's bank account; he then followed it up with another $50,000.) It was always a comfortable situation. I always wanted a more traditional setting, but I loved him so much, I just settled for what he was willing to give me."

Woody, for his part, began exploring his own dormant paternal feelings shortly after Mia adopted two-year-old Moses in 1980. The boy, who had never had a father, and the man who had never been one, tentatively, if unsatisfactorily, tested a relationship of sorts, occasionally playing chess or tossing a baseball, until the adoption of Dylan, the birth of Satchel, and most of all, the Soon-Yi affair, tore it to shreds.

Still, it took a long time for Woody to warm up to the notion of fatherhood. In 1987 he described his family involvement this way to *The New York Times:* "Mia is surrounded by kids and pets. I live by myself across the park. I don't have to be there when the diapers are changed or anything awful happens."

In the next few years, not a great deal changed about his attitude. As the court judgment in June, 1993, stated: "Mr. Allen preferred that Ms. Farrow's children not be a part of their lives together. Until 1985, Mr. Allen had 'virtually a single person's relationship' with Ms. Farrow and viewed her children as an encumbrance. He had no involvement with them and no interest in them."

On July 11, 1985, Mia adopted the newborn Dylan, and Woody slowly, and much to his own surprise, developed a deep attachment to her. Then in 1987 Mia gave birth to Satchel. Though he was Woody's first biological child, Woody remained closer to the little girl while Mia developed a stronger bond with their son. Woody was sufficiently stirred by his newfound fatherhood to confide to his biographer, Eric Lax, "Mia has brought a completely different, meaningful dimension to my life." He would bound across the park to the Farrow household every morning to have breakfast and play with Dylan and Satchel. He would do so with the same intense absorption that he does everything else.

Still, Woody wasn't about to give up the comfortable status quo—the his-and-hers households, the benefits of a big, loving family with few of the obligations, and the free time to do as he pleased. "[Mia] likes to spend tons of time with kids," he told Lax. "I like to spend . . . only a limited time with kids."

In the case of one of Mia's daughters, however, it would soon prove to be too much time. At any rate, more time than was good for anybody concerned.

"The way you treat me, you're lucky I don't stick an ice pick in your damned chest."

Tina in Broadway Danny Rose
on the phone to her lover, Lou

FOUR

Autumn Sonata

"Kristi, I have some very bad news." My mom's voice on the phone carried a gravity I had never heard before. It was early September 1991, and I had barely settled back into my dorm room at Manhattan College, when she broke it to me: John had been critically injured in a car crash. Immediately, I flew to Dublin, filled with guilt and sorrow. By the time I landed, he was dead.

I stayed with John's family for a week. The funeral and wake were oddly jarring for someone as committed to the Catholic Church as I had been. As a child, I would go to Mass every Sunday. In my senior year at high school I was a rebellious teenager who shaved my hair off at the sides, studied acting, and wore only "artsy black," including a beret. Still, I managed to go off on a three-day religious retreat called an Emaus. At Salve Regina University in Newport, Rhode Island, the college I attended during freshman year, I went to Mass almost every day. Then at Manhattan College I would attend noon Mass three times a week as well as on Sundays. But after John's death, I simply gave up on my religion. It upset me too much. During Mass I would cry steadily, so I decided that I never wanted to see the inside of a church again. I did not want to confront God about what I thought He had done. Some people turn toward religion when they suffer a profound loss, some turn away. I turned away.

When I returned home, I was numb with my loss. John had been a rare man, as beautiful on the inside as he had been on the outside, with a wonderful generosity of spirit. When we were in Ireland together in the summer of 1989 and then Christmas of 1990, I could tell the kind of person he was by the gentle way he behaved toward his family—his parents, and also his eight brothers and sisters, whom he treated as if they were his own children. He was gentle with me, too, and also funny in a goofy sort of way. What's more, we shared a love of running and were both highly competitive people who felt burnt out after trying to live up to the expectations and physical demands imposed by our Division I track scholarships. Not only did John coach me, but he was always emotionally supportive. If he couldn't be at my track meets, I would phone him immediately after I ran my races. He was the one with whom I wanted to share both my cranky defeats and exhilarating victories. So much of my identity had been wrapped up with him, and now with his death, it had been ripped away.

At the suggestion of a psychologist whom I was seeing for grief counseling, I continued with school, taking two classes a week, both of them leading to a physical therapy major. It was his idea, too, that I begin a daily journal, which I continued throughout my employment with Mia. Still, during that period, there were long stretches of time when I couldn't bear to see anyone. Sometimes, when I was home, I would—with Mia's permission—go over to her house while she was in the city and just straighten up after her family, doing wash, putting toys away, whatever needed to be done. It was healthy activity for me because when I stayed home, I simply went to sleep, exhausted by my own depression.

And Mia was sympathetic and understanding when I told her what had happened. John's death, as terrible as it was, was a bond between us. Mia is very nurturing, and she said that she could identify with what I was going through because she lost her brother Michael at a very young age (she was thirteen, he was nineteen, when he was killed in a light airplane crash). She confided that her mother never got over his death either. For years Maureen would break into tears whenever she thought about her son.

Occasionally, throughout October and November, Mia would ask me to come over and help her with the kids on a Saturday or Sunday. Sometimes I would show up for an hour, and I would teach Dylan and Satchel gymnastics on the lawn—cartwheels, tumbling—as I had been a gymnast myself before I became a half-miler. It helped me, being with them as they jumped and ran around, laughing joyfully. And Mia herself was always gentle and solicitous. "I know these days seem very difficult," she comforted me, "but a year from now you'll be much stronger, and it won't hurt nearly as much. But you must always have faith." As she did.

In mid-October Mia adopted Sanjay, a Vietnamese boy whom they guessed to be six years old. While I was falling apart, she radiated new happiness and seemed so centered and nurturing. She was also a whirlwind of activity since she and Woody were, at the same time, shooting their prophetic movie, *Husbands and Wives*.

A day or two later I drove over to Frog Hollow. It was one of those perfect, crisp fall days, with golden-red and rust-dusted leaves floating from the trees into the pond, kissed by the autumn sunlight. When I arrived, Sanjay was sitting on the beach, moving the sand around with his little hands, babbling to himself and laughing. He had no use of his legs at all, he was a paraplegic. Satchel and Dylan were standing close by, watching him. Sascha, Mia's oldest son and the twin of Matthew, came walking down the lane to meet me, along with his girlfriend, Carrie Englander, and Mia—it was the first time I met Sascha and Carrie because they were both working at a video store in Manhattan that summer.

But what stands out most about that day is how utterly delighted Mia seemed with Sanjay. In moments we were walking up to the house, where she showed me the wheelchair that she had had custom-built for him. It was bright red and cheery-looking, with a checkerboard-patterned seat cushion. "I'm so thrilled that he's here with us, Kristi," she confided. She was prepared to start building ramps leading from her stone terrace into the kitchen, and from the laundry room steps that led down to the boys' room. Mia reacted instinctively and wholeheartedly to these special considerations. They were part of what made her so pleased to adopt disabled children.

The next time I spoke to her, however, Mia appeared much less chipper. When I asked what was wrong, she told me that the family was having problems with Sanjay. Several doctors had examined and tested him, and although they had previously assumed that his babble had been a Vietnamese dialect, now they claimed that it was no dialect at all, that he had never learned any language skills whatsoever. The new child soon presented a series of thorny problems. An entry from my journal:

October 16, 1991.
Mia is in a dilemma over Sanjay. Doctors have agreed that he is retarded and functioning at the level of an eighteen-month-old. He pulls himself around on his hands. He is driving the kids crazy with his constant screaming and carrying-on. At night he shrieks at the top of his lungs, waking up Satchel repeatedly. Several doctors have looked at Sanjay, but none seem to find the real problem. Mia may have to give him up. God pray she feels no guilt and only strength.

In our next phone conversation a few days later, Mia told me that she was giving Sanjay to a New Mexico family who had actually requested a child exactly like him, one with extensive disabilities. Though she was beset by guilt and anxiety, she felt that he couldn't function in her family. After much thought, and a substantial amount of lobbying by Woody, she had decided that she wasn't equipped to handle a child as severely retarded as he turned out to be; it simply wasn't fair to the other kids. I could tell it was one of the most difficult things Mia ever had to do; she really adored this baby. She still has a photo of him hanging in the children's room.

Even though Sanjay was with Mia for a mere six days, she loved him. Woody later criticized her for taking him and then giving him up. But that, it seems to me, was a cheap shot. It pained Mia to return Sanjay. But when she saw that it was in the best interest of her other children, who are usually extremely resilient and welcoming toward new family members, she did not hesitate to do what was necessary.

The fall of 1991 also marked Soon-Yi's first semester at Drew University. While Mia was preoccupied with traveling to Vietnam to do the paperwork for Sanjay and bring him home, Soon-Yi, according to Woody in his court testimony, was having a difficult time adjusting. "As she described to me," he testified, "her mother at no time would go with her to school, as the mother of other kids did. She went up to school by herself. She called me . . . [and] said that she was 'lonely at school.' That she wanted to change her major. That it was her first time really away from home in any significant way or maybe at all, for all I know. And I would call her. I said, 'Look, you can call me anytime you want. I'll call you if you want. But stay up there. Don't change schools. It's too early.' "

Insisting that Soon-Yi was not getting any support from home, Woody told the court: "I just wanted to mention [this] because . . . so many questions were asked about my parenting, that . . . the college is only one hour from New York, Miss Farrow never, ever, ever went up there at any time."

Gee, Woody, maybe if *you* had gone to college, you'd have a better understanding that kids don't always *want* their parents to visit. My parents never came to visit *me* at Manhattan College unless it was to watch me run in a track meet. And I had college friends who would have *died* if their parents had come up to the campus for a weekend. They figured themselves all grown-up and were desperate for independence. (Not true of Soon-Yi, however. She traveled home virtually every Friday night and returned on Sunday night. So it's not as though Mia didn't see her.)

As the holiday season drew near, I found myself in a cocoon of depression. On the day after Christmas, however, I roused myself enough to drop off presents for the kids. Woody's adoptions of Dylan and Moses had just come through (on December 18), and I figured that everyone would be in a festive mood. That evening at about six I headed over to Mia's house. Woody was there, and so was Andre. And the two men and Mia were sitting in the living room by the fire, drinking wine and reading the reviews of Andre's memoir of life as a Hollywood composer, *No Minor Chords: My Days in Hollywood,* that had just been published. Then Woody slipped down onto the floor and entered into a spirited board game with Dylan. Whereas Andre, Mia had told me, was a jealous type, how did Woody feel about Mia's ex? "He didn't care about Andre either way," Mia told me not along ago. "He never ever asked about him."

I stayed for an hour that evening, admiring their tree with its twinkling lights and playing with the kids. It's odd, I remember thinking during that visit, that her home was so cozy and happy, and her relationships so sophisticated and civil: Mia and her men, past and present, sitting together, laughing and enjoying each other's wit, charm, and talent. How soon things would change.

In fact, as I would soon learn, the previous day, Christmas, had been a trying one for them. On this day, Mia told me, she and Woody got on each other's nerves in the small, thoughtless ways that most couples do from time to time. "Everything looked so lovely," she recalled. "I had set up the tables beautifully, and I had lit candles which were bathing the apartment in a beautiful golden glow. We had a choir singing Christmas music on the stereo, and a variety of Christmas punches was set out in the dining room. The kids and I were all talking about how gorgeous the singing voices were, when Woody went into the kitchen and started putting apple after apple into the juicer. The juicer's motor was so powerful and loud that it drowned out the music, and none of us could hear ourselves talk. Then Woody walked into the room, holding a pitcher of juice in his hand and asking, 'Does anybody want any apple juice?' And we all said no because there were bowls and bowls of fruit punch already sitting on the table. So Woody frowned and went straight to the sink, pouring everything he had just squeezed down the drain. It was a typical thing he would do. Everything was too nice, too beautiful. He just *had* to ruin it."

In court, Woody, too, recalled that 1992 Christmas party. "You're describing the Kennedys and Christmas," he told Eleanor Alter, accusing her and Mia of glorifying the reality. "They were not talking about the Mass and reviewing the carols. This was a consecutive group of kids eating. There was no sense of Christmas dinner about it."

In the middle of January 1992, Mia rang me at my parents' house and said in a strained voice, "Kristi, something terrible has happened. I can't go into it, but we're changing the locks at the house in the country. And we're also changing our phone number. I'll leave a set of keys for you." I said okay, and although I was curious, I didn't really probe further. Mia had set her boundaries. She was not willing to confide what that "terrible" thing was that had happened. Later, I would realize that this was a pattern with them. When Woody and Mia fought and broke up, she would run to the locksmith to get the locks changed, and she would also get a new phone number. Then she would weaken and call him—or he would somehow locate her new number and call her. A reconciliation would occur, and with renewed trust she would give him the new number and keys. Until the next time.

At moments like this I couldn't help thinking that Mia's behavior was crazy and certainly not the way *I* would conduct my own love life. On the other hand, I was just twenty-three and had had only one important relationship. How could I know how I might act or feel at the end of a thirteen-year love affair? So I always gave Mia the benefit of the doubt and all the sympathy that I could muster.

Shortly after her trembling phone call, Mia adopted Isaiah, a black crack baby. And a week later, Tam, eleven, a blind girl whom Mia and Woody first saw standing beside Sanjay in photos taken at their Vietnamese orphanage, arrived, following a year of frustrating bureaucratic red tape. Mia thought briefly about canceling Tam's adoption, but then decided that she simply couldn't in good conscience do that to this little girl's future. Besides, she felt, it would make her happy too. She immediately cut Soon-Yi's face out of a photo that hung, framed on the wall, replacing it with Tam's. Nobody noticed this seemingly bizarre act. Two days later Mia guiltily removed the picture.

With two new children in her household who were extremely demanding, Mia often asked me to help her on weekends. She seemed preoccupied. Occasionally I would walk in on her in the kitchen and see her crying. I figured that maybe she and Woody were having a hard time or thinking about breaking up. But she never mentioned anything specific to me. She never told me that Woody was cheating on her with her own daughter, and that is why she had removed the girl's image from the family photo. Not then.

That winter Mia had her hands full with the new arrivals. The timing of the adoptions seemed horrible, I thought. Here she was, expanding her family at the moment when everything that props her up personally and professionally was starting to crumble. Yet the paperwork for Tam's adoption had begun a year earlier. Isaiah was somewhat of a surprise, although she had been talking about adopting a baby (as opposed to a child) for some months. His adoption may also have come out of an emotional void; she had just lost Soon-Yi and Woody, and perhaps was looking for a new outlet for her love. Whatever her motives, I admire her grit and her capacity for caring.

That Valentine's Day proved memorable in an Addams Family sort of way. Although I didn't know exactly what transpired at the time, Mia made quite an effort to exchange valentines with Woody. He sent her a heart-shaped box filled with chocolates and a pin cushion. She sent him a valentine of another sort altogether: In a box was a family photo pasted on a big red heart. Real skewers pierced the hearts of the children in the photo, and a real knife cut through Mia's own heart. In addition, Mia had crossed out the words *love and joy* imprinted on the Valentine, and substituted *pain* instead.

When Woody received her handiwork, he later claimed, he was "stunned" and "absolutely terrified," so much so that he took it home and "put it in his Tiffany box for preservation."

In court in March 1993, Dr. Susan Coates, Satchel's psychiatrist, testified that she feared for Woody's safety after he received this gift. Mia told me: "It was not a threat. On that day of hearts, I wanted to show him what he had done to us. How do I show him this? So many wounded hearts. This was my lover. We had

exchanged valentines for twelve years, and he didn't care about
the pain he had caused. I wanted to depict the degree of pain
he had inflicted on us all. He seemed to have no concept. The
morality of the situation seemed to have totally eluded him."

Yet ironically, Mia would be roasted almost as thoroughly by
the press for having sent this valentine as Woody would be for
having slept with her daughter Soon-Yi. So on Thanksgiving 1993
I brought up the subject of the skewered heart once again. "That
valentine was meant for Woody Allen only," she responded with
passion. "It surprises me that these people would criticize. They
didn't see the pictures of my daughter. They didn't see her
spread-eagle in Polaroid photographs—photographs taken by
their lover. I thought the valentine I made was extremely appropriate. I mean, what are you supposed to do? Sit down and sip
tea and say, 'Dear, what you did was wrong'? He broke my heart.
None of us will ever be the same."

During this period, as I later learned, Mia also tore up and
incinerated scores of photographs of both Woody and Soon-Yi.
However, she was always discreet in my presence. I had only an
inkling, until she told me about Soon-Yi months later, of what
was going on.

Still, I knew that Mia was overworked. And I would come by
when I could. I was finishing up the classes I had dropped after
John died, and sometimes on school nights I'd leave my dorm
in the Bronx and take the #1 train down to her Central Park
West apartment. This vast eight-room place, with its spectacular
view of Central Park and the Manhattan skyline, may once, when
it was owned and inhabited by her mother, have been the height
of elegance, but Mia had transformed it into a big family-style
home. It was furnished in a relaxed manner, with faded floral
sofas and bookcases stuffed with books that clearly looked like
they had been read and appreciated. Except for one photo of
Frank Sinatra, and another of her three oldest sons when they
were still boys, posing with her in tuxedos, there were no clues
that this was the home of a movie star. No expensive works of
art. No priceless crystal or Aubusson rugs. No home gym or
walk-in room-size closets. Instead, there were worn Persian car-
pets, closets crammed with kids' games and arts-and-crafts mate-

rials, and walls covered in tiny cinnamon-colored Victorian-patterned paper. Hanging from the walls were the children's latest drawings and, more often, clusters of frames containing family photos.

The latest addition to the Farrow household, Tam, then eleven, had spent the last three years of her life in a Vietnamese orphanage. At eight, she had come down with the measles and lost her sight, causing her parents to regard her as a liability and abandon her. In her orphanage, Tam had been taught Vietnamese braille, but she knew no English.

To prepare for her arrival, Mia and I had learned basic Vietnamese words like water, which is *nuk*, and bathroom, which is *deedoi*. Our repertoire also included hello or *hoho*, thank you, or *hohodoe-chay*, and *kwan*, which is pants. We also had to adapt the house, making it accessible for a blind child. To do this, we put identifying stickers on the microwave so that she could make her own food, and stickers on the shampoo and conditioner bottles to tell them apart. I put a sticker on her toothbrush as well, although she had never used a toothbrush before in her life.

What we couldn't prepare for, or even expect, were Tam's tantrums. She must have been brutalized in the past, because when she first arrived at Mia's, she was deeply frightened and would kick and scream at every little thing. I remember when she came down with an ear infection; every time we tried to put medication in her ears, she'd throw a violent fit. So Mia and I would literally force her down to the ground, and I would hold her head while Mia released the drops into her ears. It was like combat for us.

At the beginning Tam was a high-maintenance child. When Mia first brought her home from the airport, her head was full of lice. The first thing Mia did was get on her hands and knees and scrub the little girl's hair and scalp over the tub three times, trying to detach the vermin and their eggs. Tam didn't acknowledge her at all during those first few days. The child would sit at the kitchen table, her head on her hands, making moaning noises for, literally, hours. After a while Tam would allow Mia to take her in her lap, and she would lie there passively while

Mia stroked her head and said over and over in a soothing voice, "Mommy. Mommy. I'm your mommy now."

Satchel and Dylan greeted Tam with enormous curiosity. They would ask question after question about her. Satchel would say, "Why is she blind?"

And Mia would reply, "Because she got sick with the measles, and she wasn't immunized, and so she lost her sight."

Dylan would stroke Tam very gently and say, "Dylan. Dylan." Then the kids would put toys in her hands, sometimes a glob of Play-Doh or Legos, so that she could feel them. They displayed great patience with and sympathy for her, even though she would often fling a toy they handed her to the floor and descend into one of her hellish tantrums.

I had a big square antique ring that my parents had bought me, and for the first three months I'd put her hand on the ring before I'd pick her up. I wanted to give her a tactile as well as an auditory cue as to who was here to take care of her. She would usually feel the ring and push it away because I don't think she liked the way it felt. But she understood the concept that that was the way I was identifying myself. And after about three months she knew my name. Instead of "Kristi," I was "Kiss." And now, of course, I'm "Chicken," because when Tam first knew me, I was changing my vegetarian diet, and chicken was practically the only thing I would eat.

As for Tam, she immediately became addicted to hot dogs. She wanted them morning, noon, and night. Fletcher, eighteen at the time and the wittiest of Mia and Andre Previn's three sons, would tease her about this in the same Pidgin English Tam herself used. "Tam fat girl," he would say.

"I not fat," she would reply, then call Mia. "Mommy!"

At other times Tam would listen, fascinated, to the computerized voice on the telephone that says, "Please hang up and try your call again." All the kids would needle her on this: "Tam loves man on phone," Fletcher would say.

"Tam marry man on phone. Maybe baby 'ninety-three," Daisy would join in.

Tam, for her part, expressed curiosity about my life. One day she told me: "Mommy say Kristi very pretty. Mommy say boy die, and Kristi cry all day."

At the same time, Mia was weaning Isaiah from his crack addiction. In physical distress, the baby would cry every night all night. Not just cry, holler at the top of his poor little lungs. He would awaken three or four times for a bottle. It was exhausting. Mia took care of him four nights a week; Lark, who is such a maternal young woman, would take him one night, and I would stop by and stay over one or two nights. Sometimes I'd hold him and walk back and forth outside the nursery, gazing out the window at the breathtaking nighttime city skyline with its magical lights and hoping that the motion of my movement would soothe him.

While Isaiah cried, the room's other inhabitants, Satchel, Dylan, and Tam, miraculously slept in their turquoise wood custom-made Goldilocks beds. Sometimes a few sentences of Mia's phone conversations with Woody would drift into the dark room. "You're so selfish," she would say to him, "it's always you first. I can't believe you've done this." Of course, I wondered, *Done what?* But I never had the courage to ask, nor was I told. Yet.

The traumas of that winter prompted Mia, a lapsed Catholic, to renew her relationship with her faith by having her children baptized. It was to be a joint ceremony with Casey Pascal's three kids. "Although we both felt that our children could grow up and learn good solid values *without* religion," says Casey, "we had talked about having a mass baptism for years. We thought we would do it at a little church in the country, but it never happened. Then, when Mia discovered the photos of Soon-Yi, she said to me, 'Something is radically wrong that this could happen. Something is drastically missing from my children's lives. I have to get them on the right road. We need something to hold this family together and give them proper values.' " Baptism, Mia hoped, would be part of that glue.

The Soon-Yi affair, said Mia in court, "underlined for me the importance of maintaining your moral roots and having a spiritual life. And I understand that this would be very important for my children. And I should not be remiss in making sure they have some sort of religious life." Indeed, when Dylan had been adopted, one of the provisions was that she would be raised in a good Catholic household.

So on Wednesday evening, March 11, 1992, the family gathered at the Church of the Blessed Sacrament on Seventy-first Street between Columbus and Amsterdam avenues. All Mia's children, with the exception of Matthew (who was working) were present. Since the older kids had already been baptized, only Soon-Yi, Dylan, Moses, Satchel, Isaiah, and Tam received the sacrament. Soon-Yi came straight from Drew, wearing jeans because for some naive reason she didn't think that everyone else would be dressed up for the solemn occasion. Despite the girl's clothing faux pas, says Casey, "it was all done properly. The children, who wore white shawls over their dresses or blazers, met with the priest before the ceremony. They all looked terrific as they lit candles, walked up to the altar one by one, and had the priest pour water on their heads. It was particularly fun to watch the little ones because they were no longer babies and were trying to look so serious about the ritual."

A variety of godparents and neighbors, including actress Dianne Weist, who is godmother to Isaiah and held him in her arms throughout the ceremony, stood beside the family, carrying lit candles. The occasion was particularly moving, and somewhat tense, reports Casey, "because the immediate family was aware of the Soon-Yi–Woody situation." Woody, she adds, was not present at the ceremony. Nor was he at the celebration Mia held for her family and guests back at her apartment immediately following it. "Considering everything, it was a happy occasion," Casey reports.

What were the baptisms really about? Mia's desperate attempt to reclaim her faith? To suddenly provide a moral center for her children? To recreate a lost family bond? I think Mia really missed church, although it was difficult for her to take all the kids to worship on a regular basis. After all, the baby had to be held; Tam had to be guided with her cane. And then there are the celebrity gawkers who make Mia feel conspicuous and self-conscious.

Religion may have offered a soothing balm from time to time, but Mia was still distraught enough to seek the help of mild antidepressants. These never affected her skills at mothering her disparate brood of kids, all of whom had special interests and needs. Between her tears and mood swings, she had to juggle appointments with child psychiatrists (to help the kids deal with Woody's romance with Soon-Yi), French tutors (for Satchel and Dylan), German tutors (for Fletcher), Vietnamese visitors (Mia wanted Tam to keep up her language skills), social workers doing home studies for the adoption agencies, and music teachers (for Tam, who plays piano).

Whatever secret dramas were being played out that winter, Woody still came by to see Mia and the kids regularly, so I figured that they were trying to work their problems through. I never dreamed, nor would I know until a year and a half later, that throughout the first half of 1992 they were really discussing a permanent custody arrangement. In the short term, they had agreed that Woody could visit the children for an hour every afternoon, and that he could stay in the country for one overnight each week.

Yet I felt that he and Mia didn't want to let go. Indeed, as they chewed over custody details and possibilities, they seemed to be desperately clinging to each other.

"Why do I hear $50,000 worth of psychotherapy dialing 911?"
Woody Allen as he kisses twenty-year-old Juliet Lewis in
Husbands and Wives

FIVE

The Betrayal

"Kristi, I've got something to tell you, brace yourself."
It was on an otherwise-gorgeous day in June, 1992,
that Mia first told me about Woody's affair with
Soon-Yi. She called me into one of the guest rooms, and I immediately began to panic. She sounded so serious, so trapped—as
if she were about to discuss something awful. Was she going to
fire me? "What did I do?" I asked gingerly. And she said, "You
didn't do anything." Then, as I stood there, trying to read her
sad, pale eyes, she told me something that would dramatically
alter our lives. "What I wanted to tell you," she said, "is that
Woody sexually abused one of the kids."

She might as well have said "The Martians have landed." For
a moment, I simply couldn't grasp the implications. Then I began
to focus. And I wondered, Was it Satchel? Dylan? "Who?" I
asked, and she answered, "Soon-Yi." Again I went blurry. I
couldn't help thinking, *I don't get it. Unless it's rape, you don't
sexually abuse a twenty-one-year-old girl. That's a strange choice
of words.*

Later that summer Mia would come to use the word *molest*,
on the advice of a child psychologist. Whether it was molestation
or sexual abuse, I don't know. Clearly, what happened between
Woody and Soon-Yi was sexual intimacy. Sexual intimacy between a young woman and the man who had been her informal

79

stepfather since she was ten years old. The two were having—
what were they having? An affair? A fling? An actual—please,
God, no—relationship?

My mind was racing in those few minutes. How could this
have happened? Soon-Yi had definitely become like a daughter
to Woody. Why, after she had turned thirteen, he would, *specifically at Mia's request,* take long walks with her in order to help
her feel more comfortable around men. Later on, he took her
with him to Knicks games—and secretly, we later found out, to
movies as well. Sometimes, during her last year at Marymount
High School on Eighty-fifth Street and Fifth Avenue, Woody
would come over to the apartment and pop into the girls' room
in the evenings to inquire (in what we thought was a paternal
way) about her homework. During a difficult and lonely first year
at Drew University in Madison, New Jersey, Soon-Yi—secretly
once again, as it turned out—telephoned Woody on a regular
basis for solace and support whenever she felt fearful and
isolated.

Of course, I have to wonder now, why so secretive about a
few movies? Why so furtive about a couple of phone calls? I'm
sure that, to Mia and the world at large, Soon-Yi would have
seemed the last likely choice for a love match with Woody.
Here's a man who is brilliant, intellectually curious, and quick-
witted. He has chosen a young woman who, quite frankly, is
slow to grasp things (her IQ was tested and is 94). Why, she
acts like a kid and in person looks no older than sixteen.

Yet that wasn't all. Barely had I caught my breath when Mia
dropped her next bombshell. She said, "And furthermore, Woody
has taken explicit pornographic pictures of Soon-Yi. They are
absolutely horrible."

Mia then told me about the day last January 13—a month
before that fateful Valentine's Day—when she discovered the
photos and then the affair itself. She had gone to Woody's apartment to pick up Satchel after Satchel's appointment with his
psychiatrist (I couldn't imagine then why a regular five-year-old
boy was in therapy but felt it was not my place to ask). The
sessions were always held there because that's the way Woody
wanted it. On this particular day, says Mia, Woody was not

around. He was at his office/editing room in the Beekman The-
atre building, so when Mia got off the elevator, she stepped into
the vestibule leading into his penthouse and looked under the
umbrella stand for the key, which he usually left there for her,
the cleaning lady, or his assistant. Then she let herself into the
apartment.

Heading for the blue room, Woody's office, to wait for Satchel,
Mia immediately rang Woody at the Beekman. As she hung up
after their conversation, she just happened to pass by the fireplace, where she spied a stack of colored Polaroids—six photos
thrown on the mantel as carelessly as if they were picture post-
cards. They were in full view of whoever cared to notice, including the maids, who would surely come by to dust later that day:
Soon-Yi, nude, posing in a reclining position on Woody's couch,
her legs spread wide open.

"He left them out on the mantel?" I asked, incredulous, as
Mia nodded.

"Yes. He wanted me to find them."

My eyes welled with tears. I felt sad for her, and personally
horrified. Amazingly enough, the very night before she discovered the photos, Mia said, she had been sitting in her living
room with Fletcher, Woody, and Soon-Yi, and they had all been
chatting animatedly about pulling up their Manhattan roots and
moving to Paris, where they had vacationed in the summer of
1990. Woody spoke about how exciting such a change would be
for all of them, and especially for Soon-Yi, who, he pointed out,
could attend art school there. Yet less than twenty-four hours
later, what had seemed like a prospect, a possibility, would seem
to me a mere pipe dream that had gone up in smoke.

I didn't understand how Woody could have so little regard for
Soon-Yi, or for Mia, for that matter, to have left those photos
out on the mantel. Mia says bitterly: "He wouldn't care if the
maids saw them because they wouldn't dare say anything. Besides, Woody never cared what *anybody* thought about him, especially somebody whom he considered as low as a maid. I
believe that he subconsciously left those photos out for me. He
wanted to destroy me. Not only did he want me to know that

they were having an affair, he wanted me to see it for myself in an ugly, obscene, disgusting way."

Grabbing the photos, Mia phoned Woody immediately in a scattershot effort to confront him. "I found the pictures," she said, her voice colored with hurt and anger. "Get away from us."

Then she reached Soon-Yi at home, crying, "What have you done? I found the pictures." Soon-Yi replied, "What pictures?" and hung up on her mother. With supreme effort Mia composed herself, waited for Satchel, and hurried home, taking the photographs with her.

On entering her apartment, Mia recollected: "I left Satchel in the hallway. I saw the baby-sitter in the next room. I saw Sascha coming toward me, and I asked him to call his father, Andre Previn, quickly. I blurted out that Woody had been sleeping with Soon-Yi. I didn't know what to do."

Passing Soon-Yi's room on the way to her own, Mia pushed open the half-closed door and abruptly walked in, to find the girl sitting at her desk, crying. Mia strode over to her, asking sharply, "What have you done?" Then she shoved the photos under her daughter's nose. Soon-Yi glanced at them for a split second, then stubbornly turned her head away, refusing to acknowledge them—or Mia. This infuriated Mia even more. "I just took her head and made her look at them," she said. "I just pushed the chair over—it was between us—and went into my room to wait for [Andre's] phone call." Moments later she spied Woody as he arrived and headed down the hallway to see her. Closing her door, she screamed, "Get out of our house, and get away from us." But Woody pushed his way into her room. There, behind closed doors, they screamed, whispered, accused, cried, lied, vowed, and tortured each other for hours.

That night, when then-seventeen-year-old Daisy, Mia's third-oldest daughter, arrived home, she entered through the back door as usual. What was definitely *not* usual is that Moses, thirteen at the time, met her there, a grim look on his face. "Don't go in," he cautioned, his voice not more than a whisper. Then he told her about the Polaroids and added that Woody had been sleeping with Soon-Yi. In response, Daisy started laughing. "I thought it was a joke," she says. Peering into the kitchen, she saw Mavis Smith, the housekeeper, sitting hunched over the huge wooden family dining table. A heavyset Jamaican woman, Mavis, who was about fifty, had worked for Mia for years, and for Mia's mother before that. At that moment her body language spelled trouble, and her expressive face wore a look of extreme gravity. Daisy now knew there was nothing funny about her brother's words.

The house was curiously quiet. Soon-Yi was up in the girls' loft, sobs racking her thin, childlike frame. Woody was in Mia's bedroom with her. For hours the two remained behind closed doors while a crazy, intense drama played itself out.

Surely, confronting Woody had been even tougher for Mia than talking to Soon-Yi. After all, he was the adult; he knew better. In the privacy of Mia's room, he immediately confessed, "I am in love with Soon-Yi, I want to marry her." Mia told me that she thought he was saying this to make his behavior seem more legitimate and less swinish. Whatever the reason, she replied, "Fine. Take her. Leave, go."

Then Woody reversed himself. "He told me 'No, no, no, I don't want to be with her, I want to be with you,'" said Mia. "'I'm in love with you. Soon-Yi was a terrible mistake. Please, Mia, let's use this incident to find a deeper relationship between us. I want to be with you. I want to marry you. Let's work it out.'"

Mia had always wanted to marry Woody. Now was her chance, and in a moment of confusion and weakness she agreed. "Okay," she told him, "stop seeing Soon-Yi, and let's get married. Just promise me you'll never sleep with my daughter again."

Woody gave her his word, muttering that Soon-Yi was an aberration, a tepid little affair, that she didn't mean anything to him and would have lasted only a few weeks more at any rate. He told Mia that the affair had been going on, she said, "for several months" (although he later refuted this, saying that it had begun only two weeks earlier), and when Mia inquired whether her daughter might be pregnant, Woody said no, he was sure that he never came inside her.

In the middle of the conversation Sascha let his mother know that Andre had returned her call and was on the phone. Now Woody really flipped out. He began rolling around on the floor, holding his stomach as though he had a gigantic bellyache, and begging her not to tell Previn. Andre, for his part, wanted to know what that whining noise in the background was. But Mia wasn't concerned with Woody's tantrum. She got right to the point. "I said that Woody was screwing Soon-Yi," Mia testified in court. "That's exactly what I said, and [then I asked] what shall I do?" Luckily Andre brought Mia back to reality. As she explained, "He said, 'Get him out of the apartment.' "

Incomprehensibly, Woody refused to leave. "I said, 'Get out!' a million times," Mia told the court. "I said, 'Just leave us alone.' He was saying, 'Let's use this as a springboard to a new relationship,' and I didn't know what that meant." Mia went to run her bath, and while she did, Woody, instead of leaving, visited Soon-Yi in her room. The pair talked for about twenty minutes behind closed doors. Then Woody returned to Mia, repeating that Soon-Yi had been an aberration. When Mia cried to him, "What have you done to Soon-Yi?" she claimed that he replied without flinching, "I think I gave Soon-Yi a little confidence. I think this is good for Soon-Yi."

Mia was distraught. "But what about Soon-Yi and me?" she flung back at him. "What about her principles? To lead her into a betrayal of her siblings, of her mother, of her principles into a situation of this magnitude, how can you suppose that this would be good for this child?"

Woody, she claimed, responded, "She's not a child, she's a young woman." When he refused to leave her room, she simply stormed into the bathroom to take her bath. And finally Woody left the apartment.

But not for long. Daisy recalled to me that when dinner was served, not only did all the children, as usual, come in and sit down to eat, so did Woody. He had returned to the apartment, let himself inside, and as if nothing had happened joined them at the table. And one by one, the older kids, who all knew by now what was going on, took their plates and left the room. They wanted him to know how they felt.

Woody still refused to take the hint. Finally, Mia called him into the hall. "You can't just come in here and sit down like nothing happened. Get out of here," she said. "Then he said,

'Come into the living room.' And we went into the living room. I started crying again. There was another hour or two of talking, and I was begging him to leave the whole time, and finally he left."

For a moment I couldn't help wondering why Mia had confided Woody and Soon-Yi's betrayal to the older children so quickly. Why hadn't she had the sense to keep it to herself until she had digested it, regained control of her emotions, and figured out the best way to handle it? But I realize that she was consumed by her own rage and at that moment, on January 13, 1992, she was too emotional to keep a cool, controlled head. In fact, she did not mention anything about the situation to either Dylan or Satchel until April, when Dylan finally revealed to her therapist that she had, in January, overheard Soon-Yi threatening to kill herself. "Then," says Mia, "I wrote down, word for word, what Nancy Schultz wanted me to say to her." And, per the shrink's instructions, she told the child, "Daddy is playing 'girlfriend' with Soon-Yi." Satchel did not find out about the affair until later when Dylan, in fact, told him.

The whole story was shattering to me. Woody rolling around on the floor, pleading with Mia not to tell her ex-husband about his behavior? The two of them making wedding plans? Woody insisting that his affair with Soon-Yi plumped up her confidence? Nothing made sense. Whom *did* Woody love? And how could Mia let him off the hook so easily? Did this scene not resemble a romance novel gone mad? Or a gloomy Ingmar Bergman movie as parodied by *Saturday Night Live*? During their custody battle more than a year later, Woody, in recollecting that afternoon, would dismiss his own words. He would say that he had simply been humoring Mia, that he hadn't meant a word he said, that he did not love her at all.

Mia, for all her willingness to let Woody dictate the terms of their unspoken contract with each other, remained unimpressed with his testimony. "That's not true," she told me with simple conviction. "I know he loved me."

It's hard to imagine that in the deepest recesses of his heart, Woody, too, doesn't have regrets. He forfeited a big, boisterous,

lively family, and a mature and accomplished woman who collab-
orated both on his life and his work, for the love of a quiet,
unformed schoolgirl. I couldn't believe it when I read what he
said in *Time* magazine that August: "The heart wants what it
wants. There's no logic to those things. You meet someone and
you fall in love and that's that." How could a mature man say
this about *that* particular situation?

I also couldn't help thinking that so many of the Woody Allen
movies I loved—*Manhattan, Hannah and Her Sisters,* and *Husband and Wives*—seemed like a bizarre blueprint for his future.
How strange that long before Woody acted on his obsession with
Soon-Yi, his pictures spoke about older men and *their* obsessions
with young girls. I remember a group of friends at college rent-
ing his 1977 movie, *Manhattan,* where Woody as Ike, a cynical
forty-two-year-old New York television writer, has an affair with
Tracy, a seventeen-year-old high-school girl (Mariel Hemingway). When Ike muttered, "She's got homework. I'm dating
a girl who's got homework," we all cheered.

But by the time I saw *Husbands and Wives* in September,
1992, I was shocked. Here Woody drew on the breakdown of his
own relationship with Mia for material. Worse, he seemed to
have translated his fascination for Soon-Yi to the screen. Yet as
a professor in a stifling marriage, Woody onscreen was able to
rebuff his eager young student (Juliet Lewis). In real life he did
not travel the moral high road.

Since the Woody–Soon-Yi affair, I've read interviews where
Woody insists that such similarities are rubbish. "Movies are fic-
tion," he told *Time.* "The plots of my movies don't have any
relationship to my life."

He always was a comedian.

Nobody except Daisy Previn laughed about Soon-Yi, however.
Having an affair with a young woman barely out of her teens
who happens to be your lover's daughter is no laughing matter.

From the beginning, Soon-Yi had been a demanding child.
First of all, Mia had to do battle to adopt her, even lobbying in
Washington to help overturn a federal law limiting the number
of foreign adoptions per family (Mia had already filled her quota

with Lark Song and Daisy, two babies from Vietnam). Then, when Soon-Yi arrived, it was with heavy-duty emotional baggage. Her childhood held the kind of twists and turns that made Dickens seem like Mother Goose. In a letter to Nancy Sinatra, her friend and former stepdaughter, Mia wrote the following shortly after the adoption:

> My children are a continuous joy. The latest is Soon-Yi (aged 6, 7, or 8—we're saying 7). She's from Korea—was found abandoned in the streets of Seoul—with rickets, malnutrition—even her fingernails had fallen off, she had lice and sores everywhere. Now she speaks English and is learning to read, write, play piano, dance ballet, & ride a horse. She is also learning that people can be believed in and even loved. These are golden times and I am aware of that every single second.

Only months before her transplantation to the world of Manhattan private schools and privileges, Soon-Yi, age six, was running with a pack of wild ragamuffins, stealing to stay alive. Her mother had been a prostitute, Mia was told, who had beaten Soon-Yi savagely before abandoning her. One of her mother's favorite cruelties would be to make Soon-Yi kneel in the doorway while she would swing the door into the little girl's head, banging it severely.

Mia worried that the transition for Soon-Yi had been too shocking, that going from the most sordid type of street life in an Asian culture to a protected, privileged family life in America may have been too much of an upheaval for the little girl. She always mused that had Soon-Yi stayed in Seoul, she would have led a simple life, perhaps working in a shoe factory, perhaps as a prostitute like her mother. But at least she would have been able to understand that life.

Now, Mia felt, her daughter was being abused again—this time by Woody, the man whom Mia had loved and trusted. Could Soon-Yi have concluded that it was okay for her, too, to love and trust him? Or was this a classic Freudian situation—a jealous daughter fighting her glamorous, beautiful mom for the love of a man, and perhaps, more important, for her own sense of self? Or, possibly, an angry and confused daughter misdirecting her fury toward her *biological* mother by lashing out against her adoptive mom? Whatever the girl's motives, Mia maintained that Soon-Yi was too impressionable, too much under Woody's sway to have been able to make a clearheaded decision about whether or not she genuinely wanted a romantic involvement with him.

Muddying the girl's judgment even further was the fact of her intelligence. As Mia's sister Tisa Farrow noted: "She has a double-digit IQ. It's not like she's a drooling idiot, but she's very naive and very immature." Here was a physically and emotionally tattered child from an exotic, war-torn culture who was dropped into the middle of a sophisticated American world. It must have further disoriented her. Still, Soon-Yi was tutored from the fifth grade right through her senior year at Marymount by Dr. Audrey Seiger, a specialist in learning disabilities. In addition, in order to graduate from Marymount, Mia told me, Soon-Yi took a curriculum adapted for slower students.

To her own credit, Soon-Yi herself refuses to be seen as a victim. "I am not a retarded little underage flower who was raped, molested, and spoiled by some evil stepfather—not by a long shot," she told *Newsweek* in August 1992. Still, I couldn't believe her statement; it sounded like something concocted by Woody. "I'm a psychology major at college who fell for a man who happens to be the ex-boyfriend of Mia. I admit it's offbeat, but let's not get hysterical. The tragedy here is that, because of Mia's vindictiveness, the children must suffer. I will always have a feeling of love for her because of the opportunities she gave me, but it's hard to forgive much that followed."

That's a cool one for you. I have had several conversations with Soon-Yi, and frankly she was always so aloof that it was impossible to assess her intelligence. Maybe this was her way of compensating for not being able to comprehend everything, her way of protecting herself.

In every family some children are outgoing and mix well; others are private and solitary. In the Farrow clan Soon-Yi was always the outsider, distant from the others, shy, and scared. One peculiarity. She was markedly afraid of adult men, and as

a child would hiss and spit at her father, Andre, and others.
Her distrust and fear toward men was one reason Mia originally
encouraged Woody to take Soon-Yi for long walks once she entered her teens.

Soon-Yi's relationship with her brothers and sisters was always
prickly. With Fletcher, the youngest Previn boy, it was downright
hostile. Fletcher is probably the closest to Mia, and in the press
it has been said that she favors him. But that is not the way I
see it. Fletcher is the kind of kid who has always angled to spend
time with his mother. For a while he even asked for play dates
with Woody. He is the rare teenager who truly *likes* being with
adults. Unlike the twins, Matthew and Sasha, he adored visiting
with his father and often spent summers in England and Germany with Andre (he is now at a preparatory school near Hamburg, Germany).

The animosity between Fletcher and Soon-Yi was a predictable
sibling rivalry of sorts. Don't forget, he was three when Soon-Yi
was adopted and had up until that point been the favored youngest. But frail little Soon-Yi, coming from another background
and not speaking the language, absorbed Mia's attention. No
doubt, competition for Mommy helped create tension between
them. It came to a "head" when Soon-Yi was nine and Fletcher
six. She showed Fletcher what she thought of him by pushing
his head into the toilet bowl and actually trying to drown him.
(In her court testimony, she even acknowledged, "And I *hate*
Fletcher.").

While marginal, Soon-Yi's relationship with the other kids was
somewhat warmer. As she grew up, she was closest with Matthew, who is fairly reserved himself; and Daisy told me that in
the year or so before Soon-Yi left the house to pursue her romance with Woody, Daisy, too, became much closer with her.
But it was a long time coming, this sisterhood. For the first
eleven years Soon-Yi, who had always shared a room with Lark
and Daisy, maintained clear emotional and physical boundaries.
While Lark and Daisy slept in a loft that held three beds, Soon-
Yi—coming into the family when the other girls were older and
had already developed a rapport—chose not to join them, but
to sleep alone in the guest bed under the loft. However, Soon-

Yi genuinely loved the little ones whom she had helped nurture, and she phoned them throughout the bitter summer of 1992, even after choosing to estrange herself from her mother.

If truth be told, for the past few years Soon-Yi had been most preoccupied *not* with her siblings but with Woody himself. Mia's court testimony during the custody proceedings suggests a relationship between Soon-Yi and Woody, or at least a keen mutual awareness, long before the end of December when, they both claim, the affair began:

ALTER: (showing Mia a photo of Soon-Yi and Woody at a 1990 Knicks' game at Madison Square Garden): *Miss Farrow, when did you first see this photograph?*

MIA: I think in August of 1992.

Q. *And when did you become aware that Mr. Allen had taken Miss Previn to a basketball game in January of 1990?*

A. Oh, the day before he was going to—I was aware that he was taking her.

Q. *And can you describe what she's wearing?*

A. She's wearing a skirt. She's got black leggings on or tights. She's got a long-sleeve sweater. She's got her hair back in a ponytail. Seems to have no makeup on. She is looking at Mr. Allen. She's holding his hand. (After objections from Abramowitz about whether or not they are holding hands)

Q. *Miss Farrow, now, did you know that Miss Previn had been to Mr. Allen's apartment during the week alone at any time in 1990?*

A. I didn't know that.

Q. *And did she ever tell you that she was visiting Mr. Allen at his apartment—*

A. No, she did not.

Q. *—during her junior year at Marymount?*

A. No, she did not.

Q. *Did she ever tell you that she was going to his apartment in 1991?*

A. No, she did not.

Q. *Did Mr. Allen ever tell you that Miss Previn had been at his apartment alone, not with Dylan or Satchel, in 1990?*

A. No. He didn't tell me.

Q. *Did he tell you—did Mr. Allen ever tell you she had been there during 1991?*

A. No.

Q. *Have you subsequently learned that Miss Previn was at Mr. Allen's apartment alone during those periods?*

A. Yes, I have.

Q. *And when did you learn that?*

A. I learned in the deposition of his doorman and his building manager, I think, this May that she had in fact visited him during the week alone in 1990 and 1991.

(After objections from Mr. Abramowitz)

Q. *Now, did you know that Miss Previn had been at Mr. Allen's apartment during spring break of 1990?*

A. No, I didn't.

Q. *And when did you first learn that?*

A. From the deposition of his housekeeper, Colette . . .

Q. *And during the spring break and summer of 1990, was Soon Yi employed?*

A. Yes. She was.

Q. *And can you tell us where?*

A. In the summer of 1990 she first worked in Bergdorf Goodman and then for Mr. Allen—with Mr. Allen in *Scenes from a Mall,* a movie that he was doing in Queens.

Q. *And did Soon-Yi tell you about a friend that she had made while she was making* Scenes from a Mall?

A. Yes, she did.

Q. *And what did she tell you?*

A. She said that she had this friend who was about thirty years old, who was an extra in the movie, as she had been, and she said she wanted to meet with this friend on occasion.

Q. *And did there come a time when you asked to meet this friend?*

A. Yes.

Q. *Did she tell you what the friend's name was?*

A. She didn't tell me. She told the other kids.

Q. *And what occurred to make you ask to meet that friend?*

A. Soon-Yi would leave the house at 9:30 in the morning some Saturdays, some Sundays all dressed up as if it was nighttime, tight miniskirt, a lot of makeup at 9:30 in the morning, and say she was going to meet this friend at Bloomingdale's because the friend worked [there]. And I asked her, "Well, what do you do when your friend is working, just stand there all dressed up?" I didn't understand, and I asked if I could meet this thirty-year-old woman. I didn't feel comfortable. I found it an incomprehensible situation.

Q. *How often did Soon-Yi tell you that she was meeting this friend on Saturday and Sunday and be all dressed up?*

A. Many times. It seemed for a while there every single weekend. I mean, a dozen, more than a dozen.

Q. *Did you ever meet the friend?*

A. No.

Q. *Now in the fall of 1990, Soon-Yi was in her senior year at Marymount?*

A. Yes.

Q. *And that's after the summer that she worked at Bergdorf?*

A. Yes.

Q. *And she was meeting her friend on Saturday and Sunday. Is that correct?*

A. Yes.

Q. *And do you recall a time when you overheard your other children teasing Soon-Yi?*

A. Yes. Around the fall or summer of 1990 through 1991.

Q. *What did you overhear?*

A. That they were teasing her about her clothes, about her makeup, about her crush on Mr. Allen. Lark told her that she was going to get raped going around dressed like that at 9:30 in the morning. One of them said she looked like a slut. They would tease her a lot about—that she looked at Mr. Allen the way she looked at him, the way she followed him, the way she was always next to him whenever he was in the apartment. She got a lot of teasing for that, especially from Jesse and Lark and Daisy.

Q. *And then did there come a time when Daisy and Lark told you of a conversation in their room—something that Mr. Allen said in their room—*

A. Yes. They said that Mr. Allen said to Soon-Yi that bare legs were sexy.

Q. *And after that statement was made, did you notice any change in Soon-Yi's dress?*

A. Yes. Soon-Yi never wore leggings or tights or anything. I used to say this in winter, when she did go out in the mornings, "It is freezing, you know, why don't you wear tights? Why don't you wear trousers or something?" She would always wear bare legs. I didn't know about that statement until 1992, though, but it is absolutely true that she wore bare legs for her whole senior year.

In fact, for the longest time, the girl's transformation was evident to everyone—except Mia. Whereas once Soon-Yi had been a drab little mouse who wore Victorian granny dresses, she began to covet skimpy, tight-fitting outfits. "And it was not only her clothes, but her manner," Casey told me. "She became so much more confident toward the end of high school. More secretive, with a secret smile on her face. Something was going on. Instead of being shy, she was a whole other presence."

Soon-Yi's seductive new way of dressing, her self-assurance, and her sudden fascination with basketball eventually tipped even Mia off. She testified in court:

Q. *Now, in the spring of 1991 Soon-Yi was in her senior year at Marymount, correct?*

A. Yes.

Q. *Now, during that period did you have occasion to observe Mr. Allen in her room?*

A. Yes.

Q. *And can you tell us with what frequency?*

A. Daily.

Q. *And do you know what they were doing or talking about generally?*

A. I saw her showing him slides of her paintings, her drawings—showing him her drawings, talking. . . .

Q. *Was there a pattern?*

A. Yes. There came a time when he would go into Soon-Yi's room, the girls' room, and be standing in there, and when the children were asleep, on my way to my room, I would see him in that room, and he would leave then. . . .

Q. *Now, what was Soon-Yi Previn doing during the summer of 1991?*

A. She was working in a children's day camp in New York. In the city . . . She would come on weekends to Connecticut with Mr. Allen on Saturday mornings. He would always come up, as I described. Because Soon-Yi was in New York, she would come up with him on Saturday mornings.

Q. *And when would Mr. Allen leave?*

A. He would leave usually Sunday afternoon.

Q. *And did Soon-Yi Previn leave with him or did she stay?*

A. She would go back with him. There might have been a couple of times when he came for one day and left the same day, but that was the usual pattern.

Q. *Was there a time in the summer of 1991, when you called Mr. Allen concerning your concern about Soon-Yi?*

A. Yes.

Q. *Can you tell us when that was and what happened?*

A. I can only tell you that it was in the summer of 1991 and Soon-Yi was working at a day camp as a counselor, and I had called in the evening to say good night to the kids.

Q. *Where were you?*

A. I was in Connecticut, and I reached Fletcher. When I asked for Soon-Yi, he said she had told me that she was going to her friend Siobhan [a girlfriend from school]. And so I called Siobhan because it was late. It was like eleven o'clock, and Soon-Yi never did that, and I called

Siobhan, and Siobhan didn't know anything about it, and
then I called Mr. Allen. I told him how worried I was
and everything.

Q. *What did you say to him?*

A. I said I was worried, I couldn't find Soon-Yi. This was
not like Soon-Yi to disappear like this. I told him I called
Siobhan, and Soon-Yi wasn't there, where did he think
she could be, and I was worried.

Q. *What did he say?*

A. He said he couldn't imagine where she was and, you
know, don't be silly and all that, and she'll be okay. Then
within fifteen minutes she called me, and she was home.
She was home, and then I said, "Well, where were you?
How could you do this?" She said she had been with
yet another friend who I didn't know. . . .

There has been much speculation about the date when the
affair between Woody and Soon-Yi began. The exact date is of
special interest to Mia not for prurient reasons but legal ones:
She contends that *if* their sexual relationship began before the
adoptions of Dylan and Moses were finalized on December 18,
1991, then the adoptions were made under false pretenses and
should be overturned. Woody officially insists that it began *after*
December 18. Soon-Yi, says Mia, first admitted that the relationship had been ongoing throughout her senior year of high school,
but then thought better of it and (like Woody) backpedaled.
Attorney Alan Dershowitz, who worked first as a mediary and
then, briefly, for Mia, cited December 1, 1991, Woody's fifty-
sixth birthday, as the date that Woody and Soon-Yi first had sex
together. Of course, the extensive testimony above lends greater
validity to Soon-Yi's first admission. What's more, Mia isn't alone
in recalling Soon-Yi's weekend shopping expeditions "to Bloomingdale's." Daisy and Lark recall them as well, and regard them
as little more than smoke screens concealing their sister's assig-
nations with Woody.

Even Casey Pascal weighed in about the date Soon-Yi's affair
with Woody began. "I asked her how long it had been going
on," Casey remembered, "and she said it started when she went

to Drew, which was in September of 1991. Then it occurred to me that it would have been a perfect time when Mia, Satchel, and I were in Hanoi and Bangkok, trying to get through the red tape in order to adopt Tam. Actually, I also noticed something odd about her attitude at about the time that Woody was shooting a movie in Stamford—it was *Scenes from a Mall*. She would drive up with him in the car, and she always had this little smirk on her face."

Leslie Salter, a scenic artist who worked on *Scenes from a Mall* and also built the loft, cribs, and baby furniture in Mia's nursery, told me that she would not have been surprised if Soon-Yi's relationship with Woody started around the time of *Mall*. "This was the world she really wanted to be a part of—lights, camera, action!" says Salter. "She wasn't like the other children. She was caught up by the fame."

Other Woody-watchers agree. Don, Woody's then-driver, observed Soon-Yi during her senior year at Marymount in the spring of 1991, walking the ten blocks down Fifth Avenue to visit Woody at his apartment on her lunch hours. And once, on the way up to Frog Hollow in Woody's limo, Lark's ex-boyfriend Jesse, when waking from a brief nap, noticed Woody resting his hand intimately on the inside of Soon-Yi's leg. At the time Jesse knew that this was unusual but shrugged off the signal. After all, who wants to voluntarily step on a hornet's nest?

It wasn't as if Mia were deaf and blind to the sudden interest Woody and Soon-Yi were showing in each other. According to her court testimony, when her attorney asked her if she ever discussed with Woody or Soon-Yi the nature of their relationship, or "the way they treated one another," she replied:

A. From time to time in the 1990, 1991 time frame, and I had one conversation with Soon-Yi, but I had a few with Mr. Allen.
Q. *Tell us first what you said to Mr. Allen.*
A. The ball game thing was what brought it up. Someone at work said to me that it was in the papers that [Woody] had been holding Soon-Yi's hand at a ball game. . . . I asked if he had been holding her hand, because he didn't

have that relationship with any of my kids. He never held any of their hands, except the little ones. And he said, oh, you know, he was scared walking in, because there were so many people, that he might have grabbed her for a minute like he does with Elaine of Elaine's restaurant. Elaine's is crowded. He would hold her hand sometimes to be led out. I said, "[Soon-Yi] is only seventeen and has never had a date or phone call from a boy. I don't think you should hold her hand. She has a crush on you, and she might misinterpret that. . . ." He said, "Don't be silly," but I said, "Don't do it because she might misunderstand." And I went to Soon-Yi and said, "Soon-Yi, if Woody was holding your hand, and I understand he grabbed your hand for a minute when you were walking into the ball game, then don't misunderstand that in any way." She said no, of course not. Then Mr. Allen invited Soon-Yi to more ball games, and I said to him, "Could you not invite some of my other children? Why just Soon-Yi?" He said, "Well, Soon-Yi is very interested." I said, "Well, so is Lark, so is Moses. Daisy is interested and maybe Matthew would like to go. . . ." So he did bring a cluster of them . . . then asked if he could bring Soon-Yi again. I was happy he was paying attention to Soon-Yi.

As time went on, Mia explained, Woody was in Soon-Yi's room more and more in the evenings. Not only would he take her to Knicks games, but also, occasionally, to Michael's Pub while he played his clarinet on Monday nights. On Sunday nights during the school year of 1990 and 1991, she pointed out, when she returned from Connecticut, Woody would be in her apartment, watching basketball games on TV, often together with Soon-Yi, although he had never *ever* waited at Mia's house for her to return from Connecticut before. And Mia gradually became suspicious. "I would question him about this just to be sure. I had a subliminal feeling. . . ." she said.

But on each occasion that Mia would voice her suspicions or express her anxiety about Woody's attention to Soon-Yi, he would dismiss it. "On each occasion," she told the court, "he said, 'Don't be silly,' and he would give me a hug, and he would say, 'You silly, remember you were jealous of your sister once?' He said, 'I can't believe you are saying this!' and stuff like that. I would say, 'Yes, forgive me. It is very stupid of me, and I'm sorry.' Even the night she was missing, I said, 'You wouldn't know where she'd be, would you, because she talks to you?' And in the back of my mind [I wondered], she *couldn't* be at his house? He would say, 'You silly, don't be absurd, I don't know where she is. I have *no idea* where she is, and you shouldn't be worried,' and that he loved me and wouldn't dream of those things, he kept saying to me. I put it out of my mind."

The duplicities involved in this sub rosa courtship cut Mia to the quick. But nothing hurt her more than her daughter's press interviews and subsequent court testimony. She couldn't get over Soon-Yi telling *Time,* in a written statement in August 1992, "I don't go home because Mia can be and has been violent toward me. I will not go into details, but her treatment of me was hardly maternal, even given our current problems. She is not who she pretends to be, certainly not the kind of mother [people think], and while my brothers and sisters are still dependent on her, they will say things and pretend to feelings I know full well not to be true."

That same week, again in a prepared statement released to *Newsweek* by Woody's publicist, Soon-Yi continued her emotional hatchet job. "I don't think you can raise eleven children with sufficient love and care," it read. "Take it from one who's lived through it—it can't be done. Some of us got neglected, some got smothered. Anyhow, there's problems." She also characterized Mia as "hot-tempered and given to rages that terrified all the kids. They can't speak freely because they're all still dependent on her. But they could really tell stories, and I'm sure one day they will."

All this is simply not true. I lived in that household and Mia is *not* hot-tempered *or* given to rages. And the children are *not* neglected. Moreover, I knew Soon-Yi, and she does not speak in the same way that those statements were worded. She would never make the distinction that Mia "can be and has been" violent. Nor would she ever use or think of phrases like "hardly maternal," "pretends to feelings," "sufficient love," "given to rages." She would never even say, "one who has lived through it." Both Mia and I feel that although these statements were signed by Soon-Yi, the words and attitudes had Woody written all over them. In fact, after reading these quotes, Fletcher suggested to his mother that her attorneys pull up some of the more difficult vocabulary words and question Soon-Yi on their meaning in court. He, too, was sure she wouldn't have the foggiest idea of what they meant.

In the spring of 1993, at the height of the custody hearings, Mia came home from court one evening looking especially drained and doleful. When I pressed her about what had gone on, she told me that while Soon-Yi had been testifying, her slim, childlike body was contorted with rage as she recollected her life in the Farrow household. For more than five hours she went on about her miserable childhood. It was as if she were clubbing Mia with her dissatisfaction, her anger, her petulance. I believe that the only way Soon-Yi was able to justify her actions was by converting her guilt toward her mother into black rage.

"I inherited the motherhood baggage that Soon-Yi carried," Mia told me. "Her mother starved and beat her. Then Soon-Yi was abandoned and put in to a state orphanage. If in one year the child wasn't claimed, she would go into a permanent orphanage." This is where she was when Mia found her. Mia had her moved into one of the best orphanages in Seoul, where she was taken care of by the nuns for a year until Mia was allowed to claim her. It was, said Mia, "a small, nice place that the nuns were very proud of."

It wouldn't be surprising if Soon-Yi, like most teenagers, had some grounds for dissatisfaction at home, even if they were minor. Although Woody charged that mother and daughter had had some communication breakdown early on, Mia told me that this was absolutely not true. "Soon-Yi was always icy cold, and it was always difficult to get close to her," she said.

Yet, as distant as Soon-Yi was, my experience of Mia is that she is by nature affectionate. She'll hug you, be open with you, kiss you good-bye, be free with comments like "I love you." No doubt Mia had been busy with the babies—perhaps too busy to meet all of Soon-Yi's needs as she entered college. Or perhaps it didn't even occur to Mia to try to plumb Soon-Yi's emotional life, since the girl had been so closed off for so long. As Soon-Yi told the court, she may have been lonely enough to come home from college every single weekend during her first year, but somehow she and Mia never discussed that loneliness.

Soon-Yi also failed to tell her mother other crucial bits and pieces of her life: like the fact that when she came home on weekends, she often spent time in Woody's apartment. Or that at Drew she spoke to Woody by phone every day. Between September and December 18, 1991, the two phoned each other more than 135 times. And this, avows Woody, was *before* their relationship became seriously sexual.

After the affair was out in the open, both mother and daughter suffered roiling emotions. On the day when Mia first confronted Soon-Yi, Soon-Yi threatened suicide. Mia was so worried that the next morning she phoned her friend Casey. "And at her request, I went up there that day," Casey told me. "First I went into Mia's room. She was so upset, but she asked me if I would go in to talk to Soon-Yi, who was crying in the next room. Mia said, 'I'm so furious, so upset, I can't talk to her. But I want her to understand I still love her, even though she has done this.' So I went into Soon-Yi's room, and I asked her, 'How could you do this to your mother?' And Soon-Yi said, 'I never meant to hurt my mother.' I asked, 'What did you think would happen when this came out?' and she replied, 'I never thought any of it would come out.'"

Casey was further struck by the fact that Soon-Yi refused to let Woody accept all the blame. "She kept saying to me that it wasn't all his fault," recalled Casey. "I can't imagine that Woody didn't make the overture, and she might have responded and said, 'This is an opportunity.' All I can say is that the child I knew would not have seduced him."

The weekend after Mia discovered the photos, she invited the older children including Soon-Yi, Moses, Lark and her boyfriend Jesse, Matthew and his girlfriend Priscilla, and Sascha and his girlfriend Carrie to sit around her kitchen table. There Mia spoke eloquently, dramatically, almost as though she were a minister delivering a sermon. She told her children that they must not be diminished by this catastrophe. "We've seen firsthand that there are terrible consequences to terrible actions, and how important it is going through life that we not hurt anyone, even one who has so hurt us," she told them. "[I told them] that through this thing we've defined ourselves to ourselves. And that what we've learned from this definition of ourselves as people and as a family [is something] that we should hold close and carry through the rest of our lives. I told them that they'd seen the full measure of my love for Soon-Yi, and that it is unshakable, and by extension they've seen my love for all of them. I thanked them for giving meaning to my life, and told them that even my darkest hours have not been without light because of them." And how did Soon-Yi respond to Mia's attempt to impose order on the familial chaos? She abruptly left the room.

A few days later, Mia and Soon-Yi had yet another run-in, one that prompted mild-mannered Mia to uncharacteristic violence. First, she tried to make amends with her daughter. She murmured that she knew the affair wasn't Soon-Yi's fault, and that she would forgive her and happily welcome her back into the family's bosom. But Soon-Yi wasn't having any of her mother's forgiveness or solace. Staking out her newly acquired territory, she admitted that she and Woody had been meeting on Saturdays and Sundays throughout her senior year in high school (she has since denied this). "The person sleeping with the person," she told Mia, "is the person having the relationship."

And Mia simply lost control. "I just pounced on her. She was sitting by the phone on the floor. I kicked the phone into her legs in front of her. I slapped her in her face and on the shoulders about four times, and I started crying, and the housekeeper came in, and I went into the kitchen with the housekeeper. Later I said to Soon-Yi—she had a few more days left until she was going back to college—could she find a friend to stay there with, because I think it was too hard on both of us to be living in close quarters like that under the circumstances."

Soon-Yi packed up and left the house, as it turned out, for good. Mother and daughter saw each other only once since then, at the family's mass baptism in March. Although Mia sent Soon-Yi many notes and her childhood doll during this time, Soon-Yi didn't respond. In court, however, she smirked and dismissed the doll as an absurdly sentimental gesture on Mia's part.

Mystified and hurt, Mia still goes over and over in her mind her years with Soon-Yi. "She was always so icy cold, even as a child," she told me, as if to try to make sense of the ashes of their relationship. She dwells on memories of Soon-Yi's Marymount graduation, at which her daughter stood up, beaming, and said, "Thanks, Mom, for making it all so great." And in return, Mia, with a full and generous heart, wrote this inscription. It accompanied a childhood photo of Soon-Yi, dressed up in a native kimono, that appeared in her graduation yearbook:

A mom couldn't dream of a better daughter. You are a miracle and my pride and joy. I am profoundly grateful for every minute along the way. Congratulations. Bravo and three cheers for our Soon-Yi.

These days she is Woody's Soon-Yi. Mia feels that her daughter is a woman completely under his influence. In court Soon-Yi was asked why she taped her phone calls to Mia and the Farrow household. Soon-Yi answered with a beat: "Because I wanted to hear their voices over and over again."

"Well, whose equipment was it?" Eleanor Alter wanted to know?

"I don't know," Soon-Yi replied. "I guess it was Woody's."

But she said it was her idea to tape the calls. She also insisted that it was *her* idea to pose for those nude photos, lying spread-eagle on a bed, with her crotch completely exposed. No doubt about it, Woody has got her trained.

Now, of course, Soon-Yi lives on the Upper East Side. She is probably the only student at Drew University who owns a co-op. If Woody ever does cut the affair off, she'll have something for herself. A nice little something just a skip and a jump away from his own Fifth Avenue penthouse.

The price tag? One family.

"That was fast—it probably helped [that] I had the hiccups."
Sally (Mia) to Roger after sex in
Radio Days

SIX

Summer Under Siege

In the six months following Mia's discovery of Soon-Yi's affair with Woody, the intricate fabric of her life began to unravel. By the summer of 1992 her relationship with Soon-Yi was, as you might expect, permanently scarred. Yet they weren't the only family members affected by this furious passion play. The Soon-Yi–Woody love match was beginning to damage everyone. Mia and Woody rang each other at all hours, sometimes three, four, or five times a night, and the venom flowed.

Sometimes, too, he would come over to her apartment, begin harassing her, and refuse to leave. Often Mia would be shocked at the charges he flung at her. "I'm going to take those kids away from you, and you're going to be left with nothing," he would say. Or he would curse at her in a manner totally at odds with his public image.

After one mean and angry exchange in July, 1992, I suggested to Mia that she start taping Woody's phone conversations. I said, "You just have to do it." Mia had only a video camera. So Fletcher went out and bought all this recording equipment, including a suction device for the phone and a little tape recorder. But we decided against using it and put the whole kit and caboodle in a closet, promptly forgetting about it, for the time being anyway.

Still, the calls kept coming, often in the middle of the night.

Once Fletcher told Woody to stop phoning, that he was waking everybody up at ungodly hours. Another time, when Woody came over to Mia's apartment, he refused to leave despite her weeping insistence that he get out. Fletcher, overhearing their exchange, marched into her room, carrying a stun gun. He ordered Woody out immediately and chased him into the hall. Woody didn't even wait for the elevator; he fled by the stairs. I could just imagine him running out the door, crying, "Don't shoot me! Don't shoot me."

Woody, for his part, defended his actions in court. They stemmed in part, he said, from the fact that he was worried about Mia's mental state. "When [Mia] hung up on me, I called her back because I thought she might be suicidal," he explained darkly.

His thoughts were not totally unfounded. In April, in the depths of her despair, Mia had gone so far as to write a suicide note to Woody. "At the time I was so depressed," she told me in an attempt to explain the circumstances. "I was crying all night. I couldn't sleep. And then I took this antidepressant that my doctor had prescribed and became very jittery. My mind started to gallop."

In that heightened state she went over to Woody's apartment. He wasn't there, he was at the cutting room, she knew; still, she let herself inside. "And I couldn't bear the pain anymore. So I wrote this suicide note. Then I called Woody to tell him what I was going to do. I went outside and stood by the edge of his terrace, and I looked down. But I couldn't jump. All I could do was think about the children. I couldn't put them through any more pain than they had already gone through." Letting herself back inside the apartment, Mia lay on the couch and cried.

Woody, meanwhile, had heard the desperate note in Mia's voice and rushed home. "And he was very sympathetic," Mia admitted. "But later he would put his spin on the incident in court, trying to use the suicide note as proof that I was an unfit mother."

Between February and May, Mia insists, Woody had actually gone to great lengths to have her hospitalized. He contacted both Dr. Buckley, the psychiatrist who Mia was seeing to help her get through Woody and Soon-Yi's betrayal, and also Dr. Kahn, her medical doctor, telling them that Mia was violent and needed treatment. They in turn contacted her and described him, she says, as "malicious" and "manipulative." (Both later gave affidavits of these incidents to the court and offered to testify on her behalf, if necessary. It wasn't.).

By June, Mia had calmed down considerably. "Kristi, you know me," she told me. "Through it all, I never let down my banner. My concern was my terrible depression. But I never showed violence, *or* tried to show the kids the pictures of Soon-Yi."

Still, there was an unbearable heaviness of spirit that filled her household. Moses in particular had plunged into a deep depression. Angry at Woody's betrayal of his mother, the boy refused his invitations to have lunch or play ball. After learning of the Soon-Yi affair, Moses fired off this letter to Woody:

> . . . *I know what you're trying to do to Mom and Dylan and Satchel, I know what you want, you want to bring Mom to court, and take Dylan and Satchel away from her and us, I don't know who will win, but I do know that you can't force me to live with you. . . . You have changed over the last months, you have become more hostile and anxious. All you want is the trust and relationship you had in the beginning of the time, you can't have those worthy things because you have done a horrible, unforgivable, needy, ugly, stupid thing which I hope you will not forgive yourself for doing. You probably think that Mom is telling me to say these things like before, but she didn't, these are my thoughts and feelings toward you . . . If you take us to court, you are the one who is going to be sorry. I hope you get so humiliated that you commit suicide. And about seeing me for lunch, you can just forget about that. You brought these things to yourself, we didn't do anything wrong. Mom is a GREAT mother, and she always finds the time and patience to play with us. All you did is spoil the little ones, Dylan and Satchel. You tried to communicate with me, but you were going too fast for me, I couldn't let you just yet, I almost*

gave in to you, but your needs interfered with that. . . . *Everyone knows not to have an affair with your son's sister, including that sister, but you have a special way to get that sister to think that that is okay. Unfortunately Soon-Yi, who was that sister, hadn't had a serious relationship before and probably thought that, okay, this is a great chance to see what a serious relationship is like. That's probably why she did it. I just want you to know that I don't consider you my father anymore. It was a great feeling having a father, but you smashed that feeling and dream with a single act.* I HOPE YOU ARE PROUD TO CRUSH YOUR SON'S DREAM.

Woody read this heartfelt note, and instantly accused Mia of putting Moses up to it. In court he picked out words like *needy* and phrases like *you've changed over the last few months* as Mia's. "I was amazed when I read it," he said, "because that day and the prior evening the exact same arguments were given to me by Miss Farrow." Not true, insisted Moses, who later confided to his psychiatrist that he had not wanted his mother to see the letter at all.

By summer everything seemed, to me, to have fallen apart. Even I was suffering, having sprained my left ankle while training for a simple road race. Woody was surprisingly concerned about it over the phone, and Mia said to me, perhaps for the first time, but not the last, "Watch it, Kristi. He'll get you."

That summer I did all the cooking. The family rarely ate together during those tension-filled months, whereas during the school year they always had. In the winter, all the kids who were at home in the apartment were expected to sit down at the dinner table, whether they ate or not. Here the family gathered together and discussed the events of the day. When boyfriends and girlfriends visited, they always joined in the mix.

But in Bridgewater the mix was different. Mia was always on the phone, deep in emotional discussions with Woody or legal discussions with her lawyers. More often, the older kids stayed in the city during the week, going to summer jobs and generally avoiding the black cloud that hung over their mother's home. At

Frog Hollow I would feed Satchel, Dylan, and Tam in the TV room while they watched a videotaped movie like Disney's *Beauty and the Beast* or *The Brave Little Toaster*. Then I would bring Mia's dinner upstairs to her. Occasionally Mia would descend into the kitchen, looking like a teenager in her khaki shorts and white T-shirt, and she would eat with me at seven or eight o'clock. Usually she would just have a bite of pita bread and hummus (a crushed-chick-pea spread), or I'd make pasta for us. When Woody, whom I now perceived as The Enemy, would drive up in his limo once or twice a week, he would usually be carrying, along with his bag of toys for the kids, a big barbecued chicken. It is such a New York thing to do. But Woody did it for survival, not style. You see, he brought his own dinner, he later claimed, because he feared Mia might poison him.

On that humid June morning six months after Mia discovered the Soon-Yi affair, and only moments after she had told me about it, she announced that Woody was about to pay a visit later that day. And for the first time she gave me a new kind of instruction: "From now on, Kristi, I want you to keep a very close eye on him when he's with Dylan. I want you to follow him around and be very careful, because I'm suspicious of his behavior when he's with her."

I didn't know any reason to be suspicious, nor did I really believe that Woody was capable of doing anything salacious, so I took it perhaps more casually than I should have. I figured that Mia had a right to be upset with him; at that moment, she had a right to be wary.

Still, the business of taking sides and spying on my boss was sticky. Although I was employed by Mia and sympathized with her, back in 1992 I was being paid by Woody. So the first day he arrived in Bridgewater after Mia's confidential revelation to me, I watched his limo pull up in the gravel driveway and felt sick to my stomach. I would rather not have known about his relationship with Soon-Yi. Now I was required to police him, and I *didn't* want to do it.

I stood in the kitchen as Woody walked into the house, and for a moment I was paralyzed. Usually when he arrived, I would gather the children, calling, "Daddy's here! Daddy's here," and then I'd bring them over to him. But not this day. On this warm, golden June afternoon I let him find the kids on his own. And then I began to follow them around.

Immediately I sensed that he knew that *I knew*. We kept making eye contact. Woody would look at me, I would look at him, and then he would avert his eyes. My discomfort was acute. Neither of us, however, said a word.

Woody can often be that way: To the point. Dismissive. Chilly. Skipping over pleasantries and abandoning small talk. However, having spent some time alone with him and his kids, I must concede that he can also be charming. He's able to get the digs in me just by the soft, smooth way he talks to me. "Kristi, this . . ." he says soothingly, or "Kristi, that . . ." When he speaks, he works my name into the conversation, and he does it so sweetly that he manipulates the anger and hatred right out of me. When I see him, I can be friendly with him and eager to do well for him. Then I leave, and I get angry at myself for responding to his charm. After Woody's betrayal with Soon-Yi, Mia would always say to me, "You be careful, Kristi. He's flirting with you, he likes you. Watch out, or you're next." But I frankly never sensed *that* kind of danger.

During the summer of 1992 Woody was unfailingly courteous to me. But things were rough between him and Mia. At Frog Hollow, and in their happier moments, they would discuss—what else?—his work. *Husbands and Wives* was finished but hadn't been released yet. Woody had already written *Manhattan Murder Mystery*, which he was still planning as a vehicle for Mia, and he would often bring up the script, asking her questions like "Who do you think would be good to play the part of Mrs. House?" In less constructive moments—and there were many—he and Mia would bicker openly, which had not been true the previous summer. In July I wrote in my journal:

This afternoon I stood in the living room by the window and spied. Mia and Woody were having a fight, and I was so afraid that after their constant angry phone calls to each other over the last few days, things might get too crazy. She pushed him and banged her fists against his chest like a woman who has been so deeply hurt. Which is what this is all about. Yet tonight he walked down to the lake where Mia, Sophie [the tutor], and I, were reading the *Times,* and he said good-bye. He touched her head and stroked her hair, affectionately trying to calm her, but what a thing he has done! We all look at him like he's crazy, a monster. As he slowly turns his head in our direction, a little half-smile on his face, he tries to make eye contact with us—any of us. He wants everything to be normal again. Which it is not. How could it ever be?

And how could Mia be continuing to see this man who has destroyed her relationship with one daughter and is now trying to completely destroy her life? How could she even stand to look at him? If I had a lover who cheated on me—and I'm not talking about with my *daughter*—I couldn't even sit across a table from him. But to have him do it with my child! This is the most insulting thing that could happen to anyone.

Sometimes I would see Woody and Mia taking their endless walks through the fields—Woody all covered up and buttoned down, Mia with her natural-color straw hat protecting her fair skin, both seeking shelter from the sun and gesturing angrily as they spoke. Then, in the evening, they would go out for dinner. When they came back, if Woody stayed in Bridgewater, it would be in Mia's guest room.

He was still phoning her ten times a day. Instructed by Mia, I would say, "She's not here." Trying to conceal his impatience, Woody would challenge me: "I just spoke to her, Kristi, put her on the phone," At that, Mia would pick up her extension upstairs in her bedroom, and soon I would hear her crying, mewling like a sick kitten. Once in a while I would talk to her till ten or eleven at night, just listening and letting her vent her distress and disappointment.

This Woody, she assured me, was not the man he portrayed onscreen. Sometimes in their private exchanges, Mia said, he would attack her appearance, other times her acting ability. He would tell her that she was not as beautiful as everyone claimed, and that she was not such a terrific actress either. He would also insist that she was who she was—a star—because *he* was nice enough to give her these jobs. I guess he forgot about *Rosemary's Baby* and Frank Sinatra, and the fact that Mia basked in major stardom B.W. (before Woody).

It's difficult for me to imagine Alvy Singer, Virgil Starkweather from *Take the Money and Run,* or any of Woody's screen characters being so viciously, aggressively cruel as this. Yet according to Mia, the real Woody berated her for years—long before the Soon-Yi rift. When they first started to date, she said, they would go to Elaine's or some other trendy restaurant. Mia, who was unfamiliar with the variety of pastas that were available, would invariably make some slip, saying, for instance, "fungilli" instead of "fusilli." And Woody would return nastily, "Are you trying to be cute by saying that? You mean you don't know the names of the pastas?"

Often, whether they were dining alone or with friends, Mia claimed, she would make a comment that Woody regarded as silly or inconsequential. He would toss her an impatient look and mutter, "Well, some people have it and some people don't." He belittled her so much in front of others, Mia said, that when they went out together, she would sit quietly, afraid to say a word.

Then there were his absurd tests. "Once," Mia told me, "we were driving in the city, and Woody asked me where William Buckley lived. Now, he had at one time told me Buckley's address, but I had forgotten it. Woody didn't like this and started yelling at me, saying that I was stupid, and again that I wasn't 'cute.' And he said that if *I* thought I was 'cute,' I had a real problem."

Woody clearly had difficulties with what he referred to as Mia's "cuteness." Despite this, and despite what she regarded as his low opinion of her, he refused to allow her to work for other directors. "He said there was no point in my doing other movies unless the director was Ingmar Bergman," she said. "He didn't like other directors, and he said I would be ruined if I did other films, and that I should be grateful for the work that I have. Besides," she added sadly and perhaps more to the point, "I thought I couldn't get any other work."

Working for other directors would have meant added income for Mia. This might have been especially helpful since Woody paid her only a modest salary, and one that was not equal to the going rate for leading ladies (Mia received around $200,000 per picture, but Michelle Pfeiffer, Goldie Hawn, and even newcomers like Sharon Stone are paid in the millions). Yet, Mia complained, Woody also worried that if she appeared elsewhere, it would make his own movies less exclusive. Mia said she was offered *Father of the Bride* opposite Steve Martin, for instance, but turned it down at Woody's request (Diane Keaton, of all people, took the part). Moreover, he let her know that whatever she was being offered was only because of her affiliation with *him*. But Mia never argued or fought back. She just accepted his view of things. There were times when I couldn't believe what a piece of putty she was. But somehow I understood.

Three things struck me as odd that summer. The first was that even with Mia's agony over Soon-Yi and the demands of her two newest kids, she wanted to foster yet another child, a crack-addicted baby named Tunisia, taking care of her until such time as the mother was well enough to claim her. Tunisia had been little more than a pound and a half when she was born, and at somewhere between nine months and a year she was still so tiny that the Family Services people were dressing her in doll's clothes. Sometimes Mia and I would sit on the beach like two little girls playing house, and we would make up lists of baby names we liked. Topping our list was the name Harper (for a girl) Farrow. Riley was also up there. And Peyton.

For a brief moment I was supportive of this foster-child plan, knowing that it would distract Mia from her own anguish. Clearly, saving these small babies satisfied her heart and soul. In fact, one morning I found a book about Vietnamese orphanages on her shelf and copied a beautiful poem in it for her. Later she took out the book and said, "Kristi, I want to show you something." And she turned to a photo of twenty-five premature babies, all tucked into shoeboxes like dolls, and she pointed to one shoebox, saying, "That's Larky, in that shoebox over there. It was taken before I adopted her." Mia recalled how she and

Andre first went to the airport to pick up Larky, and they were so moved when they took her home that they wept.

But the moment I had my wits about me, I voiced concern about her adopting again. Didn't Mia think she had her hands full with her other children? And was the possible arrival of Tunisia meant to be a diversion from the pain at hand? Or was it a way to test her own capacity for love at a moment that felt bleak and loveless? At any rate, when Mia mentioned this foster sister to Satchel and Dylan, they were enthusiastic. But they told their mother that they didn't want any baby whom they would have to give back; they wanted one whom they could grow up with. Eventually, Mia withdrew her foster-child application. Little Tunisia and her doll clothes went elsewhere.

The second odd thing is an incident that occurred during the Fourth of July weekend, 1992. I remember walking slowly into the house on Saturday afternoon. It was silent. "Hellooo," I called, but I heard nothing. I wasn't working on this particular day. I just stopped over to see if Mia needed anything. When I entered the living room, I heard something coming from upstairs, and I headed that way. At the top of the stairs I saw Woody and Satchel playing on the floor of the children's room and then noticed that the bathroom door was closed. Woody barely looked up when I entered.

"Could you get her out of there?" Woody asked in a pleasant voice. He meant Dylan, of course. "I've got to leave soon. I've got to go back to the city," he continued.

"I'll try," I promised him, then called into the bathroom, "Dylan?" No response. I knocked on the door. Still no response. Then, I said, "Dylan, why don't you come out? Daddy has to go back to New York soon. He's here to see you. Why don't you come out?" Again there was no response.

Woody was getting impatient. So I suggested that we pick the lock with a coat hanger. He nodded with approval, and I headed into Mia's room, took a hanger from her closet, and straightened the end. I returned to the nursery, handing the hanger to Woody. He jabbed, twisted, poked, and finally failed miserably at picking the lock, so he returned the wire to me and said challengingly,

"You try." I inserted the wire into the lock, turned it, and heard it click open.

"Thank you, Kristi," Woody said. "How did you do that?"

"It's all in the wrist," I replied, feeling slightly smug about my dexterity. I opened the bathroom door, and Dylan walked out. Without saying a word she joined Woody and Satchel.

One thing for sure. Dylan certainly hadn't been sitting on the toilet, doing her business. Nor was this the first time that she had locked herself in the bathroom when Woody was there. In court Mia testified about another occasion when "Dylan locked herself in the bathroom for four and a half hours. I came home [while she was locked inside]. She let me in, and eventually came out with me."

I flashed back to other times, the times when Woody would arrive and seek Dylan out, and she would run away from him, shrieking, "Hide me, hide me." Or times when Dylan would complain of headaches while her father was around, although she had only once, to my knowledge, suffered one when Woody was *not* present. On this occasion, oddly enough, his spirit *was* very much there: Satchel, returning from a visit with his father, had brought home a huge bag of toys from Woody for Dylan In the middle of tearing into her gifts, Dylan raised her hands to cradle her head in them, moaning loudly, "Oh, I have such a headache. Oh, my head, my head hurts." Mia and I, who were both observing this, exchanged glances.

As I left the house that July Fourth afternoon, having picked the bathroom lock, I wondered, Why had Dylan needed to secure that door? She had done something like this as many as six times before. Looking back now, I think that I never felt the urgency to watch over the kids like a hawk. I also knew that there would be moments when Woody would be alone with them. He was their father and had every right to spend private time with his kids. Or so I thought.

The other thing that was odd about the summer of 1992 is that right up until August, Mia and Woody were going out to dinner and logging big chunks of time together. I was touched by the desperate lengths she seemed ready to go to to forgive Woody, and, if it were humanly possible, to put the Soon-Yi incident, the nude photos, and Woody's traitorous heart behind her. During this period Mia was still entertaining the notion of getting back together with him. She claims that the only reason she was considering it was that she wanted to make a deal with him: If he stayed away from Soon-Yi, she would marry him. In return, she wanted Woody to promise *never* to go near her daughter again. And he did promise.

Their continuing relationship was so foreign to me that, at the time, it was difficult to understand and impossible for me to judge. I think if Mia and Woody had not been international stars, merely an ordinary couple, I would have dismissed them as crackpots and kept my distance from them while I did my job. But because they were celebrities and eccentrics as well as artists who had created work that I loved, I allowed myself to become enmeshed with them and swept up in their drama. Mia's heartbreak became my own. When Woody promised not to see Soon-Yi anymore, I, too, prayed that he held to it.

But it was one promise that Woody didn't keep. I noted in my journal that summer that Woody claimed that he was no longer seeing Soon-Yi. Mia and I certainly thought that the affair had ended. She had sent Soon-Yi to work as a counselor at Camp Meadowlark in Maine. But at the end of July she received this letter from the camp director. It was dated July 21:

[i]t is with sadness and regret that we had to ask Soon-Yi to leave camp midway through the first camp session. Although we rarely contact parents of staff members, we want to share some information regarding the situation. . . . Soon-Yi had a most difficult adjustment to camp and country living. Throughout the entire orientation period and continuing during camp, Soon-Yi was constantly involved with telephone calls. Phone calls from a gentleman whose name is Mr. Simon seemed to be her primary focus and this definitely detracted from her concentration on being a counselor. . . .

The obsessive "Mr. George Simon," as it turned out, was Woody, who also occasionally called himself, "Max." He phoned

Soon-Yi between six and eight times a day—as obsessively as he had always phoned Mia. The camp director was clearly *not* amused. Soon-Yi was sent back to New York City, where she promptly disappeared, refusing to tell Mia her whereabouts.

During this time Mia would rail at Woody, "Where is my daughter? What have you done with my daughter?" He would shrug and plead ignorance. Soon-Yi left a phone number with a New Jersey area code—possibly someplace near Drew. From time to time she would call Satchel and Dylan and say to them things like, "Woody did a good thing for me, not a bad thing."

Later, according to Mia, Woody attempted to explain his deception by claiming that he was in touch with Soon-Yi simply to placate her. (He was *also*, poor guy, very busy placating Mia.) After all, Mia and I theorized, if Soon-Yi got fed up and returned home, she might have admitted that she and Woody had been seeing each other while she was in high school *and* before she turned eighteen (which, because of a disputed birth date, was either in 1988 or 1990). If that were the case, Woody could have been brought up on charges of statutory rape. He also might have been forced to forfeit custody of his children. He must have been aware that if Soon-Yi were to admit that their affair began *before* the adoptions were finalized in December of 1991, then the adoptions themselves could have been declared fraudulent. Whatever his concerns, throughout the spring and early summer of 1992, Woody was working, on one hand, to keep Soon-Yi happy and quiet, and on the other, to keep Mia happy, perhaps so that he could gracefully break up with her.

While they tantalized each other from time to time with the dream—or nightmare—of reconciling, the couple continued to haggle over legal separation points: Mia would still be in Woody's movies, and he would remain financially responsible for Satchel, Dylan, and Moses. In return, he would be awarded supervised visitation with the kids three times a week for about two hours at a time, but no overnights. There was never any question of custody, although the couple had made a verbal agreement that if Mia died before Woody did, he would *not* then seek custody. It was an odd agreement, going so far as to set down the terms for vacations (together, yes!) and other vestiges of family life.

Sometimes, I thought, it really did seem like this relationship could be saved. "Let's put the incident behind us," Woody would say time and again as he stroked Mia's head and gave her a half-smile. But he would turn around, and there would still be Soon-Yi, carrying with her the bloom of youth and the threat of a jail sentence.

One highly-charged family dinner stands out in my mind. Sascha, who had a summer job as an intern for a cable TV music channel, and Carrie were staying with Mia that weekend. So was Moses. The rest of the older kids were either asleep or away. (Matthew, a law student at Georgetown, was working as a paralegal and living at the Central Park West apartment. So was Lark, then a nursing student at New York University, who that summer was doing office work at a nursing agency. And Daisy was visiting a friend in Canada.) It was among the most emotional nights of the summer, and it followed a visit from Andre to see Mia. During his visit, Soon-Yi called the house. And Mia, as she had been doing for weeks, cajoled and pleaded with her daughter to come home. "Please, I love you, please come home," she cried.

Andre was shocked and dismayed at Mia's desperation. "You can't keep begging her to come back," he told Mia. He and I both attempted to talk her into cutting Soon-Yi off. We felt that Mia had to give Soon-Yi an ultimatum: Either stop seeing Woody and come home, or choose to be with Woody and take the consequences—the loss of her family. We were concerned because every time Mia got on the phone, she would fall into the same emotional sea. We also felt that her good intentions were betraying her, that Soon-Yi was simply feeding off her own new-found power. She would taunt Mia about Woody and then, after each phone call, she would tell Woody everything Mia had said.

Never mind our counsel. On this particular night, immediately after Andre left, Mia picked up the phone to call Soon-Yi and put to right their disastrous earlier conversation. Mia dialed the number somewhere in New Jersey that Soon-Yi had given her when she returned from Meadowlark (Soon-Yi would not tell her mother where or with whom she was staying), and Mia heard a disconnect message. Now, she realized, she could not get in touch with her daughter at all, and she collapsed into tears, starting to shake with an intensity that summed up all her frustration.

By that time I had become used to Mia's fragile emotional state. I actually felt quite helpless when she would break down. Still, I would quietly put my arms around her—she's so small and thin, like a child—and I would summon up my most religious and faithful self for her. And although I myself rarely prayed during that period, I would say calmly, as I did now, "It's okay, God is going to get us through this, we just have to pray a lot."

And Mia replied, "Kristi, life is so hard, it's so hard, you don't know." I looked at her, and her face seemed so grave and as full of turmoil as any I'd ever seen. A tear rolled down her cheek, and in mere seconds she was bawling in my arms.

Before long, everyone else started to cry—Sascha, Carrie, Moses, and even myself. We were all standing there in a little teary-eyed knot, hugging each other. Then we headed down to the lake with a bottle of wine, and we sat in the grass drinking and rehashing our thoughts about Woody, Soon-Yi, and Mia's broken heart.

A little while later I went up to the house to prepare an impromptu dinner. I set the table as prettily as I could with floral napkins and Mia's hand-painted Mexican plates. Finally, Mia, Moses, Carrie, Sasha, and I sat down for a special pasta dinner. And Carrie said, "Let's make a toast." She turned to Mia and raised her wineglass. "First I want to thank you, Mia, for giving me your son, because he's so wonderful and I love him so much," she said. "And I want you to know what an inspiration you've been for me. I love you."

Then Mia made a toast to Carrie, and Sascha toasted his mother. Even shy Moses stood up and said, "Mom, I love you. And I know things have been really hard. I know I don't talk very much, but I've always been behind you."

Mia was so moved. Tears ran down her lovely face as she raised her glass and said in the most tender voice, "To Moses, the prince."

And then I made a toast to Mia. "After John's death, I couldn't live for myself," I told her, "so I decided to live for you and to give you everything I could. You've been an inspiration to me with the way you are devoted to your children, and with the way you live. I was once just a girl who cared only about winning races and having fun. But you've really changed me as a person." I may have sounded corny, but I meant every word.

It was a festival of sweet emotions and shared goodwill. We were coming off such a low point that we needed the tears and the toasts and the expressions of love and support to sustain us. In the months to come Mia would look back on it and ask, "Do you remember that night where we all sat around and toasted each other and had a great dinner?" It was an evening to remember. We called it our Night of Celebration. It was the one time during the entire dread summer where we allowed the weight of the ugly events that had brought us to this point to be lifted, even if briefly.

Then there was the matter of Dylan's birthday party on Saturday, July 11, 1992. Woody was to be present, and so Mia worried beforehand for two reasons. The first: She feared that he might monopolize Dylan's time, taking her away from her other guests. The second: Five of the older children were coming up from New York City for the occasion, and they wanted to avoid seeing him. Mia and Woody had a discussion about it, and he promised her that during the festivities he would stay away from Dylan, allowing her to enjoy her party and her brothers and sisters. This, Mia felt, was especially important because the older children were all returning to Manhattan on the five P.M. bus.

Come the party, and, contrary to his word, Woody was all over the little girl. The other kids had no time to spend with her and felt excluded. So did Casey, her husband, and their kids. They had brought firecrackers and sparklers which Woody, said Mia, "did nothing but insult"—to the point where the Pascals left early. Then Woody took Dylan down to the lake, completely isolating her from the rest of the guests. Afterward, Mia and Woody exchanged words. "You never left her side," she said to him. His lack of remorse sparked her anger even further. He cared little that Dylan's sisters and brothers hadn't had a chance to spend time with her. As Mia said later, "The whole day he had never taken his eyes off her, which he did all the time anyway. But that day he promised he wouldn't."

That evening Mia composed her now-famous note. After trying unsuccessfully to shove it under the guest-room door where Woody slept, she tacked it to the bathroom door. It read: CHILD MOLESTER. MOLDED THEN ABUSED ONE SISTER. NOW FOCUSED ON YOUNGEST SISTER.

An omen, witting or un-, of things to come.

"I'm doing a sociological study of perversion. I'm up to advanced child molesting."

Fielding Mellish (Woody)
in Bananas

SEVEN

Allegations and Abuses

66 I can't really talk right now," Mia said when I phoned her from Boston on Thursday, August 6, 1992, "but I have to tell you that Woody molested Dylan." I had been up in Beantown visiting Mark Page, the lead guitarist in my old college band (I played the guitar and was the band's vocalist), and I had had a weird, nagging, ESP type of feeling that something was amiss back at Frog Hollow. But I never expected this.

"What???" I screamed into the receiver, then when her words sank in, I added, "Oh, God." There was a long silence before Mia picked up the conversation. In a quiet voice she told me that she was on her way to her doctor's office to have Dylan examined, but that I should call her later.

I was left in the dark as to the particulars of what happened, but I was worried on two counts. One was my selfish fear that this alleged molestation could have occurred on what I thought of as "my watch." My second thought, of course, was about Dylan herself. How was she? And what had really happened? I called Mia again that evening, but this time she was on the phone with her lawyer.

The next afternoon, when I had completed the three-hour drive from Boston to Bridgewater, I headed over to Mia's to pick up Monica Thompson, who also helped with the children. I used to drive her to the bus station from Frog Hollow. On

125

this day Monica, a large black woman of about forty, was going home to Jamaica for her vacation and not planning to return until September. So I beeped the horn, and she came out, lugging her bag. A grim look on her face, she slid into the seat beside me. I didn't say anything at first, but as soon as we pulled out of the driveway, I asked her, "Monica, what happened? What's going on?"

She shrugged and said, "I don't think anything happened. I think Mia is exaggerating. She's trying to make you feel bad for not staying with Dylan the entire day."

The alleged molestation, Monica said, had occurred two days earlier, on Tuesday, August 4, 1992. However, Monica knew only the sketchiest details of what had supposedly transpired. Although she had been working for Mia for seven years, they weren't close at all, and so I played dumb and agreed with her. Yes, I said, Mia must have been stretching the truth. And no, I didn't remember leaving Dylan alone with Woody. Then, without asking—or answering—any more questions, I drove back to Frog Hollow, my foot on the gas pedal the whole trip. My conversation with Monica would one day come back to haunt me.

When I arrived at Mia's, Sophie Bergé, the kids' French tutor, was standing by the fridge in the kitchen, pouring juice for herself. Frail, dark-haired, and around my age, Sophie, who was studying acting at the Circle in the Square in Manhattan and lived in SoHo, always seemed so calm. "Sophie," I asked, trying to contain my own curiosity and sense of urgency, "is it really true?"

And she replied in her soft voice, "Yes."

Then I sprinted up the stairs to Mia's room. The door was closed. I didn't even knock, I just pushed it open. Mia was sitting on the beige carpet in the adjoining nursery, wearing her standard tan shorts and a white T-shirt, and her face was red, with tears staining her cheeks and lashes. She was on the phone to her mother, talking with a frightening intensity. As she spoke, she motioned to me and pointed to a tape that was sitting beside her on the floor. Getting up, she put the tape into the video machine and pushed the play button, then took the phone and, dragging the cord behind her, turned around and walked into the adjacent nursery, allowing me to watch the tape all by myself.

It is chilling. It begins with Dylan sitting on Mia's bed. Mia, holding the video camera, is not in the picture, but we hear her asking Dylan questions like, "Where did Daddy take you?" And Dylan answers, "He took me to the attic." Mia asks several more questions while Dylan sits on the bed. Then the scene shifts to the lake. Now we see Dylan lying in one of the lounge chairs by the water. Mia asks her questions like "Where did he touch you?" And Dylan, whose legs are slightly open, says, "He touched me here, and he touched me here, and he touched me here." Each time she says this, she points to her genital areas. During this scene, Dylan seems manic and distracted, and there are many interruptions. She gets up from her chair often. Occasionally, too, Tam runs into the picture to play, blocking Dylan from view. Finally, one distraction too many, Mia stops the tape. When she starts it again, Dylan tells her that she wishes that Andre were her daddy. "Mommy, it hurts there, it hurts there," she says and holds her genital area. Mia pauses, she sounds very upset, and Dylan says something about Woody putting his finger inside her. Dylan says again, "It hurts." Toward the end of the tape Dylan repeats her claim that Woody has taken her to the attic and has told her that if she doesn't move, if she lies very still, he will take her to Paris and put her in his next movie. Then she says, a serious expression on her face, "I don't want to be in the movie, and I don't want to go to Paris." The tape closes as Dylan looks at Mia and asks, "Mommy, did your daddy do this to you?"

Woody tried desperately to dismiss this tape by suggesting that it had been doctored. Experts checked it and concluded that this was not so, with one exception—there was a splice, Mia explained, that cut out some tape inadvertently capturing Dylan's private parts, and which, Mia felt, was "inappropriate" to show. The tape had undeniably, however, been stopped and restarted several times. I suppose it's possible that in the interim Mia *could have* told her daughter what to say. Some viewers have watched it and said that it looks rehearsed, as if Dylan is acting. But she's a very melodramatic child, and it seems farfetched to me that Mia would have coached her as to such minute details. I was with Mia several times while she actually tried to get Dylan to recant her story, and each time the child would refuse.

I remember one specific moment when we were standing in the kitchen in Connecticut. Mia had just had a strained telephone conversation with Woody about the alleged molestation. "Please just give me two weeks to investigate this," she had begged him. "Please hold off. Don't call lawyers or anything yet." And Woody replied in a voice so loud that I could hear it through the phone, "I will not hold off! This is absurd, and I can't even believe that you're accusing me of this!" After they hung up, Mia went downstairs and asked her daughter once again, "Dylan, you've got to tell me, is it true?" and Dylan said, "Yeah, it's true." Then she ran out of the house.

Now, I witnessed that. But I didn't know what to make of it. A part of me hoped that Dylan had made the story up. After all, nobody *wants* to think that Woody Allen would be capable of such a heinous act. What's more, as I've mentioned, I felt responsible for the events of August 4, since Dylan was in my care that afternoon. Still, I had been puzzled by the vigilance with which Mia herself had been watching for signs of molestation; it had sometimes seemed as if she were *willing* the incident to happen. For instance, take the child-molester note that she tacked onto the bathroom door after Dylan's birthday party. Of course, Mia said that she was referring to Soon-Yi. In light of events to come, her accusation seems eerily prophetic. But of what? Of Woody's actions? Of her own vindictive need to make the punishment fit the crime?

On August 4, the day in question, Mia had gone out clothes shopping to New Milford with Tam and Isaiah, and Woody had driven up from Manhattan to play with Satchel and Dylan. Not long before his arrival, Mia's friend, Casey, also came by with *her* three children and baby-sitter, Alison Stickland, in tow. I was present, and so was Sophie Bergé, the French tutor, who baby-sat all that summer as well. The truth is, when we retraced our steps that day, there were only fifteen to twenty minutes in which Dylan was out of my sight, Sophie's, Casey's, or Alison's. Of course, those are the suspect "twenty minutes" when, Mia alleges, the molestation must have occurred.

From my point of view, everything seemed normal on August 4 except for one thing. That afternoon, for reasons nobody has ever been able to explain, Dylan, at age seven—an age when all children usually have a well-developed sense of modesty—was wandering around in her billowy white sundress, but without her underpants. Nobody knew where they were. Nobody was ever able to locate them. Nor did Dylan ever admit that she knew where her panties were. She said that she didn't remember what had happened to them.

Yet maybe the answer to this is less sinister than it seems. Maybe Dylan's panties had been wet or soiled from playing at the beach, and she had just chucked them under a bed or into the laundry. Or maybe when she changed clothes in the middle of the day, she simply forgot her drawers and didn't notice that she was putting on a dress rather than sweatpants, which she often wore without undies. Still, Dylan's missing underwear and her distracted willingness to run around half naked seemed, at best, odd. It was the first thing that Mia noticed when she returned home from shopping.

That evening, Woody and Mia went out for dinner as usual; not even his affair with Soon-Yi had altered that ritual in their lives. Nothing seemed ominous that evening either. Yet much later, when they returned home, they had a squabble over Tam. It began when Woody went upstairs to the children's room to read to Satchel and Dylan. As usual, he ignored Tam—or tried to. This time, as he related his evening tale to the kids, Tam began to cry and shout. As Mia recalled, she screamed, "I don't like him." Mia, who told the court that Tam was scared of Woody "because he never spoke to her and just kept appearing," was unable to calm the child down or move her out of the room—at eleven she was a big girl—so she asked Woody to hurry his story and leave. He refused. Finally, when he had concluded, the pair made their way downstairs. Mia testified under oath: "He said something angry to me like 'Look what you've done,' or something to that effect. And I said that he always blames me. 'Why is it always my fault?' Something like that."

While Mia and Woody were tangling over Tam, something else was preying on Casey's baby-sitter's mind. After Alison Stickland left Frog Hollow on the afternoon of August 4, she told Casey in passing, "I had seen something at Mia's that was bothering me." What she claimed to have seen was this: In the television room that afternoon, Dylan was sitting on the sofa, and Woody was kneeling on the floor, facing her, with his head in her lap.

Casey phoned Mia the next day, August 5, and, in passing, related Alison's remark. Mia immediately took Dylan aside and asked her "whether it was true that Daddy had his face in her lap yesterday." In court, Mia related Dylan's response:

> Dylan said yes. And then she said that she didn't like it one bit, no, he was breathing into her, into her legs, she said. And that he was holding her around the waist and I said, why didn't you get up, and she said she tried to but that he put his hands underneath her and touched her. And she showed me where. . . . Her behind.

That's when Mia brought out her video camera, and she began to tape Dylan. She also called the child's psychiatrist, Dr. Nancy Schultz, who had been treating her for severe shyness, and Satchel's psychiatrist, Dr. Susan Coates, who was seeing him for identity problems. Twenty-four hours after Mia first started to videotape her daughter, the little girl allegedly confided to her mother that she and Woody had been in the attic on August 4. There, she claimed, he had inserted his finger into her vagina.

At this news, Mia immediately contacted Eleanor Alter, who calmly advised her to take the child to her local pediatrician, Dr. Kavirajan. Mia did so. First, she spoke to the doctor privately, describing to him what Dylan had told her had occurred the previous day. Then Dr. Kavirajan took Dylan into his office alone. Here, he asked the child to tell him what had happened. Dylan hesitated, then said merely that Woody had touched her.

"Where?" asked Dr. Kavirajan.

"On the shoulder," Dylan managed to say, then immediately, nervously, asked to leave the room to rejoin her mother.

In the car on the way home, Mia asked Dylan gently but firmly, "What is the truth? What you told me? Or what you told Dr. Kavirajan?" And Dylan replied, "What I told you." Then she hesitated and added, "But I don't like to talk about my privates."

The moment she got home, Mia called Dr. Kavirajan and told this to him. He noted that Dylan's reaction was a common one in children who had been molested, and that Mia should bring her back in the next day.

Before this second visit, Mia explained to Dylan, "If you tell the truth, it will help Daddy." According to the court judgment, Mia also told her daughter, "We wanted to help Daddy, he forgot to act like a daddy." So in Dr. Kavirajan's office on August 6, Dylan repeated her original accusation of abuse. That evening, said Mia, "when I put her in the bath, she wouldn't sit down. In the bath she said her vagina hurt." On August 9, a purely external physical examination showed no evidence of sexual abuse; even so, Dylan was so reluctant to have it done that she had to be sedated.

A few days later Mia and I brought Dylan to St. Luke's-Roosevelt Hospital in Manhattan for an internal examination under the auspices of the New York City Child Welfare Administration. Mia was so convinced of the abuse that she seemed anxious and eager for this delicate internal exam to take place. Yet again Dylan flipped out, crying and insisting she didn't want it done. Frankly, Mia would have gone against her daughter's wishes, and she actually begged the doctors to sedate the little girl. Mia had been told that the hospital had instruments of such sensitivity that they could detect all sorts of foreign substances and vaginal bruises. Well, St. Luke's refused to knock Dylan out against her will, which is too bad in one sense, since Mia felt certain that the tests would have offered closure, for better or worse.

In court Mia was asked if she had ever suggested to Dylan that she had to tell her story the same way each time, "if you love your daddy." No, she said. "I told Dylan when she has to go to these interviews with strangers to be honest and tell them what happened in the attic. And each time I hope it will be the last time [that she has to do these interviews.]."

Every day during this period Mia conferred by phone with Dylan's psychiatrist, Dr. Schultz, who was on vacation in Europe. She also spoke with Satchel's doctor, Susan Coates, telling her that despite the wealth of detailed description from Dylan, "Let's hope it is her fantasy." Dr. Coates immediately let Woody know about Dylan's accusations. Then, as she was required to do by law, she notified the New York City Child Welfare Administration. She also suggested strongly to Woody that he not see Dylan again, for the time being.

What I didn't know then but have discovered since is that Mia's concern over what she considered Woody's inappropriate behavior with Dylan was not new. It did not crop up as a revenge fantasy, a contrived bit of hostility sparked by his romance with Soon-Yi. In fact, the relationship between Woody and Dylan had seemed to her unnaturally close almost from the beginning. It also stood out in contrast to his behavior toward the rest of the children. "He paid no attention to any of them at all," said Mia. "Those that were more aggressive would call him on the telephone and ask if he would spend some time with them, take them out on a Saturday afternoon, spend an overnight at his house, and those that were shyer made no contact with him, and he made no effort to get to know any of them. That was true of Moses too."

Although Woody had been initially cool to Mia's idea of adopting Dylan, choosing not to participate in it, he nevertheless became enamored with the baby within months after the tiny blond infant was first delivered into her mother's arms in July, 1985. By the time Dylan was a year old, Woody began his pattern of coming over to Mia's apartment twice a day to play with her. Every morning he would wake her up by lying at the foot of her bed, slipping his hands under the blankets, and massaging her little legs and belly. He would "kiss her and whisper things. Just caress her awake," said Mia. Then he would carry her into Mia's bed and get into it with her. This ardent behavior, understandably, began to disturb Mia. Woody continued it, however, until

Dr. Schultz, in connection with Dylan's therapeutic situation, asked him not to.

On a trip to Paris when Dylan was two and a half, Mia became further disquieted about his devotion to the little girl. At the time, as Mia testified in court, she told Woody, "You look at her in a sexual way. You fondled her. It's not natural. You're all over her. You don't give her any breathing room. You look at her when she's naked." Woody often played with and read to the child in his bed while dressed only in undershorts, and he let her suck his thumb. According to Mia, he displayed little or no understanding of boundaries. From 1989 onward, when Dylan was four, she explained, "He was draped around her all day long, following her, wooing her, demanding her attention, demanding her affection, physically all over her all day long. It was relentless, and I think it immobilized Dylan."

"He used to wrap himself in Dylan," says Lorrie Pierce, the children's piano teacher who one day watched, fascinated, as Dylan tried to squirm out of her father's grasp. "He was holding her and kissing her, kissing her, kissing her," says Pierce. "At the time I thought he was just an overly affectionate father, I tried to explain it away to myself, but now I realize I was uncomfortable with it from the start."

The consequences of Woody's intense affection were dire. During custody hearings, Mia described the evening dinner scene, from the time Dylan was three, this way:

> Usually the children would be at the dinner table, and she would hear the key, and [Woody] would just push the doorbell, sort of announcing he was coming in, and he had his own key. I mean, Dylan would start screaming, and on one occasion just jackknifed against the table and fell flat, hitting her head on the floor. The whole high chair just fell to the floor, and she would run every single night into all of the other children's rooms, and she would just scream, "Hide me, hide me," and there was—it was a strange combination of tremendous excitement and clearly fear. I mean, it was beyond what she could deal with.

Although Lark was not present during this incident, she told me that the hide-and-seek game that Dylan and Woody played seemed odd to her. "Dylan always seemed motivated by fear when she used to run into the girls' room, chased by Woody," she admitted.

Woody, however, chose to interpret the dinner-table hysteria in a different way. Under cross-examination by Eleanor Alter, this dialogue took place:

Q. *What would you do when she yelled "Hide me, hide me!" and run away?*
A. I'd stalk after her in an affectionate, paternal way, pick her up, and kiss her.
Q. *And what would she do?*
A. She would hug me and kiss me and giggle.
Q. *Do you recall her asking other children to hide her—the older children, Daisy and Lark?*
A. In a playful way, in a playful way. Strictly a playful way.
Q. *How often did this happen?*
A. It happened a couple of times. I'd ring the bell to come over in the evening, and there was a brief period of time where it happened a couple of times, where she would run and squeal into the other rooms and hide, and I would come after her.

At bedtime, too, while Dylan watched a videotape on television, or if Woody read to her, he would, according to Mia, "just twine himself and twine himself around her, very often putting his head in her lap and just be draped around her, completely around her and nuzzling her and kissing her and kissing her stomach, rubbing her all over the body." Concerned, Mia broached the subject with Woody and suggested that he back off. "Maybe this is too much for her," she told him. " 'That's why she runs away from you all the time. Don't compliment her so effusively, so continually, because, look, it is stopping her from talking.' I would say, 'Why don't you let her come to you sometimes?' because he would pounce on her all the time, and she would enter a room that he was in, and in order to deflect it, she would be a dog or start barking or—she kept him away by being an animal. She came into the room like an animal. She would be on all fours. She would pretend to have antlers, scurry away, not meet his eyes. That was the entering-the-room part." When her attorney asked if Dylan acted that way when Woody was *not* around, Mia said no, not ever.

Mia also claimed that Dylan, in her overexcited state, often grabbed at Woody's penis. ("We don't do that," she would reprimand her daughter.) Woody countered by saying that Mia had been reading sex education books to the kids as bedtime stories, and for weeks Satchel and Dylan walked around the house in a state of extreme kiddie arousal, giggling, pointing, and, apparently, touching.

At Frog Hollow during the summer of 1992, Mia forbade Woody to go upstairs in the morning until the children were awake because she found that he would enter their room while they slept and just lie there on the floor until they opened their eyes. "I thought it peculiar," she remarked.

She was also troubled by how Woody behaved when Dylan went to sleep. She detailed this in court:

> What I saw was that [Woody] would put his hands on either side of [Dylan], sometimes holding her arms down and trying to get eye contact with her. I saw her move her head from side to side just not wanting eye contact, and she would sing; she would do *non sequiturs*; she would just make sounds, and he would say, "Dylan, I want to say good night. I'm saying good night." He would insist on a good night, whatever good night he was expecting from her.

After a while, Mia says, she told Woody outright that his behavior with Dylan violated the child's needs and boundaries. "His approach to her was meeting his own needs rather than being respectful of what Dylan needed," she explained. "I told him that he was intimidating her. I told him that he was making her thought-fragmented; that she was a forthright, direct, clear-thinking child, but that I could see that when he continually pressed himself onto her that she would be evasive. I asked him not to put his thumb in her mouth. I asked him not to take her into bed. He would wait for her when he spent the night in my country house. He would just wear Jockey shorts to sleep in, and he would wait for her to come into bed and then be all over her, and I asked him not to do that. I asked him not to put his head in her lap. There was this wooing quality to his relationship with her that excluded everyone else, and it was overpowering and relentless."

While lavishing attention on Dylan, Woody would at the same time ignore the other kids, including his high-strung towheaded biological son. You could say the patchy relationship began even before Satchel's 1987 birth. Then, Woody commented to *The New York Times* about the new addition-to-be: "I hope it's a she—that would be very important to me."

Too squeamish and disinterested to participate in Mia's Lamaze class, Woody was only too happy for Casey to act as his stand-in. After Satchel's birth, Dylan remained Woody's central focus. Of course, this was in part because Satchel was a difficult, colicky baby who felt secure only with Mia and who would screech uncontrollably when Woody tried to hold him. "Satch demanded attention," says Casey. "But Woody didn't pay much to him. His role was to take care of Dylan because Mia had to spend so much time with the baby. He screamed for hours on end. I don't know how she did it. Poor Mia. Her whole philosophy at that point was 'If I try to satisfy all Satchel's needs now when he's an infant, maybe he won't turn out to be as neurotic as his father.' "

Woody, rather than spending time developing a rapport with his difficult child, doted on the placid one, the "she." His motive, he claimed, was to redress the household balance of power. "[Mia] was always breastfeeding Satchel," complained Woody. Worse, he added, "From that point on, she spent less time with Dylan. I objected to that. And I believe that I overcompensated in that area. I found myself spending more time with Dylan because I found her, in a certain sense, bereft of her mother. There were times I would come over in the morning and find Dylan, having awakened in her own room and crawled down the hall, crying outside Mia's room. And Mia would be inside with Satchel, [with] the door closed."

Mia, for her part, claimed that she always keeps her door open, and that not once did she ever hear her daughter weeping in the hallway. I can attest to her open-door policy with her kids. In the time I spent with her, I *never* saw her bedroom door closed, even when she had the flu and was lying in bed, inert and burning up with a fever.

What Mia felt that Woody didn't understand was how her household always became integrated after a new arrival. "I said that every time I had a baby, the other children were jealous, but that it becomes a unit," she explained during her trial. "I said to him continually, 'Leave Dylan with me and the baby. I will read to Dylan while I nurse the baby. She will get used to [him], and it will be fine eventually.' He expressed concern that I was spending the early days with the baby and not with Dylan, and I kept saying no, it's to do with a family, and everybody gets together and learns to share the time and share me."

But Woody was impatient with that notion. And he was also frequently irritated with Satchel, whom he had named after the famed Negro League pitcher, Satchel Paige. A strikingly bright baby, he was, by nine months, already conversant. In the mornings Woody would come into the children's nursery and try to awaken his son, who slept in the bed beside Dylan, and Satchel would scream at him to go away. When Woody refused to leave, or to leave him alone, Satchel would start kicking his father. Woody took offense and backed off. "It was a terrible relationship," testified Mia, who went on to add that Woody at one point deemed Satchel "a completely superfluous baby." Once, she related, when the child wouldn't stop crying, Woody told him to shut up, "or I'm going to break your fucking leg." (In court Woody categorically denied that this interaction had taken place. It is "absolutely untrue," he claimed.)

Satchel was little more than two when Mia and Woody put him into psychiatric treatment. Sure, Woody, who had been in psychoanalysis for twenty years, emphatically believed that this was the path to personal enlightenment and urban nirvana. Sure, he worried about the boy's dependence on his mother. But they sent him to a therapist for other reasons. "Satchel," Woody explained under oath, "started to exhibit some gender problems." From the age of one, he noticed, his son "was always identifying with the females on the videotapes that were shown to him. Always saying he wanted to be Cinderella, Snow White. Wanted to wear women's clothes. And it alarmed Mia and myself."

Woody blamed Satch's so-called gender problems on Mia, suggesting that she was smothering her son. Naturally, she didn't react well to that. To the contrary. "Mia flew into a rage on the few occasions I said that," he recalled. "She said it was not her fault, that it was probably genetic in some way." I, of course, think that Satchel *had* to be affected by the fact that he was constantly surrounded by females—Tam, Dylan, Larky, Daisy, Monica, and myself. And for at least some of the time, Mia functioned as both mother *and* father.

At any rate, Satchel entered a course of therapy with Dr. Coates, a gender-identity specialist, and according to Woody, the child was greatly helped. "The business of wanting to wear female clothing and identifying with the female character in all stories, and the constant saying, 'I want to be a girl, I'm a girl deer, I'm a girl animal,' eventually dropped away," he said.

Shortly afterward the couple asked Dr. Susan Coates to evaluate Dylan. The little girl was unusually shy, they both agreed. In addition, claimed Woody, "She was having problems distinguishing between fantasy and reality." Mia fiercely disputes this. "I never saw such a problem with her," she told me, pointing out that it was something Woody put into the shrinks' heads.

At the time that Dylan went in for her evaluation, Mia told Dr. Coates that she worried about Mr. Allen's behavior toward the child. Dr. Coates had an occasional chance to observe it in person. Once she was at the apartment when Woody greeted Dylan, who had just come home from school, and, as Mia tells it, the doctor expressed concern to Mia.

"It was Heathcliff and Cathy," said Mia, referring to the passionate lovers in the novel *Wuthering Heights*. "There was a coming together and an embrace and loving words, and it was just very intense, and one would have said romantic, kind of. I would probably ask Dr. Coates to describe that specific [encoun-

ter], because it didn't stick in my mind. I can only tell you that
all of them were like that."

In court Dr. Coates, while pointing out that she was not a
child-abuse expert, merely said:

> I understand why she was worried, because it [Mr. Allen's
> relationship with Dylan] was intense. . . . I did not see it as
> sexual, but I saw it as inappropriately intense because it
> excluded everybody else, and it placed a demand on a child
> for a kind of acknowledgment that I felt should not be
> placed on a child. . . .

As a result of Dr. Coates's evaluation, in April of 1991 Dylan
began therapy with Dr. Nancy Schultz.

Over the years Casey Pascal has observed Woody interacting
with his adopted daughter. "From the beginning I thought that
the way he acted with Dylan was inappropriate," she says. "All
along, I said to Mia, 'What's going on?' And Mia would say,
'Woody just loves Dylan so much.' But I thought it was all one-
sided. It was all coming from Woody, who was dumping his
attention on Dylan, and she couldn't handle it. She would be
sitting there, looking off into space while he was whispering in
her ear. She wasn't responding the way my children respond
when they're being cuddled or tickled. But Woody didn't seem
to notice, and that's what I thought was really strange. He followed her around, and she wasn't even nice to him. Sometimes
she looked like she wanted to be anywhere else."

Whatever excuses Mia made to outsiders, she was deeply concerned about Woody's seductive behavior toward their daughter.
Says Casey: "We always discussed the fact that Dylan shouldn't
be allowed overnights with Woody until she was twelve or thirteen." That is, until she was old enough to know what was going
on, and to be able to get up and leave, if necessary. "Nobody
wants to believe that Woody molested his daughter," Casey adds.
"And it's so easy to believe that it *didn't* happen because that's
what you prefer to believe. You want to say, 'The only way I'll

believe it happened, deep down, is if I see it.' Yet honestly, I always believed it would happen eventually. *Always*."

If Mia was so suspicious of Woody's behavior toward Dylan that she was refusing to allow her overnights with him, why, then, did she stay with him? There was a time, when Dylan was two and Mia and Woody were talking about adopting another child together, that Mia herself began to have grave doubts about their love. At one point she noticed that Woody was not just bestowing extravagant attention upon the little girl, but thoughtful little presents as well. He was courting her, she felt, in a way that he had once courted Mia herself. "It wasn't the presents per se, it was the notion that he [once] would do little things for me, bring little things for me, tokens, and that had stopped," she told the court. "I was hurt and a little perplexed that that element had gone from our relationship."

It was after Woody seemed to have transferred all his affection to the child that Mia became convinced that she should no longer be involved with him. She had tried maybe three times before that to leave him. "But I never had the courage to say anything about it or do anything about it until I was pregnant [with Satchel]," she told me. "And each time before, he would not stay away, so after a week I would recant my decision. Yet when I had this new life inside me, I had a strength, a vision. And so I said to him, 'I don't think we should continue this relationship.'"

Actually, her words were stronger than that. "I told him that I wanted to leave him," she said, "because he was cold and cruel, and I couldn't take the emotional abuse anymore." She explained that she longed for a more conventional union with someone who was kinder. But Woody wouldn't let go. He argued that marriage was just a piece of paper, saying to her, "Do I not behave as if we're married?"

What an irony that back then Woody *refused* to leave Mia. And Mia herself didn't have the strength to really call it quits. "I wanted him to go away. We weren't married, so we couldn't even get a divorce," she said in court. "He wouldn't go away, and then finally, after a few months I lost my resolve, and I'm emotionally dependent on him, or was, and I went back into the relationship."

They never discussed breaking up again. Mia put up with their "sexually and romantically diminished" life together. Until January 13, 1992, that is, when she found the Polaroids of Soon-Yi.

With all her misgivings about her own offbeat and frustrating union with Woody, and her doubts about his behavior toward her daughter, why did Mia allow Woody to adopt Dylan in the first place? In court Eleanor Alter asked Mia the same thing:

Q. *Did it occur to you at the time that if you believed Mr. Allen was acting in an inappropriate manner toward Dylan, that it would not be a good idea for Mr. Allen to formally adopt Dylan?*

A. Can I answer that in two parts? One: I thought he was addressing those concerns seriously [with] two, if not three, psychiatrists. Two: I believed I would be with him for life anyway.

Q. *Did you have any concern for Dylan's physical safety prior to the time that you let him adopt Dylan in 1991?*

A. Safety? I had concerns but I felt reassured by the psychiatrists in attendance [Nancy Schultz and Susan Coates] that everything would be okay ... That he was addressing his behavior, and indeed those things that I had objected to were curtailed, stopped. It was much improved.

Still, back in the middle of 1991—long before Mia was aware of Woody's romance with Soon-Yi, long before she might have toyed with the notion of revenge—she agreed to Woody's adoptions of Dylan and Moses. She did so, she said, *only* after he assured her that "he would not take Dylan for sleepovers ... unless I was there. And that if, God forbid, anything should happen to our relationship, that he would never seek custody. And he gave me his oath that he would never do either of those things."

Was she interested in clinging to Woody's name and power? Making certain she had a movie role every year? Insuring a hefty financial legacy for her kids? Nothing so premeditated and Machiavellian, according to Casey. Mia put up with Woody despite her doubts, Casey suggests, "because she was told all the time that it was her imagination. Woody told her constantly that she was misreading everything, and that he was a loving father who was simply showing his affection to his child. Don't forget, her whole life was involved with him—her business, her children. But she didn't *live* with him. If they had been living together, she probably would have left. But there was so much space between them that she always had time to recover. Their relationship was not so defined. There was time for her to go home and say, 'Yes, I was imagining things.'"

There was no imagining the hideous scenario that was unfolding during the second week of August 1992. While an indignant Mia begged Woody for more time to examine Dylan's molestation charges, an even more indignant Woody threatened that if she didn't drop them instantly, he would go public with his affair with Soon-Yi. He later insisted in court that Mia had "brainwashed" Dylan.

> I believe she had been brainwashing the child all along for the last weeks or month [before August 4]. She had told me on the phone several weeks earlier that she had something nasty planned for me. That I had taken her daughter, she was going to take mine. And she put a "child molester" note on my door. I believe she was brainwashing Dylan at that time, planning to do that nasty thing she had planned for me. . . .

When Woody's attorney, Elkan Abramowitz, wondered aloud how Mia could have brainwashed her daughter *before* August 4 to accuse Woody *after* August 4 of doing something to her *on* August 4, Woody explained:

> I don't think she brainwashed her to say I did something on August 4. I thought she brainwashed her, and the opportunity presented itself on August 4. That became the date that the fruits of her brainwashing came to fruition. . . . I

think she was telling her [before August 4] that "your father did a dirty thing to Soon-Yi." That "he did a terrible thing to her." That "please be careful. Does he ever touch you? Does he ever put his hand on you?" I think she was speaking to her in that way constantly. And to the other kids around there who're also reinforcing this.

Woody explained that the fact his head was in his seven-year-old daughter's lap was "a normal paternal thing, as it was not in any way sexual." He also claimed that Mia, after receiving the phone call from Alison, had boasted to Monica, "There, now I got him."

"And," Woody said in court, "she said it with relish."

So, in a nutshell, here it was. Mia thought Woody had violated two of her daughters. Woody thought Mia had accused him unjustly and "with relish." They were at an angry impasse.

Woody held off until August 13. That day, during yet another sub rosa settlement discussion at which attorneys for both sides were present, Woody decided to go forward immediately with his legal battle for custody of Dylan, Satchel, and Moses. Papers were filed later that day in the state supreme court in Manhattan. We thought he was doing this to call into question Mia's still-secret child-abuse accusation. Both Woody and Mia were now caught up in a public process which, it seemed, carried them along like a furious tide.

I'll never forget that afternoon. Barely was the ink dry on the legal documents than a sheriff's car arrived at Frog Hollow, and a big, burly, mustachioed lawman strode up the driveway to serve the papers on Mia in person. The doorbell rang, he announced himself, and Mia, exhausted and tense, simply panicked. Thinking that he had come to take her kids away, she began to scream, "Don't let him take the kids, Kristi, please don't let him take my children."

Her hysteria and terror were contagious. I, too, was stricken. And there we were, like two chickens without our heads, running from room to room, locking all the doors, and Mia was crying, "Kristi, don't accept the papers! Don't touch the papers!" But the doorbell kept ringing and ringing. Finally, I opened the door and said in my most officious way, "Mia is not here." Meanwhile, she was standing right behind me, looking the sheriff straight in the eye. Without blinking, she told him, "I'm her sister." I looked around at her, feeling confused and crazy. Mia's face stared back at me, a desperate intensity in her blue eyes. "She's her sister," I said. It was like a bad episode of *I Love Lucy*. If I weren't so scared, I would have laughed at the absurdity of it all.

The sheriff, with little sense of humor and less tolerance, simply slapped the papers into my hand, wheeled around, and headed for his car as Mia cried to me once more, "Don't accept the papers." I ran up the walkway after him, feeling as if I had a smoldering coal in my hand, and I tried to stuff it through the top of his window. But the glass wasn't open wide enough. The sheriff quickly sped away in a cloud of dust as the papers fell to the gravel driveway. By the time we actually looked at them later that afternoon, the news had already hit the wires.

We always felt that Woody broke the story as a counterattack. He feared that the tabloids would get wind of the molestation investigation, and so he tried to put his own spin on events by announcing his split from Mia and his battle for the children first. By charging her with being an unfit mother, he was like a second-rate prizefighter who took a below-the-belt swipe before the starting bell rang.

Mia's molestation charges and Woody's lawsuit together unleashed a media circus that did not let up for an entire year. Mia was so overwhelmed by the mob of hungry reporters and photographers who had suddenly flocked to Bridgewater, stationing themselves at the top of the hill, right outside her driveway, that, with the exception of three visits to the doctor with Dylan, she didn't leave the house in Connecticut for three weeks. Not once. I was her lifeline to the world. I went to the grocery store. To the video store. The bookstore. The post office. I faxed letters and memos for her to her attorneys from my parents' house, and she received all her faxes through them. We didn't leave the house until the Bridgewater Fair arrived on August 28.

And in some ways it was very exciting. Not only would I meet actual reporters like Roseanna Scotto, but I was constantly pursued by photographers and TV camera crews as I went about Mia's business. Occasionally, at night, I'd catch a glimpse of myself on the eleven o'clock news. My phone started ringing off the wall. My college roommate, Colleen Tracy, called the very first night and left a message: "What are you doing on TV, you little movie star?"

However, Mia's own doubts about her future quickly began to filter down to the children. One day shortly after Woody let her know that she would not be in *Manhattan Murder Mystery*, the movie he was preparing to shoot that fall, Satchel and Dylan decided to pitch in and lend their mother a hand. They set up a little stand in front of the house, which they piled high with pine cones and acorns. As I walked by, Satchel called to me, "Kristi, we're helping Mommy because she doesn't have any money. Want to buy a pine cone for fifty cents?" "Yeah, Kristi," added Dylan, "want to buy an acorn?" "Sure," I answered and bought one of each. Recently, Mia and I recalled that pine cone stand and had a good laugh, but at the time the incident tugged at my heart.

It was a period of heightened emotions and heightened tensions. There was high comedy too—although that's not the way we looked at some of our crazy plans back then. For instance, at one point we seriously thought that the Connecticut police might indict Woody. For three days the state police said, "We're going ahead with it." We were wild-eyed with fear that there would be another big press explosion. So Mia instructed me: "This is what you have to do. Pack one warm-weather suitcase and one cold-weather suitcase." Then she tried to decide where we would escape in the event that Woody was indicted. Among the possibilities: Lieutenant's Island, off Cape Cod, where my old high school girlfriend Laura German's family had a house; or Mike Nichols's place just down the road. Mia also thought about going to stay at her friend Skip Stein's villa in the Bahamas. Or Frank Sinatra's in Palm Springs. She found that idea especially appealing because Frank apparently has so much security there, although Mia wondered whether Frank's wife Barbara would welcome our arrival quite as much as Frank. In the end, she took both the cold-weather and warm-weather suitcases to

Mike's house and left them both in the breezeway leading to his kitchen. Then, if Woody was indicted and went to jail, we were ready to flee to avoid the media zoo.

Mia lived in fear. And she fed on local rumors. At one point she heard through the law-enforcement grapevine that there may have been a fix in at Yale, and that the Connecticut police were investigating to see if this was true. Nothing immediately came of it, however. Unless you count what we considered to be the bungled nature of the investigation by the noted Yale–New Haven child-abuse team. It that had been brought into the case by the Connecticut police because of its success at uncovering instances of child abuse. Despite its reputation, incredibly enough the team never even called a child psychiatrist to interview Dylan.

As you can imagine, we were all getting stir crazy. Finally, on the 28th of August, the day we had planned to go to the Bridgewater Fair, I walked outside and strode to the top of the hill. Emerging from the house could mean being "shot"—by a photographer, of course. But the word "shot" has a double meaning, the second being "to hunt game, as with a gun." Very appropriate to our situation, I thought. Of course, Mia has been so anti-press, dating back from the days when photographers hounded her and Sinatra, that I couldn't help sharing her feelings. The only difference was that Mia was a movie star and I was only her friend and helper—a protective figure who just happened to be in the way of the photographers/marksmen. But I often forgot this and, swept away by the intensity of the situation, I, too, ran from the cameras as though the men behind them were desperate to capture my image as well. I still feel uneasy when I see a stranger, even a harmless tourist, holding a Nikon.

On this particular day I made a deal with the photographers and reporters who had been staked out, twenty strong at least, for weeks. We agreed that they could take photos of Mia going into the local Bridgewater bank to cash a check if, in return, they would keep their distance from the kids and ask no questions whatsoever.

So we gathered the kids together, and I told Mia to change out of her black T-shirt and jeans into her white T-shirt and jeans because they looked more cheerful. Then we all got into the Suburban, Big Red, and drove Mia to the bank. She held Isaiah and took Satchel by the hand as she walked inside. Dylan and I stayed in the car, and I covered the window with my red windbreaker to protect her from the photographers' lenses. Afterwards we fooled them. While all the reporters scurried off to the fairground entrance to wait for us, we faked them out and drove back home.

The next morning at eight-thirty, we sneaked away from Frog Hollow. First we took Tam and Sophie down to Mike Nichols's farm, where we planned to swim in his pool later on (although he was not home). Unfortunately, Tam was in the middle of one of her terrible screaming fits. First in the car, and now at Mike's farm, she pitched and rolled, screamed and spit and tore at my T-shirt and face. Mia and I had to carry her into Mike's barn. We brought her to a lounge area right off his indoor riding ring, where she clawed my arm and kicked cabinets, booting magazines and ashtrays off the table. Kim, one of Mike's helpers, said, "Don't worry, we'll take care of her. Go to the fair." So as soon as Tam calmed down, we took Isaiah, Satchel, and Dylan, and piled them into Big Red. Then we headed for the fair.

Only one reporter, Paul Adeo from the *New York Post*, saw us there. I said, "Please, Paul." Already, I was getting to know the press. "Please keep your distance. This is our first day out." He was very respectful. He took only a few pictures, and then he left.

A good thing too. Suddenly, Mia started to feel ill. Her chest was rising and falling, and she began breathing heavily. All the color drained from her face. In moments she turned ghostly white. I thought she was going to faint. "Mia, are you all right?" I asked. Clearly, she wasn't, but she was desperate to appear perky and upbeat. Steadying herself, she finally said, "Kristi, I feel like I'm going to collapse. I can't take this anymore. I've got to get out of here." She began to shake uncontrollably. But the remarkable thing is that, as she had promised the kids, she went on the Ferris wheel anyway. She felt it was the least she could do for them. They hadn't been away from Frog Hollow in three weeks.

Not for lack of trying, however. Once, desperate to go out but reluctant to stir the beast in the road, Mia and I packed a picnic lunch of fruit, cheese, ham and bologna sandwiches, and we took Moses, Tam, Isaiah, Satchel, and Dylan on a hike about a mile into her property. For a few hours we sat by a stream not far from a road, watching the butterflies light onto the oaks and the ants march in a single column through a stray Oreo. The kids were so happy to be out of the house. But whenever we would hear a car whiz by, Mia would automatically duck or shield her head with her hands. It was nerveracking—as though she expected the entire New York City press corps to suddenly swoop down on her in our leafy hideaway.

Another time we weren't quite so lucky. Again, Mia was wearing her uniform in those days: black jeans and a black T-shirt that was way too big for her. She had developed a habit of buying them, six at a time, and now almost always shrouded herself in black because, as she herself put it, she felt as if she were in mourning. I myself wore black all the time too, and so did Sophie Bergé, the French tutor, who was also with us. That day, as we decided to escape Frog Hollow, we looked like three old Italian widows in our oversize black uniforms.

We had been mapping out various contingency escape plans but arbitrarily chose to go with plan A. This involved my driving out onto the road and picking up Mia, Sophie, and the children, who had already sneaked through the woods and past the photographers, and were hiding behind a cluster of bushes about two hundred yards from the house. I would serve as the decoy, leaving the property solo in the hope that the photographers wouldn't follow me.

Mia and I gave each other the high sign. Wandering out into the cool, shady yard, I watched the group head into the long, velvety grass. Silently I asked God to please just let us get out, unencumbered, for a little while. After all, the kids only wanted to go to Toys "R" Us. Moments later I stood up and padded slowly across the cold slate path in my bare feet, holding my shoes in my hands. I boosted myself up into the bouncy driver's seat of Big Red. The car seemed so huge and empty without the children crowding into it. I turned the engine over and backed out of the garage. As my sweaty palms squeezed the wheel, my heart soared. "We're going to make it," I said to myself, and began to hum the "Mission: Impossible" theme song.

It was always the same when I rounded the corner of the driveway that August. The road was lined with reporters and photographers who had become familiar to me: Paul Adeo from the *New York Post,* Patty Vine from *A Current Affair,* and Rick Maiman from Sigma Photo Agency, among several others. This day was no different. Yet as I turned out of the driveway, I tried to remain as relaxed as possible. Thank goodness Tam wasn't with us. More than once that summer she had had fits like the one that had overcome her the morning we visited Mike Nichols's stable. A few times she ran out into Mia's yard and at the top of her lungs screamed, "AAAaargh!" Sometimes I'd put my hand over her mouth to stifle her scream. The press, only two hundred yards away, must have thought that Mia and I beat Tam. To muffle her shrieks, we later got into the habit of putting a coat over her and shoving her into the car before we headed up the driveway. She would claw, kick, and scream like the devil. To this day I have scars where she scratched me. Then eventually she would tire herself out, and an hour later she would be lying in my arms, sleeping as soundly as a baby.

We certainly didn't need any fits today, I thought as Big Red rumbled up the hill. As I glanced into the rearview mirror, I saw Paul Adeo's car and Rick Maiman's behind it. Damn! They were gaining on me. I approached the designated bushes. Mia popped her blond head out from behind them and waved to me. I continued on past her to the corner, the press cars all close behind. Then I slammed my fists down onto the wheel in disgust. It wasn't working.

I tried to back out onto the road, maneuvering Big Red around to return to the house. Five or six cars were now behind me. Finally I turned and headed back to where Mia and the children were hiding. "Forget it," I yelled angrily at her blond head. I sat idle in the road for a moment. I hadn't been this angry in days. "Why can't you just let us go out, for God's sake. You guys are driving me crazy," I screamed through my teeth at the cars behind me. The trip to the toy store had been effectively aborted.

I headed home and parked in the driveway, waiting for Mia to return. A few moments later I could hear the children chattering at the top of the meadow. Slowly, they made their way down through the clover-dotted grass. "I'm sorry," I told Mia.

The kids seemed happy enough. But as we returned to the house which was fast becoming a prison, Mia asked in a small voice, "Oh, God, Kristi what will become of us?"

"You have to make your own moral choices. Otherwise you're like a robot or a lizard."

Leonard Zelig

EIGHT

Mia's Older Kids

When she speaks about motherhood, Mia sounds more like a blissed-out Catholic schoolgirl than a movie star or wispy femme fatale. Just ask her, and she'll tell you that the glamorous work, the fancy friends, and the dashing, accomplished beaux are nice, but what really matters are her kids. "My children have given real meaning to my life," she once confessed to me. "I've always told them, 'You must look into your deepest soul and find something that you can give to the world that will be meaningful—not for yourself, but for other people. Until you can do that, you can't be truly happy. You can't live without giving.' All I can tell you, Kristi, is that I found a loving way, through my children, so that I can give back to the world."

With eleven children, four natural-born, one black, two Korean, three Vietnamese, one blind, one with cerebral palsy, and one—Soon-Yi—learning disabled, Mia has created a great, boisterous, multicultural, multiethnic brood.

Woody and his sister Letty Anderson, forty-nine, who is an executive in his newly formed production company, Sweetland Films (and whom Mia helped when she, too, decided to adopt a child), managed to deride Mia's family as often as possible. Woody, in court, said, "This was not a traditional household at all, as I went through it. A household with many children, with

153

an adoption that could come and go, with kids sleeping in bunk beds, with kids from different parts of the world . . . it was more like a foster-home feeling. I did not perceive this as a traditional family."

Letty took it one step further. "Mia favors her biological children while treating the older adopted kids as servants," she has said. Interestingly, Monica Thompson, in her sworn testimony, echoed this accusation. I believe it is sheer nonsense. It simply shows that Monica was influenced by Woody and his sister, and that Letty has never had the slightest sense of who any of the kids were, most especially Mia's oldest daughters.

Mia adopted Lark Song in early 1973 and Summer Song in late 1974. When she was a little girl Summer changed her name to Daisy—Daisy inspired by Mia's performance opposite Robert Redford as F. Scott Fitzgerald's golden flapper with a voice "full of money" in the 1974 Francis Ford Coppola–Jack Clayton adaptation of *The Great Gatsby*.

Immediately Mia provided her girls with illustrious, pedigreed godparents: Lark, who didn't have a godmother, made up for it with her royal godfather, Yul Brynner. Daisy's godparents were Samantha Williams, wife of *E.T.* composer, John Williams, and Tom Stoppard, the British playwright who wrote *The Real Thing* and *Rosencrantz and Guildenstern Are Dead*. (As for Soon-Yi, her first godmother was actress Natalie Wood, and after Wood's 1981 death, Rose Styron, wife of William Styron, the author of *Sophie's Choice*, stepped in.).

Anyone who has spent a minute in Mia's household understands that Lark is, by nature, the most maternal of young women. She stands five feet tall in her stocking feet, everything about her is bold and powerful—her build, her voice, and her personality. A little mother hen to her younger siblings, she emanates strength, self-sufficiency, and concern. Where Mia is a mild-mannered and sometimes wishy-washy disciplinarian, Lark is precise and bossy, often telling the kids in a no-nonsense way, "Don't you do that!"

Larky, as we call her, isn't merely passionate and powerful, she possesses a sharp tongue and is always ready with a quick retort. When I first came to work for Mia, I thought Lark had competitive feelings toward me, but we have since become close friends. But back then she may have seen me as an usurper seizing her position in the family as Mia's chief baby-sitter, bottle washer, and kiddie watcher. It had always been her niche, but now she was living at a New York University dorm and studying nursing. Still, she remained extremely close to her mom and occasionally came home on weekends to help out with the kids simply because she wanted to. She is, hands down, Dylan's favorite, after Mia.

Daisy takes care of Dylan and the other little ones too, but frankly with much less enthusiasm. Petite and willow-slim, Daisy is more of a true teenager—she loves progressive rock, going shopping with her friends, and wearing grunge jeans or trendy black—the "in" color for Manhattan kids. Outgoing and generous, Daisy, with her impish sense of humor, enjoys being a tease. She especially likes to joke around with Tam. "Oooh, Tam got in trouble at school today. I'm gonna have to tell Mom!" she starts in. For a brief second Tam's face darkens with anger, and then she laughs. Daisy isn't all jokes, however. She won the math prize in her senior year at the Nightingale-Bamford School and is now studying psychology at Wheaton College in Norton, Massachusetts.

As is typical in many families, Mia's boys have a harder time with baby-sitting chores than the girls do. Fletcher absolutely *will not* watch the kids. Nor will Sascha. They have no patience for it. Matthew has patience, though, and he will baby-sit sometimes. Moses does too, because he's at that age—fifteen—where he has no choice. Yet he's not always a model sitter. He agrees to play with the little kids, but he gets ruffled when they act up and suddenly gives them a swat or two.

The older kids all share terrific relationships with each other. If the natural-born children have ever had any resentment toward their adopted siblings, they have rarely shown it. Perhaps Fletcher did not appreciate little Isaiah's crying through the night during his first six months in the household. And sure, there have been times that all of the kids have wanted more attention from their mom; that happens in any family. But Mia has taught them to make room in their hearts for the others.

While Matthew and Sascha, the twins, are both easy to get along with, Matthew may be the most remote of Mia's brood, hidden and difficult to know. Having just completed his freshman year at Georgetown Law School, he has a polished, preppy look and an adult way of articulating things. During the media blitz, he spent as much time as possible with his girlfriend, Priscilla Gilman. Priscilla, whose mom is Mia's literary agent, Lynn Nesbitt, wants to be an English professor, and she is at Yale getting her master's degree. The pair are complete opposites. She is a happy, outgoing, robust person, very buoyant and with a sweet, spontaneous giggle. He is quiet and brooding. When Matthew laughs—which is rarely—you enjoy it.

Sascha, Matthew's fraternal twin, is a more relaxed type, and perhaps the most unaffected person I have ever met. He is so *himself*, never fussing with his hair or his clothes; much like his mother, he never really worries about his appearance. Sascha has a great sense of humor and he is also so pliable. If I ever said, "I have to run an errand. You want to come with me?" he would be game. "Sure. Why not?" he would reply. Sascha's girlfriend, Carrie, whom he has been seeing for three years, is central to his life. They met when they were working part-time at a video store on West Seventy-second Street a few years ago. In May 1993 Carrie earned her master's in social work, and she projects the perfect social worker's personality—nurturing and sympathetic. Yet Carrie is special on another count as well. She does a comedy routine at clubs like Stand Up New York. Not only that, she teaches stand-up comedy to patients. I hope she helped Sascha, who is a sensitive guy, discover the funny side of life, post-Woody.

If there's a "charming" gene, Fletcher has got it. Although he is highly intelligent and loves to either tinkle at the piano or fiddle with his computer, he was never much interested in school. Mia was constantly telling him not to do his homework in front of the TV and sending for the math tutor and German tutor. Like Matthew, Fletcher attended Collegiate, a private Manhattan high school, graduating in June 1993.

On Valentine's Day, 1993, Fletcher invited me to a concert that his father was participating in at Lincoln Center. Also along were two of his buddies, Walleed and George. Lark and her boyfriend, Jesse, and Matthew and Priscilla were planning to be there as well. And throughout the concert, while the jazz trio played "Over the Rainbow," with Andre at the piano, Fletcher sat in his seat, drawing zany cartoons of Dad and the other players, which he then passed around to all of us. Very teenlike, true. But when I went off on a European holiday, he sent me a bon voyage present of an elegant Parker fountain pen and a beautiful Victorian-style note which he had scripted on his computer. It clearly took a great deal of his time, and it was such a sweet gesture. That's also the kind of person he is.

As a present for my twenty-fourth birthday, Mia's kids heaped surprises on me. On Friday, January 22, 1993, the night before my actual birthday, I went out with some friends, and when I returned, I found a chocolate cake with vanilla icing that Daisy and Sascha had stayed up all evening to bake. And there was a sweet note as well, with a little drawing of a daisy beside her name.

The following night, my real birthday, Daisy and her boyfriend, James, Sascha and Carrie, Fletcher, and two friends all took me out to a Japanese dinner. There were gifts as well. Fletcher bought me a big boxful of chocolate eclairs and cookies and sweets; James and Daisy gave me a Slinky because they said that it reminded them of me (I was flattered). Lark, who was at school, left me a pretty forest-green ribbed shirt from the French Connection boutique. And Fletcher, who usually dislikes playing the piano for an audience, even serenaded me for twenty minutes.

Mia noted my birthday as well. At nine-thirty in the morning she called from Connecticut and sang "Happy Birthday" to me very, very slowly in her soft voice. Then she said, "I've left a little present on your pillow for you. Did you find it?"

I had. It was a generous check, along with a white long-sleeved button-down shirt from J. Crew. She also left a couple of long-sleeve turtlenecks—one was moss green, the other black. Then Tam and the little kids got on the phone. "Hey, Chicken," squealed Tam in her loud "outside voice," "happy birthday." At eleven o'clock that morning, a dozen white porcelain roses arrived, and for a moment my heart skipped a beat—a mystery admirer, I thought. Then I read the note: "We love you. Mom and Dad."

In a family as large as Mia's, it's only natural that some bonds are stronger than others, and that some kids get on others' nerves. Lark and Fletcher, for example, often locked horns. It was a matter of clashing styles. Fletcher is the type who would never complain, "You're stepping on my foot." He would rather stand there and take the pain, whereas Lark would immediately yell, "You are stepping on my foot, you jerk." But they are the two most extreme opposites in the family.

Lark tended to overpower Soon-Yi and even Woody. He was markedly uncomfortable with her. Soon-Yi drew closest to Matthew and, later on, to Daisy. Matthew and Sascha, of course, were best friends. Sascha and Daisy formed an alliance. And, perhaps closest of all, Daisy and Lark. Moses, the kid who bridges the babies and the young adults, is perhaps the family's major loner. Yet like his sisters and brothers, he is fiercely loyal to his mother.

In fact, whenever the children went on TV to defend their mother, it was always spontaneous and of their own making—or mine. For instance, one day in August, reporter Chris O'Donoghue from Channel 9 caught up with Fletcher on his way to the airport. Fletcher was off to Greece, where his then-girlfriend lived, for a vacation. And O'Donoghue asked him what he thought of the Woody situation. All on his own, Fletcher came out with this incredible statement:

Well, I think it was probably a last-minute attempt to detract some of the weight or validity from our side of the argument. His accusation that my mother is an unfit mother is absurd. I think he is probably a desperate person right now, and he has to say he's in love with Soon-Yi because he's trying to make the best of an already-embarrassing situation.

Then Fletcher turned and just walked away from the cameras. But nobody put him up to it.

I did, however, push both Moses and Daisy before the cameras in Bridgewater. I, too, felt that *somebody* should put the record straight after Woody and his spin doctors were setting it on its ear. So when a CNN crew showed up to tape a statement from Moses, even after Mia had said she didn't want him to appear on TV, I convinced her to let him go ahead, promising that I would run interference for him. In fact, the interview got away from us and became a half-hour grilling that neither of us was up to. In the end, I completely regretted it.

On another morning, Daisy and I drove up to the Village Store in Bridgewater to get some milk, only to discover a dozen or so photographers and TV crews milling about. And I said to her, "I wish you would come to your mom's defense and set the record straight as to the kind of mother she is." Daisy wanted to, but she was nervous. Just as she was contemplating a statement, a reporter walked up to her, not knowing exactly who she was, and asked for her comments. "I'm Daisy Previn," she began, and suddenly, as twenty reporters gathered frantically around us, she blurted out, "and any accusation that my mother is an unfit mother is completely ridiculous. She is the best mother I have ever seen." Then, almost surprised at her own vehemence, she jumped back into the car, turned to me, and said, "Let's go."

To Woody's claims that Mia is an unfit mother, Mia says, "Look how my kids are turning out. They are great. They are happy and healthy. None of them drinks or does drugs. We are a very close family."

Only one thing mars their record: Soon-Yi.

In the spring of 1993, before I left Mia's household, Daisy, Lark, and I went out to lunch at Diane's, and the girls revealed some of their feelings toward Woody, Mia, and Soon-Yi herself. Musing about Woody, they admitted how lukewarm they felt about the possibility of him marrying their mother. "I didn't care," said Daisy with a shrug, "but I actually did want Woody and Mom to move in together because the apartments they looked at together were really nice. At about the time that Dylan came, in 1985, they were sent pictures of New York City apartments by realty agents. Really incredible places. One, which was located in Gracie Square, had a spiral staircase and so many rooms that we would all have had our own bedroom. It was a huge place. It was in a building that used to be an old school." Nothing, however, came of the idea of actually consolidating under one roof.

Woody's presence in their lives *did,* however, offer certain privileges. For instance, when the girls where eleven and twelve, he would let them use his screening room. "We used to take friends there every weekend to see movies. It was fun," said Daisy.

"I thought the trips to Europe were really nice," chimed in Lark. "We stayed at really nice hotels, and Woody took my boyfriend Jesse with us one year, which I always thought was great."

When I asked if they were ever harrassed by paparazzi in Europe, both girls suddenly began to giggle. "Remember the glass doors?" Daisy said, looking to Lark. Lark nodded, and suddenly the giggles erupted into laughter. Feeling a little out of it, I looked from one to the other. "One time we were in Paris," Lark began to explain, "and Woody was holding Dylan. And there were these huge glass windows in front of the hotel. Actually, the façade was completely glass. Woody was frantically running from photographers with Dylan in his arms, and he walked right into the glass. Dylan went into the glass too—BAM! Her head went smack right into it." Well, that wasn't exactly hysterical in *my* book, I observed.

"But then he did it again," said Daisy. "He turned and started running from the photographers, and he ran into a marble pole in the lobby. I'll always remember it. It was so funny." Maybe you had to have been there.

There was one perk that Woody provided that the girls despised: the limousine. "The limo was when I was in the sixth grade. It was so-o-o embarrassing. All of us except Soon-Yi hated it," said Lark. "When we were driven to school, we used to have the driver drop us off two blocks away. I mean, do you think it would be smart to be dropped off in a limo in front of Columbia Prep?" She laughed as Daisy adamantly agreed. "Ooh, I *really* hated the limo," she echoed her sister.

Did Woody ever yell at the girls or try to discipline them, I wondered. In unison, Daisy and Lark insisted, "No. Not ever."

Still one big happy family on holiday: In 1989, Mia, carrying
Satchel, 2, Woody, wheeling Dylan, 4, and, at rear, Soon-Yi, then 17,
arrived at the London airport. (PARKER/ALPHA/GLOBE)

"I suppose you could say that we're sort of a family of hippies," Mia (pictured at home with her mom, actress Maureen O'Sullivan) once said. (STEVE SANDS/OUTLINE)

"You silly, remember you were jealous of your sister once?" Woody used to say to Mia, pictured in 1979 with her sister Stephanie, younger by five years. (DARLEEN RUBIN/OUTLINE)

Shortly after moving back to Manhattan from England in 1980, Mia, carrying newly-adopted Moses, negotiates the sidewalks of New York, with, from left, Soon-Yi, Fletcher, Daisy, and, holding grandma Maureen's hand, Lark. (GLOBE PHOTOS INC.)

"Frank had to realize that a flower is a better present than a mink," said Mia (posing in May of 1967 with her husband Frank Sinatra) of their brief generation-gap marriage. (GLOBE PHOTOS INC.)

"A lot is said about Mia's childlike quality," said her second husband, Andre Previn (pictured with, from left, Matthew, 3, Mia, Lark the infant, and Sascha, 3, in 1973). "But it's just a cloak. There's real maturity underneath." (TERRY O'NEILL/GLOBE PHOTOS INC.)

"What does that mean—to be a star?" claimed Mia shortly after winning an Oscar nomination for *Rosemary's Baby.* "I cringe from the glamour and the tinsel." Here, she confers with *Rosemary's* director, Roman Polanski, on location in 1967. (ARCHIVE PHOTOS)

"I know which directors are good for me by their concepts," said Mia (with Woody in *Hannah and Her Sisters* in 1986, left, and in a scene from John Guillermin's 1978 *Death on the Nile,* below). "You look for one who can satisfy your concept, and he yours. In a way, it's strangely sexual." (GAMMA-LIAISON AND ARCHIVE PHOTOS)

"Smile, Kristi!" Daisy took this snapshot of Isaiah and me in Central Park in February of 1993. Then we switched roles, below, and I played *paparazzi,* posing Daisy and Dylan on a slide in the playground. (AUTHOR COLLECTION)

At the height of the media blitz in April, 1993, I hurriedly carried Satchel into a waiting limo. (AUTHOR COLLECTION)

Mavis Smith, Mia's long-time housekeeper, and I took a moment to vamp for Daisy's camera in Mia's kitchen during the stressed-out days of January, 1993. (AUTHOR COLLECTION)

Tam, then 11, and I caught our breath during a December, 1992, afternoon of ice skating at the Wolman Rink in Central Park. On a February, 1993, outing, right, camera hams Satchel, 5, left, Dylan, 7, and I smiled for Daisy in the park. (AUTHOR COLLECTION)

After the custody verdict in June of 1993, I visited Mia at Frog Hollow, left. Tam stood in the foreground while Satchel, back to the camera, played on the lawn. In Miami in December, 1993, while Mia filmed *Miami*, Isaiah, bottom, and Dylan, posed with me and a friendly earthbound dolphin at Sea World. (AUTHOR COLLECTION)

In August of 1992, after being cooped up at Frog Hollow for almost three weeks to avoid the press, Mia, Isaiah in her arms, and I went out for the first time to the Bridgewater Fair. (PAUL ADAO)

A familiar moment for us, at right:
During the custody hearings, Mia,
with Satchel and Isaiah in her
arms, rushes into her building to
avoid the feeding frenzy.
(PAUL ADAO)

Our trip to Los
Angeles in February,
1993: While Mia read
for a role in *Wolf,*
Satchel, 5, and Isaiah,
13 months, left,
played on the patio
outside our Bel-Air
Hotel bungalow.
Again, while Mia
filmed *Miami* in
December, 1993,
Satchel, almost 6, left,
and Dylan, 8, right,
smothered little Isaiah
with their playfulness.
(AUTHOR COLLECTION)

Daisy's high school graduation on June 18, 1993: (From left) Daisy, Mia, Lark, Fletcher, Moses (looking dashing without his glasses), and James McDonald, Daisy's boy friend, all felt very festive. (AUTHOR COLLECTION)

One day earlier, on June 17, 1993, Sascha, Daisy, and Mia celebrated Fletcher's graduation from the Collegiate School on 74th Street and West End Avenue. (AUTHOR COLLECTION)

In front of Collegiate, I took a few moments to congratulate Fletcher, who I think may be one of the world's most charming young men. (AUTHOR COLLECTION)

Mia shared a loving moment with her daughter Daisy on Daisy's graduation day. (AUTHOR COLLECTION)

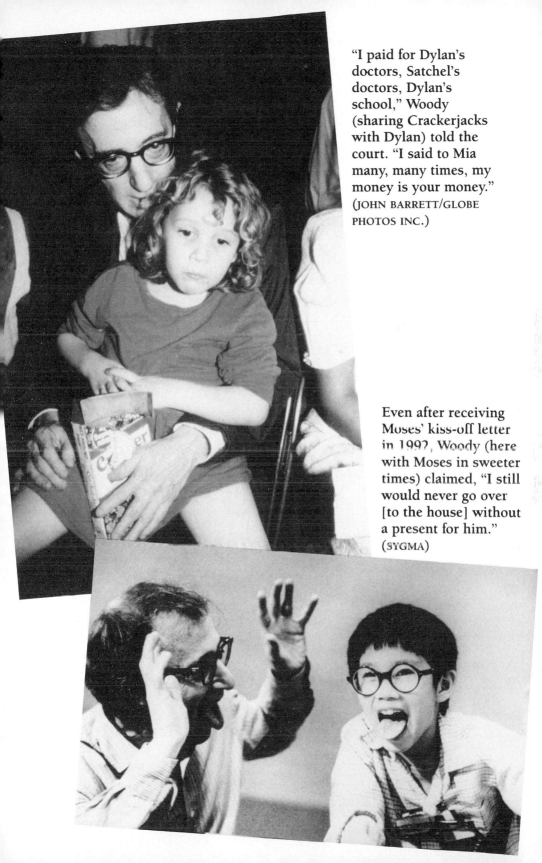

"I paid for Dylan's doctors, Satchel's doctors, Dylan's school," Woody (sharing Crackerjacks with Dylan) told the court. "I said to Mia many, many times, my money is your money." (JOHN BARRETT/GLOBE PHOTOS INC.)

Even after receiving Moses' kiss-off letter in 1992, Woody (here with Moses in sweeter times) claimed, "I still would never go over [to the house] without a present for him." (SYGMA)

"What about Soon-Yi and me? What about Soon-Yi's principles?" Mia (with Soon-Yi in 1991) asked Woody when he admitted his affair with her daughter. (GERARDO SOMOZA/OUTLINE)

"Woody was never any kind of father figure to me," insisted Soon-Yi (at age 15, crossing Central Park West with Woody, Mia, and the infant Dylan in 1985). (PAUL ADAO)

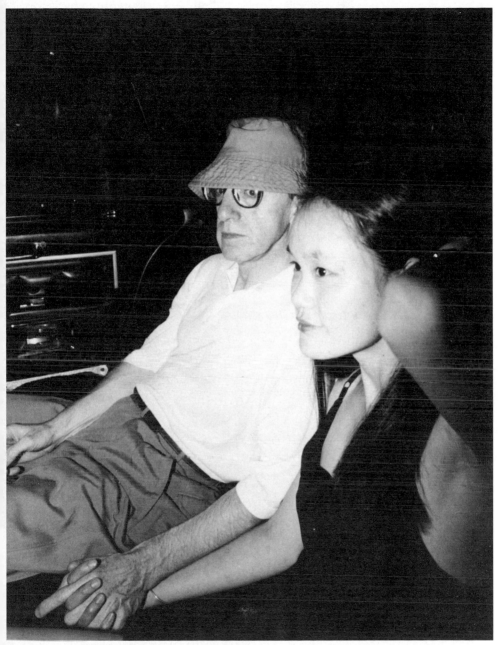

"When I first got friendly with Woody, he and Mia were finished with their romance and were just friends," said Soon-Yi, (with Woody in September of 1992). (PAUL ADAO)

MIA'S CENTRAL PARK WEST APARTMENT: Left, her hallway, looking into the children's nursery. Mia has removed all photos of Woody from the family snapshots on the walls. Below: This dream view, which looks across the park to Woody's own penthouse, is what Mia sees from her 11th-floor living room windows. (AUTHOR COLLECTION)

Mia's CPW bedroom, above: There is a treadmill at right that Woody gave her, which she rarely uses. Above it is a needlepoint family tree with Woody and Mia on top, kids below. Mia made this during *The Purple Rose of Cairo* (1985). Photos and paintings by the kids hang over the bed. The crucifix once belonged to Mia's mother. (AUTHOR COLLECTION)

In Mia's kitchen, right, the kids threw Moses a 15th birthday party on January 27, 1993. From left are Moses (standing), Satchel (back to camera), Dylan (making a face), Tam, and Mia, wearing her party hat. (AUTHOR COLLECTION)

"I think it was meant to be," Woody, pictured strolling through Manhattan, below, with Soon-Yi in October, 1993, has said of their affair. Left: The onscreen affair he created between a high school girl (Mariel Hemingway) and comedy writer (Woody) in *Manhattan* (1979) seems to have foreshadowed the real thing. (PAUL ADAO)

On April 10, 1993, the day I testified, Mia and I (looking stoic but feeling scared) left her Central Park West apartment on our way to court. (SYGMA)

Mia, accompanied by two associates, made her way through the mob of reporters into the courtroom in June of 1993. (ANDREA RENAULT/GLOBE PHOTOS INC.)

"It's unthinkable," said Woody (shown at a 1992 press conference) shortly after Mia's charges of molestation made headlines. (JOHN BARRETT/GLOBE PHOTOS INC.)

In fact, recalled Daisy, "He actually stuck up for me once when I got into trouble. If he saw that I did something that was wrong, he wouldn't tell Mom. Like, if he was sitting in the kitchen and saw me come home late, he wouldn't mention it to Mom. I liked that. It's funny, I didn't like him at first. But I got to like him more and more."

"I had no relationship with him whatsoever," shrugged Lark. "I didn't care either way. I felt that he used to be mean to Mom really quietly. He was like that. He could be very nasty. You could tell, he's so nasty to his parents. He's so cruel to them. He has even gotten the little kids doing it. For instance, he used to say to the kids, dead serious, 'Isn't Grandma stupid?' or 'Doesn't Grandma have a big nose?' But the kids thought it was a joke. They would laugh."

I brought up the image in the movie, *New York Stories*, of the Woody character's mother hovering in the sky to nag him. "Well, most characters in his movies are taken from life," asserted Lark angrily. "Look at *Hannah and Her Sisters*. As for *Husbands and Wives*, I wouldn't pay to see that movie."

Neither Lark nor Daisy hid their anger toward Woody. What about Soon-Yi, I wondered. Growing up, were the girls close? Said Lark: "Soon-Yi and I were close until I was about eight years old. Then she just changed. I thought she was going to be a nun. On her camp application she said that her marital status was 'nun.' " At that, both Lark and Daisy laughed. "She was seventeen then," added Daisy.

And what of Soon-Yi's well-publicized learning disabilities? "She worked damned hard," said Daisy, "but she had trouble. Luckily, she's a *very* hard worker." Soon-Yi did fairly well, however, the sisters reported to me. She took the SATs, untimed, in a special test situation provided for learning-disabled students.

The sisters recall with bitter amusement how suspiciously Soon-Yi initially regarded Woody. "She *hated* him at first, she just hated him," said Lark. "But all that changed during her junior year at Marymount." After Satchel was born, added Daisy, "She went ga-ga over him." Soon afterward, they observed, her behavior began to change. By her senior year at Marymount, said Lark, this once-shy, scared little girl "became almost snobby."

More than that, even. "She was much more confident and her style was different," recalled Daisy. "She went from wearing 'Little House on the Prairie' clothes to wearing *very* fitted clothes. We *all* noticed and used to tease her."

But the girls' relationships changed after the nude photos were discovered in January 1992. "There was only one week left of vacation after Mom found the pictures," said Daisy. "That week Soon-Yi didn't come down from the loft at all. She simply wouldn't show herself. I went up there every night to talk to her. I was *so* nice to her. Before she decided to stay with Woody, Soon-Yi was scared that she would be cut off financially. So I actually wanted to get a job to send her money. I told her, 'If you need money, call me. I'll get a job and send it to you.'"

Yet since Soon-Yi moved out of the house and chose her relationship with Woody over that with her mother, the sisters haven't seen or spoken to each other. Daisy has regrets. When I asked if she would speak to Soon-Yi now if Soon-Yi phoned, she quickly answered, "Yes."

Lark was not so generous. "No, never," she burst out. "It's unspeakable. I'm sorry, Soon-Yi has been here since she was seven years old. She has got to have some morals. She has lived in this society in New York City with Mom, and she has to know that it's a wrong thing to do. You don't have an affair with your mother's boyfriend, who is also your sister and brother's father. I think she is brainwashed, but she *must* know right from wrong."

"Yeah," Daisy countered, "but I blame Woody more."

Did the girls think any of the other kids would reconcile with Soon-Yi? Daisy was cautious. "I don't know, but I don't think so," she said. "Moses was so hurt by the whole thing." Then she paused for a moment. "Kristi, I don't think I want to talk about this anymore."

"Yes, Kristi," Lark added. "I wish we didn't have to talk or think about it anymore. Ever."

And with that, we were on to other things. Like college and boyfriend trouble. The usual.

"I'm reminded tonight of the farmer who had incestuous relations with both his daughters simultaneously. . . ."
Fielding Mellish in Bananas

NINE

Of Shrinks and Things

As Woody and Mia locked horns over whether or not Dylan had been molested, the child herself began a traumatic year, one marked by endless interviews with policemen, social workers, doctors, and, most especially, psychiatrists. She had always been a shy and dreamy girl with a fragile emotional nature, but within days of the alleged abuse, Dylan vigorously protested her own therapy. Her regular therapist, Dr. Nancy Schultz, was brought up to Connecticut in Woody's limo for sessions on August 17, 18, and 21. Whereas it was usual for Dylan and her more outgoing brother, Satchel, to kick and scream before their sessions—also known, surrealistically, as "playtimes"—during this last appointment they both poured glue in Dr. Schultz's hair, took a scissors and cut her dress with it, and ordered her to leave. There was nothing subtle about their message: Loathing, if not of the person, then at least of the process.

Mia, too, had begun to mistrust the clinical psychologists, in part because Dr. Schultz and also Satchel's psychiatrist, Dr. Susan Coates, were being paid by Woody. He had relied on them so often that they seemed almost like family. Both Woody, who himself was seeing two therapists in 1992, and Mia phoned Dr. Coates to pour out their own problems, to seek advice about the kids, and to discuss various family crises. Almost from the moment Mia found the nude pictures of Soon-Yi and discovered

165

her affair with Woody, Soon-Yi was shuttled into a therapeutic situation with a shrink of her own as well. So at one point, excluding both Woody and Mia and whatever treatment they sought, Dylan, Satchel, Soon-Yi, Moses, and three of the older children were in therapy simultaneously. And the costs must have been exorbitant. At a going rate of $125 an hour, that would have run $875 a week for one session per child. Twice-a-week treatments, which are the usually prescribed course of therapy, would have added up to a whopping $1750 weekly.

But money was not Mia's major concern. Drs. Coates and Schultz were. Mia might from the beginning have done well to suspect the fact that the therapy sessions themselves were *not* held, as is customary for non-celebrity patients, on the neutral turf of the therapists' office, but either at Woody's apartment or, during the summers, at Mia's country house. That alone blurred the boundaries that could compromise a therapist's objectivity and analytical distance. It was compounded by the fact that the doctors were chauffeured back and forth for each visit in Woody's sleek black $95,000 Mercedes—doubtless for princely fees as well. No wonder that Mia became concerned that the psychiatrists had been co-opted by the business Woody had brought them, and the perks he provided. Moreover, as she told the court:

> I learned that Dr. Schultz had told [New York] child welfare that [on August 17] Dylan had not reported anything to her. And then a week later, either her lawyer or Dr. Schultz called [New York] child welfare and said she just remembered that Dylan had told her that Mr. Allen had put a finger in her vagina. When I heard that, I certainly didn't trust Dr. Schultz.

It's a wonder that Mia didn't consider Woody's own history of psychotherapy and despair of the psychiatric process altogether. After all, the man had been in therapy for approximately twenty years when he took up with Soon-Yi. His own history and faith in psychoanalysis was so well known that former New York City Mayor Ed Koch once observed: "What he is, he's the analysand, representing millions more. Let me put it this way. If I were building a statue to Dr. Freud, and I were going to put it in New York, and the statue was going to be Freud in his office, it would be Woody Allen on the couch."

Yet was Woody, the perennial patient, disturbed enough or confused enough, honest enough or guilty enough to discuss with his therapist the fact that in the fall of 1991 he was developing a sexual desire for his lover's daughter? Well, no. (I wonder what the hell he *did* talk about?) Confessed Woody under oath: "When I recognized that I had feelings for [Soon-Yi] beyond friendship, I acted on them fairly quickly afterward." And when did he tell his therapist about this? Before or after he had seduced Soon-Yi? "My guess is after," he told the court. *After?* When it was too late to contemplate, too late to put on the brakes? Woody admitted that he also failed to mention this involvement to either Drs. Coates or Schultz until after Mia first told them about it.

In the fall of 1992 Dylan began going up to Yale to be evaluated by the prestigious Child Sexual Abuse Clinic at the Yale–New Haven Hospital. At the request of the Connecticut State Police, who were also evaluating her with respect to criminal charges that Mia filed against Woody, the child's therapy with Dr. Schultz was put on hold during this period. Eventually, Mia chose a new therapist for her, one who had no psychological or financial links to Woody.

Dylan's first session at Yale was on Wednesday, September 22, and every Friday thereafter she would meet with the Yale–New Haven team, who would talk to her for an hour or so. None of us knows what her responses were; not even Mia has seen the records, which were sealed and have since been destroyed. I was interviewed at Yale for three hours. I sat in a room with two psychiatrists facing me, and for a brief moment I felt like I was in a Woody Allen movie. But then, no joking, I had to provide them with a blow-by-blow description of my life with Mia. I emphasized to them how caring she was, and how she devoted all of the day and night to the children. "Although it was an unconventional household," I told them, "it was a very special and unique family."

Dylan, at one of her first sessions, told the Yale team: "I love my mother. That's all I have to say. I love my mother and I hate my dad." She confided that she had begun to feel this after she learned about Woody's affair with Soon-Yi. "I'm like, why me?" she said. "Why do I have to solve this problem?" On October 2 Mia admitted to the Yale team that she had told Dylan: "If you don't want Daddy to be your daddy anymore, he doesn't have to be." Throughout the grim days of that fall and winter, she would, in fact, constantly reassure Dylan with these same words.

Then on October 30, Dylan dropped a little bomb in New Haven: She recanted her testimony. When Mia brought her for her session that day, Mia explained to the social workers that Dylan had not wanted to come. In addition, as Mia testified, Dylan had earlier confided to her that Woody "didn't do anything; nothing happened." Later that afternoon, however, Dylan reversed herself and *denied her denial*. As Mia explained, she had simply gotten sick and tired of being grilled round the clock by a bunch of strangers. Instead—and understandably—she longed to stay home and watch cartoons on TV.

The task before Yale–New Haven was to answer two major questions? Was Dylan telling the truth? And did the Yale–New Haven team think she had been sexually abused? For six months a group including Dr. John Leventhal, a pediatrician, Dr. Julia Hamilton, a Ph.D. in social work, and Jennifer Sawyer, another social worker, with an M.A., pondered the evidence and on March 17, 1993, they concluded that Woody had *not* abused his adopted daughter. And no, Dylan, they believed, had not told the truth.

The Yale–New Haven Report had concluded, among other things, that: 1) Dylan was so enmeshed with her mother that she felt herself to be "her mother's problem solver," and, 2) Dylan's telling about the touching could be construed as a way to protect her mother and banish her father.

While Woody understandably praised these findings, Mia and

the court questioned them. Even Judge Elliott J. Wilk wrote in his judgment:

> Responsibility for different aspects of the investigation was divided among the team. The notes of the team members were destroyed prior to the issuance of the report, which, presumably, is an amalgamation of their independent impressions and observations. The unavailability of the notes, together with their unwillingness to testify at this trial except through the deposition of Dr. Leventhal, compromised my ability to scrutinize their findings and resulted in a report which was sanitized and, therefore, less credible.

Judge Wilk added: "Unlike Yale–New Haven, I am not persuaded that the videotape of Dylan is the product of leading questions or of the child's fantasy."

Dr. Stephen Herman, a clinical psychiatrist called to testify on Mia's behalf, has impressive credentials. He did a pediatrics residency at the Mayo Clinic, an adult residency at Montefiore Medical Center in New York, and a two-year fellowship in child psychiatry at the Yale Child Study Center in New Haven. Board-certified in both adult and child psychiatry, Dr. Herman noted that it was "unfortunate" that Mia, and not an objective and trained evaluator, videotaped Dylan's testimony, mainly because the way she focused on specific things could possibly "set a tone for a child about how to answer. I think it could raise anxieties of a child." In short, he said, "I don't think it helps matters, I think it complicates matters."

This criticism of Mia aside, Herman took exception to a number of significant Yale–New Haven findings. First, he pointed out that the team's methodology was flawed in several ways. "To destroy written notes in a case which is clearly going to have legal ramifications is a mistake," he said, "particularly when you have a team approach and when you are combining notes in this case from three different individuals."

Next, Dr. Herman felt, there were problems regarding the interviews with the principals. "If you are going to come to a conclusion that a child should have visitation with a parent," he pointed out, "it's extremely important in your evaluation to be able to justify why that visitation is important, and one of the ways to do that is to bring a child and parent together." However, Woody and Dylan were never interviewed together. Moreover, Yale's Dr. Leventhal chose to see Mia alone; yet when he saw Woody "alone," it was with his coterie of attorneys. "There is no clinical justification for it," said Herman. Furthermore, Dr. Leventhal *never* interviewed Dylan at all, even though he is a pediatrician who has spent a great deal of time at the Yale Child Study Center, the child psychiatry division of Yale. "I would have thought that in a case such as this in which many of the conclusions are predicated on the fact that this is an 'emotionally disturbed child,' that he would have at least seen her in a formal interview and assess for himself rather than relying on other therapists' reports," observed Dr. Herman under oath. In addition, the reports that Leventhal *did* rely on—both Dr. Schultz's and Dr. Coates's—were without any diagnosis; Coates's without any formal evaluation.

Dr. Herman, under oath, discussed other serious mistakes in the Yale report. One was the inclusion of a comment from Dr. Schultz that she feared that Dylan was "psychotic." Said Dr. Herman: "Dr. Schultz has testified that she never felt that Dylan is or was psychotic, and Dr. Schultz's notes, to my reading, nowhere reflect her concerns that this child is psychotic. In the Yale report it's given as a historical fact, and that to me is a major glaring error." In the same way, the Yale team accepted Woody's notion that Dylan doesn't know reality from fantasy, whereas Herman points out that nowhere in the report is there evidence of this.

Herman went on to challenge the report's conclusion that Dylan was inconsistent about where she was touched. "There are also a number of areas of consistency which the report does not focus on," he stated.

When members of the team asked Dylan if she ever wanted to visit her father, they noted ambivalence both in her body language and the manner in which she answered this question. Her ambivalence was interpreted to mean that *yes*, she did indeed want to see him. But Herman disagreed with that. "Now, if you are a clinician and you are exploring ambivalence with a child, the appropriate response," he explained, "is not to say it looks like you want to go. [It] is to say it looks like maybe part of you wants to go and part of you doesn't want to go, or it looks like maybe you are confused about whether you want to go."

In response to Yale's accusation that Dylan wasn't credible because "she told the story in a manner that was overly thoughtful and controlling," Herman says that this does not necessarily bear on the truthfulness of her statement; it is, instead, "personality characteristics."

As to the team's dismissal of Dylan because the way she talked about the events in the attic made them seem "like a minor transgression," Herman replied: "It could be a child's way of coping with something which is very serious and upsetting, and the child could present it in a very understated or contained way."

As to the report's conclusion: "It is our expert opinion that Dylan was not sexually abused by Woody," Herman noted in court:

I think it's very dangerous to conclude that a specific person did or did not abuse a child unless there is some kind of overwhelming corroborative evidence to support that: either a very believable witness or it's incontrovertible fact, or you culture out a sexually transmitted organism [that is, a sexually transmitted disease such as gonorrhea] from the alleged perpetrator and it's the same one that is cultured from a child. Absent that, it's very difficult for a clinician to know.

Furthermore, one could easily read this report, in my opinion, and conclude that Dylan was abused, and I can just as easily look at this data and say, "Well, she consistently said, 'He touched me here in this way . . .'" over and over again. She's very upset. She's very angry." Children, whether they are or aren't disturbed, can be abused, too, and can tell the truth even if they are disturbed; and because a child is disturbed doesn't mean that she's fantasizing.

Dr. Herman wasn't alone. Judge Wilk, in his report, wrote: "I share his reservations about the reliability of the [Yale–New Haven] report."

On weekends during the fall of 1992, the police would stop by Frog Hollow to talk with Dylan, bringing with them anatomy dolls. They would show her the dolls and ask her to point to the areas where her father had allegedly touched her. I remember in December, 1992, that Sergeants John Mucharino and Bea Farlickus arrived with the dolls, and on this particular day Dylan actually placed the male doll's penis inside the female doll's vagina. When they asked her how she knew what went where, she recalled a time when Soon-Yi was baby-sitting for her and Satchel and had taken them to Woody's apartment. There, Dylan and Satchel watched TV while their sister and father disappeared. After a time, Dylan explained, she wandered upstairs toward the bedroom. Peeping through the door, she saw Woody and Soon-Yi lying naked on top of the covers. "And he was doing compliments, and they were making snoring noises, and he was putting his penis into Soon-Yi," she told the policemen (Mia placed the episode at some point in the spring or fall of 1991).

Then, a week and a half before Yale–New Haven completed its investigation, Dylan confided to Mia that one day while she had been climbing up the ladder to a bunk bed, Woody had put his hands under her shorts. Mia told the court that this time Dylan "was illustrating graphically where in the genital area" this was.

Those who *didn't* believe Woody wondered, Was Dylan creating these highly damning and sexual stories because she had been asked leading questions by Mia? Or was it because she was so upset by her father's relationship with Soon-Yi? The consensus by some was that she had identified with her sister whom she had actually *seen* having sex with Woody and so perhaps believed subconsciously that she might be next.

I have no idea whether or not Woody actually abused his daughter. Nor can I explain why she would tell a story like that and stick with it, even when challenged by Mia time and again. All I know is that after August 4, Dylan began to behave strangely. Was it because Woody had actually touched her? Or because Mia kept pressing her as to whether or not Woody touched her? This is how I testified in court:

> Q. *Now, after August 4, can you tell us, did you see any change in Dylan's behavior?*
> A. Yes. She had a tendency to cover up her private areas even with me, who she knows very well, and I would be changing her in the morning or changing her out of her bathing suit, and helping her get dressed, and she would sort of cover herself up. She was really private. Even when she was in the bathtub, she would do it.
> Q. *Did you say anything to her about it?*
> A. I said, "Dylan, I am a girl, and you are a girl." I said, "You know me, it's okay." And she just insisted on covering herself up. She would not let me see her.

In court Woody's attorney, Elkan Abramowitz, interrogated me about the children's bathing-suit baths, as if to suggest that these may have contributed to her undue modesty. It had always been a tradition that the little kids—Satchel, Dylan, and Tam—would take bathing-suit baths together in the huge gray enamel whirlpool bathtub that is the pièce de résistance of Mia's otherwise ordinary-looking Central Park West bathroom. It's a big Jacuzzi, and the kids play in it, it's how she sometimes gets them to take their baths. How could I remember when this started? And how could I know if it contributed to her sense of privacy?

Dylan's bizarre behavior goes beyond her modesty or lack of same. One night in the fall of 1992, for instance, all the kids were lying in bed in Mia's Central Park West apartment, and I was telling them the story of Aladdin and the genie who lived in the magic lamp. On that night the moonlight was streaming into the room, casting spooky shadows, and I was being highly dramatic. The kids were all lying in their beds, listening intently as I reached the part where I said, "The genie has come out of the lamp, and he wants to know what you would wish for." First came Satchel's turn, and he giggled and said, "I want Kiddie City in my backyard." Then Dylan spoke. "I wish Woody Allen would leave us alone forever," she said. Not "Daddy," but "Woody Allen"—which is the way she always refers to him now.

I remember an afternoon not long afterward when I was feeding Satchel's pet chinchillas, who live in a cage in the study, and Mara Thorpe, the court-appointed guardian for Dylan and Moses, was interviewing the family. "How do you feel about Woody Allen?" she asked Dylan. As an answer, Dylan marched over to the window, where a pink vase full of dried roses sat. She took the roses out of the vase and clutched them to her chest as she lay down on the floor like a slain princess being prepared for burial. And she said in a serious little voice, "Woody Allen killed me." It was chilling.

At a moment like that I couldn't help thinking that either Dylan is totally reflecting Mia's feelings about Woody, or he *did* molest her. Last spring we drove by Woody's apartment, and she said, "Oooh, oooh, Woody Allen lives here." And I asked her, "What is it about Woody Allen?" She replied, again with tremendous gravity, "He took my sister away."

Under oath, Dr. Herman was asked whether Woody's relationship with Soon-Yi could be termed psychological abuse. "I think a situation such as this—if a child were fragile or psychiatrically ill, or even if she weren't—might be of such emotional detriment to the child that one might say that it's an abusive situation in the sense that it is causing psychological harm on an ongoing basis. It's a bizarre situation, it's an inappropriate one, in my opinion, and it's not one that the best family therapist in the world can straighten out and make sensible to a child."

But it got worse. Think about it. Not only did Dylan suffer the loss of Soon-Yi and the loss of her father that fall. She also suffered continual examination by a revolving doorful of strangers. To make matters even graver, the first days of school were hellish for both her and Satchel. On the very first morning, September 23, Mia and I took them by cab, first depositing Dylan at Brearley on the Upper East Side and then Satchel at the Montessori School on the Upper West Side. When we got there, Mia spoke individually to all their teachers, begging them to be watchful and never, ever to let the kids out of their sight. She especially warned them not to let Woody into the school. She was convinced that he was hatching some terrible plan to try to kidnap the children, and for that reason the whole first week of school was nightmarishly tense for us. In fact, Woody did come to see Dylan at school in October, but the principal phoned Mia and told her about it. Immediately, Mia got a court order restraining him from contacting Dylan in any way.

In those days Dylan was much more quiet and cautious than she seems to be now. Whereas Satchel will barrel up to you and tell you exactly what's on his mind, she would internalize everything. Perhaps locking herself in the bathroom during Woody's visit on the July Fourth weekend had been one way she had been able to handle the intensity of his scrutiny. Perhaps complaining that she didn't feel well and was going to lie down, like a little old lady with a stomachache, headache, or whatever, had been another way of absenting herself from his monsoon of attention.

In the year following the alleged molestation, Dylan's delicate nature was aggravated further, and maybe more severely than even the sturdiest child could stand. From the first day of school that September, there were photographers waiting outside Mia's building and reporters yelling her name on the street, "Dylan! Dylan!" they'd scream at her. Or sometimes they would yell, "Hey, over here!" Every so often Dylan would turn to me and ask, "Kristi, how do they know my name? How do they know who I am?" or "Why are they always waiting for us?"

I would usually invent a reply. "Oh, that man with the beret and the camera *loves* me and keeps trying to take pictures of me," I would tell her. I couldn't stand seeing her childhood snatched away by the media. And by the ugly reality of her father and mother's breakup.

"Love is most complex emotion. Human being [is] unpredictable. No logic to emotions. Where there is no logic, there is no rational thought. Where there is no rational thought, there can be much romance but much suffering."

Dr. Yang in Alice

TEN

Picking Up the Pieces

When I came to live with Mia in the fall of 1992, she was in mourning for her lover and her daughter, but didn't know it. She would lie in bed all day, talking on the phone to her lawyers. Occasionally she would watch TV. "Kristi, I can't believe any of this," she would murmur through her depression. I would bring in her lunch—sometimes a tuna sandwich or a cupful of Ramen prepared soup—and she'd pick at it and then talk on the phone some more. Or sometimes she would just sleep. Mia spent day after day in the strikingly nunlike bedroom of her Central Park West apartment, and more than once I thought that the room's plain white walls and simple wooden crucifix hanging on the wall behind her headboard helped give her strength and, at least, comfort.

When she was up and about, her tension level often soared. On September 23 I wrote in my journal:

Today was the kids' first day of school. Mia was so upset all morning, so afraid Woody might engineer a kidnapping. When the kids came home in one piece this afternoon, you could see the sheer relief on her face. "You can't put yourself through this kind of stress every day," I told her. "You must relax, or you'll get sick." I worry about her.

179

Sure enough, by the next day the entire household was struggling with the flu or a cold. I alone seemed to be in good physical health. Which was fortunate, since I had emerged by default the family disciplinarian.

Even before Mia fell into her depression, she was a lenient mom. She never got angry and never lost her temper, and I always thought her as gentle as Bambi. If the children whined that they didn't want to go to school, Mia would beg them, "Pullease, please, get dressed." I, on the other hand, would summon a firm voice and command, like Ilse the She-Wolf of the SS, "You get in there and put your clothes on, or your butt is going to be spanked."

Of course, they were great kids and never really gave me a hard time. But because Mia was always so melancholy and exhausted, I had to make sure that they got to school on time. I also disciplined them when they became rambunctious. If one child hit another or if two of them had a fight, I would call a time-out and send the guilty parties to their rooms for ten minutes or sometimes longer. Once I walked into the living room and found Satchel lifting Isaiah off the floor by his hair. I was not pleased, and Satchel, at my directive, was sent to his bed for the entire morning.

But my gifts as a tough-love, sleep-in nanny were not the only reasons I came to stay with Mia that fall, changing a Princeton Review class I was enrolled in (I was thinking of going to graduate school the following year) so that I could take the children to school every day. Plain and simple, Mia emphatically didn't want Monica Thompson to have that responsibility. She had become suspicious that Monica was allying herself with Woody. He was, after all, paying her a salary of around $45,000 a year. And at a time when all our imaginations were running wild, Mia felt that Monica might nab the children, drive to Kennedy Airport, and hop on a plane, delivering the kids to Woody in, say, Paris, his favorite city outside of the Big Apple. This obviously was preposterous; but at the time, these ideas were very real to us. After all, when your lover has run off with your daughter, and you believe that he has molested his own daughter as well, you can easily judge him capable of just about anything.

My presence reassured Mia that the children would not be spirited away. Or, at least, not easily. I was big, strong, young, and she knew that I could be tough. If anything ever happened, God forbid, I would kick, scratch, and with my runner's training, be able to defend the kids. So every day I would get up and take them to school. Whereas during the previous year or two, Dylan especially had a problem separating from her parents, now that she was older, she attended school with enthusiasm. On dropping her and Satchel off, I would go to Central Park and study. After picking the children up in the afternoon and delivering them safely home, I would hurry to the Review class. On weekends we would usually all go to the country.

That fall we didn't know whom to trust. Certain information, we felt, was being leaked to the press, and other information to Woody. Monica, for instance, had told him that Mia had smacked Moses when he couldn't find the dog leash; although this in itself wouldn't have been such a crime, Mia emphatically denied it. There weren't too many suspects in the house who had access. One was Mavis, the housekeeper, a divine woman who had worked for Mia for thirteen years, and for Maureen O'Sullivan before that. No way, we decided. Her allegiances, we felt, would be with Mia.

So we figured that Monica, the only other possibility, must have been the culprit. She had given a critical deposition about Mia to Woody's lawyers in August; then in September she gave a glowing review of Mia to social workers, but, finally, when it came time to testify, the glow had faded for her. Clearly, her days with Mia were numbered. It's a wonder Mia kept her on as long as she did.

Mia and I decided not to let *anyone* other than ourselves enter Mia's room, even to straighten it. Maybe that was paranoid of us, but Mia was convinced that during the previous spring, while she and Woody were still on speaking terms, he had entered her apartment when she wasn't there and took inventory on every single prescription in her medicine cabinet. Presumably he was gathering information just in case the custody battle went to court. (Mia said she knew this because Woody had, in fact, submitted such information to court, claiming that two prescriptions for antidepressants which were in her medicine chest suggested that she was an unfit mother.)

A rumor had been passed to Mia from a Los Angeles detective that her house was bugged. Every day for three months we would check for bugging devices. We would look behind the dressers, in drawers, under the bed, and into the mouthpiece and receiver of the phone. When Mia wanted to have an important conversation with a friend, she would tell him or her on the phone, "Meet me at S." That meant Scaletta, a restaurant on Seventy-seventh Street and Columbus.

It was cloaks and daggers all the way. On September 25 I noted in my diary:

A few days ago, almost as a joke, I suggested to Mia that if Woody were granted custody, she should gather up her children and run away, perhaps to Ireland. She got caught up in my idea—after all, she loves the country of her mother's birth. So this morning I went with Tam alone, and then Isaiah alone, to get secret passport pictures. The truth is, this is a silly exercise, since I can't actually imagine Woody getting custody—after all, he *did* seduce Mia's daughter. But he has made Mia feel like such shit all the time that she has no sense of reality, and she sometimes convinces me to see the world through her eyes as well.

I guess we *were* a little hysterical. At any rate, I came back from the passport photographer and gave Mia the kids' photos which we spread all over the bed with their birth certificates. Then suddenly, she looked at me and said, "I love you, Kristi, but this is crazy. I'm not running away. I'm standing my ground. This is my home." And with that, she threw all my paperwork in the garbage.

While we remained stateside, Mia took every security precaution. At the suggestion of lawyers and the police, we changed all the locks so that only Mia, Daisy, the three older boys, and I had keys. These were special keys that could not be duplicated. Still, we would change them every three or four months. We also changed the phone numbers and installed a special security system including two cameras at the front door (one pans across the elevator) and two at the back. A security expert from a well-known New York firm swept the apartment and the house in Connecticut, then taught us how to check for bugs ourselves.

So convinced were we that Woody was bugging us that one Sunday night before we went back to the city, Moses and I decided to create a trap for whomever he had hired to do the dirty deed. So we took a spool of Mia's off-white sewing thread, and we wrapped it around the doorknob of both cottages, real low, and between the trees of both cottages, hoping to trip the culprit up, both literally and figuratively. We must have looked so ridiculous, but at the time we thought we were two smart little detectives doing our own sleuthing. Suffice it to say we trapped nothing and no one.

Luckily, Mia didn't depend on us. She added a sophisticated security system at Frog Hollow, too. There are cameras upstairs in her room, downstairs in the living room, outside the front door, and on the side of the house. A good alarm system is in place as well. It all costs a pretty penny—Mia estimated that the cameras and the sweeps of both homes cost her between $15,000 and $20,000. Still, if we wanted to have an honest conversation about Woody or a strategy discussion about the custody case, we would put on green Wellington boots and huge parkas, and we'd trudge down to the lake, or to the end of the garden, the only places where we truly felt safe. The Los Angeles expert even discussed sweeping my parents' house. He worried that a new kind of bugging system which could have been planted a hundred yards away made even that safe haven a dangerous place. However, in the end our paranoia never spread that far.

Surely, if there had been a bugging system in place, Woody would have been better prepared when his attorneys flew in from California to cut a deal with Mia. He would have heard on tape every doubt and suspicion she had had. And he would also have known how resistant she was about making any kind of deal that allowed him to retain joint custody of Dylan and Moses. That was in late September. The evening before the meeting, I went out for dinner at Rikyu, a Japanese restaurant, with Matthew and Priscilla. "She *has* to make a deal," Matthew said, his voice full with urgency. But she didn't make it. She insisted, instead, that she *had* to be true to Dylan.

Despite the elaborate electronic protection system, Mia continued to fear for her own safety. Another wild-eyed, farfetched fantasy, I agree. But perhaps her mother put that thought into her head. Here is an entry from my diary:

Sept. 29:
Grandma called tonight (Maureen). She said that I shouldn't let Mia go out alone. She is afraid Woody might do something terrible to her. She asked me if I would escort Mia when she leaves the house at night. We spoke for a few minutes, and I assured her I was taking care of her daughter as best I could.

I think Maureen was so upset by Woody's affair with Soon-Yi that for a long time Mia was afraid that her mother might do something horrible to him. In fact, Maureen was the first to leak to the press, before the Soon-Yi relationship was in the open, that Woody was "a desperate and evil man." She may have been furious at him, and sympathetic toward Mia, but she didn't do much hand-holding during the ordeal. Of course, her advanced age—she's 83—and distance—she lives in Phoenix—made frequent visits difficult. However, Maureen did phone often and came to visit once during the summer as far as I know—but that's all.

As for Mia's siblings, Peter, an artist, rang her often and came to stay with her for four days. Prudie, an aspiring director who had worked on the production staff of *The Purple Rose of Cairo*, but had quit to raise her five-year-old son, was hardly around. Tisa, once an actress but now a nurse in Vermont, phoned at the height of the press insanity, but she, too, kept her distance. I've heard that Tisa always felt overshadowed by Mia's success, and maybe that's one reason she didn't stand by her sister in the way that I would expect *my* sister Kelly to stand by me.

The situation with Steffi, another of Mia's sisters, was more complicated. Although Steffi lives on West Seventy-second Street, not far away, Mia *never* sees her. When I first met Mia, she told me that the two of them used to be close, but Steffi didn't like Woody, and the strength of her dislike for him affected the sisters' relationship.

Later on, Mia confided to me that she had found photos of Steffi in Woody's apartment. Now, this was *long* before she discovered the nude photos of Soon-Yi; nevertheless, as any woman would be, she was suspicious about them.

After I saw *Hannah and Her Sisters* I became even more curious. After all, in *Hannah,* Michael Caine plays Mia's husband, a man who has an affair with her sister (Barbara Hershey). And Woody plays her *ex*-husband, who falls in love with her *other* sister (Dianne Wiest). So I asked Mia if *Hannah* was written with Steffi in mind. And she said, "Yes, I think it was. But I never outright asked Steffi." Then she told me that Steffi had had roles in *A Midsummer Night's Sex Comedy, Zelig,* and *The Purple Rose of Cairo* (as Mia's sister). Mia told me that she was costumed in an uncomfortable outfit for *Sex Comedy* and during lunch breaks would have to take it off. Woody would just walk away from her and go to lunch with Steffi, guiding her elbow with his hand. Mia said she used to find them together *all* the time. She would walk into a room, and there they would be, just the two of them, talking intimately. She admitted that it was strange, and that she was really uneasy about it, which was why in recent years she hadn't had much contact with Steffi at all.

I began to wonder if perhaps Mia had had the need to create her large and loving family in order to replace her large and *indifferent* one. Beyond that, I thought, *What is it with her?* Is she totally self-destructive? How could such a beautiful and accomplished woman be such a, well, doormat? Or is it ostrich? So I asked her, "Do you think they had an affair?" And she said, "Yes. I think they did. And when I write my book, I'm going to come right out and ask her. I asked her before, but she denied it and got embarrassed. And I didn't want to have a confrontation with her." *Not* want to have a confrontation with her sister over the fact that she might have slept with Woody? Not wanting to know something so important? After all, if it were true, it would have told her something critical and ugly about Woody. Had she listened, maybe the whole Soon-Yi affair could have been avoided. And the whole Dylan affair.

But of course, that's the great thing about hindsight. Instead of sharing my observation, I merely said to her, "These movies must be so much like your life and your relationship with Woody."

"Yes," she replied, frowning slightly. "I look at them and see my life on display for everyone to watch."

Not just Mia's life, apparently. A close friend of Mia's claimed that Steffi wasn't the first sister Woody had co-opted. Woody, she alleged, had romanced Diane Keaton's sister Robin; and while dating Mariel Hemingway, the youthful star of *Manhattan,* he had also become obsessed with one of *her* sisters. *Hannah,* it seemed, had resonance beyond anything I had imagined.

Writing about the things that are happening in his life, events that are obsessing him, Woody didn't seem to give much thought to the consequences of invading anybody's privacy or exposing the kinds of intimacies that might be better left hidden.

Which is why I was so happy when an acting opportunity came up for Mia that had nothing to do with Woody—or their lives together. At the end of September I wrote in my diary:

Mia found out today that she has been cast in Mike Nichols's new film, *Wolf.* So Daisy and I set out for Columbus Avenue to buy her flowers and a card. Mia had gone out to dinner with Skip Stein at Fishin Eddie's, and when she returned, there was a bouquet of flowers and a card on the dining table signed by all of the kids. She thanked us all individually. She seemed so happy and content for the first time in ages.

But Mia didn't remain content for long. Not only did she have to battle her depression and her fears, but she also had to juggle their endless legal conversations with the vast emotional needs of all her kids—needs made needier, if you will, by the splintering of the family structure in the nine months since she found the nude pictures. B.S.—or Before Soon-Yi—therapy was the

exception, not the rule, in the Farrow household. Dylan and
Satchel were in therapy, but none of the rest of the kids received
help. Mia, I believe, went to a therapist for only a short time
during her younger years. Now the opposite was true.

None of the children, with the possible exception of Dylan,
was more emotionally fragile that autumn than Moses. At fifteen,
her Korean-born adopted son occupies an odd space in the family. He is too young to hang out with the kids who are eighteen
and older, and too old to hang out with the under-tens. Not only
that, he is the only one among the teenagers who hasn't got a
father. Although Woody technically adopted him on December
18, 1991, a mere three weeks before Mia found the nude pictures of Soon-Yi, Mia, with Moses's blessing, is trying to undo
that adoption. This is a part of the intricate legal battle that the
couple is still fighting, and part of the fallout from the disastrous
series of events culminating in their 1993 court case. Matthew,
Sascha, Fletcher, Daisy, Lark, and even Soon-Yi are all the children of Andre Previn. (Previn pays an allowance of $100 a month
plus half of their school expenses until they graduate college.
Although he is not exactly stingy with his support, you can't call
him generous either.)

Too intense and sensitive for his own good, Moses has a tough
time everywhere. At school, the kids have been cruel, and since
the Soon-Yi brouhaha began, they have teased him by saying,
"Your father has sex with your sister." This has profoundly affected him.

Moses, a loner to begin with, is so quiet that you need to
cajole him into conversation. I think in part this is because he
was born with cerebral palsy. As a toddler he used to walk on
tiptoe and limp. He also has a spastic right hand. Thanks to
surgery and years of physical therapy, he now moves about with
ease, and although he wears a foot brace, you can't really tell
there is a problem with his gait unless you look. But his hand
remains rigid, and he can't pick up anything with it. Still, Moses
adores sports, and basketball in particular. On rare occasions
when he was younger, Woody would have him sleep over or take
him to a Knicks game—he has four season tickets. It was a real
kick for the boy who, in the days before the nude photos, lobbied

in his own painfully shy way to develop a relationship with Woody.

Yet Mia always felt that Woody's relationship with Moses was perfunctory. In court she observed that up in Connecticut, "He would play ball with Moses, not more than ten minutes, and then before he could work up a sweat, he would say, 'Okay, that's it, I can't—that's it for Moses.' And I heard him say to my friend Casey, 'Okay, now I have given Moses ten minutes. Where is Dylan?'" At another point Mia noted that, "He told Moses he couldn't play games or anything because he would work up a sweat and couldn't take a shower."

Despite these occasional stabs at friendship, if not fatherhood, in June, 1993, the court judgment essentially took Mia's stance, noting critically:

> Mr. Allen's interactions with Moses appear to have been superficial and more a response to Moses's desire for a father—in a family where Mr. Previn was the father of the other six children—than an authentic effort to develop a relationship with the child. When Moses asked, in 1984, if Mr. Allen would be his father, he said "sure" but for years did nothing to make that a reality.

> They spent time playing baseball, chess, and fishing. Mr. Allen encouraged Moses to play the clarinet. There is no evidence, however, that Mr. Allen used any of their shared areas of interest as a foundation upon which to develop a deeper relationship with his son. What little he offered—a baseball catch, some games of chess, adoption papers—was enough to encourage Moses to dream of more, but insufficient to justify a claim for custody.

I believe that Woody's betrayal of the family could damage Moses forever. I remember one particularly telling event that occurred when Woody came up to Bridgewater in July, 1992. You must understand that Moses is the kind of kid who can't say no even if he doesn't really want to do something with you. So when Woody said to him that day, "Let's have a catch,"

Moses agreed. But as they tossed the ball back and forth to each
other on the lawn, it was apparent that his heart wasn't in it.
Finally, he just threw the ball on the ground and stomped off.
You could see how angry he was at Woody.

Later Moses was racked with guilt. "He made me have a toss
with him on the lawn, and I couldn't say no," he told Mia apolo-
getically, "but I felt like I was betraying my family." And she
put her arms around him and said, "Don't worry about it." But
it was impossible for Moses not to worry. Although Mia always
told him that these decisions were his for the making, in subtle
ways she made it clear which ones sat well with her.

On September 22, Moses went into a tailspin when Woody
phoned him, lobbying to get his hands on Moses's psychiatric
records. In my journal I wrote the following:

A big psychiatric to-do today: Dr. Lister called Moses at
four o'clock. Then at six-thirty Woody phoned, asking for
permission to call Dr. Lister. Moses, who began therapy as
a response to Woody's affair with Soon-Yi said no. Woody
wanted to get hold of Moses' records, probably for the trial
ahead. When Moses wouldn't budge, Woody told him he
was making a big mistake. Then he tried to make small talk,
asking how Moses was doing. Later on, Mia, Moses, and I
sat around in the living room discussing the situation. She
was afraid that the court would subpoena the records and
discover Moses telling his therapist that she didn't pay
enough attention to him. During our talk, Moses decided
to call Dr. Lister and ask him to shred the records. Dr. L.
said it was impossible, but he would do his best to keep
them confidential. I would think so. Aren't psychiatric records protected by patient-doctor confidentiality?

Mia's fears that Moses may have griped to his doctor about
the lack of attention he was receiving at home could have been
correct: In a household with a crack baby, a blind child, and two
demanding under-tens, you don't have to be neurotic to feel
neglected. Satchel was emotionally needy and immature for his
then-five years. When Isaiah came into the household in January,

1992, Satchel enacted his competitive and territorial feelings by wanting to go back to bottles and refusing to remove his protective diapers at night. So bonded was he to his mother that he, like his sister Dylan, had a hard time leaving her to go to school that September.

Perhaps that is one reason why Mia chose for Satchel the Montessori School on the Upper West Side which was lax about students' comings and goings. This eventually irritated Woody, who said in court, "[Montessori] said to us that Satchel could come when he wanted and leave when he wanted; it was not a strict thing. And so Mia would bring him late to the school—I mean, after it had started—and then she would remove him early. I myself did not think this was a great idea. . . . [Now] any time he doesn't feel like going, by the record and by his own admission to me, she doesn't send him."

Satchel can be stubborn, dependent on his mother, and furiously temperamental, but when he feels secure and in control, he is an incredible child. First of all, he is super intelligent. Not only did he speak at nine months, but he has an extraordinary vocabulary. At the age of two he was tested by his psychiatrist, using WISK intelligence tests, and he scored impressively. In fact, he skipped kindergarten. In addition, he is a kid who likes other kids, and who has a marvelous ribald sense of humor.

Tam is another child who has required a great deal of emotional buttressing from her family. It is to Mia's credit that, with all that was going on in her life since Tam's arrival in January, 1992, she had the energy, love, and sense of mission required to deal with this extremely complicated and emotionally impoverished child. When Tam first arrived from Vietnam, she was wild. For six or seven months she had temper tantrums and she would kick and lash out at whoever was trying to calm her. She was like Linda Blair in *The Exorcist*—everything but the 360-degree rotating head. I cannot imagine what her life in Vietnam had been like. However, she does *not* want to talk about her parents or about her country. Nor will she speak a word of Vietnamese since she learned English. Mia regularly pays Vietnamese people to come to the house to talk to Tam because she wants her to keep up her language. But Tam refuses to say a word to them.

And don't bother to ask her to speak it, because she will tell you that she simply doesn't know how.

The one vestige of Vietnam to which Tam clings is a friendship she made in the orphanage with Teiu, another blind girl who was subsequently adopted by a family in Colorado. Mia makes sure that the two pals speak by phone about twice a month. And every summer Mia has Teiu come to Bridgewater for two weeks. "It's important for Tam to maintain her roots, her respect 'for her country, and her language," Mia told me. "The two little girls have known each other since they were two. Teiu is the only practical friend that Tam can maintain. Luckily, it's easy for Teiu's parents and me to keep their friendship up. Tam loves Teiu, the friendship gives her a great wealth."

After one of Tam's worst temper displays during the summer of 1992, one where we had to physically carry her up the stairs in Frog Hollow, then put her in Mia's bedroom and turn on the air-conditioning to drown out her screams, I took her for a drive in my car, and I said, "Look, Tam, Woody is trying to take away Satchel and Dylan. You have to know that Mommy is in the movies, and a lot of people know her and are watching her to make sure that she's a good mommy. And you have to be a good girl, because if you're yelling and crying and thrashing about and biting us, it's going to look like Mommy is a bad mommy and like you are unhappy here. Do you think it's better or worse than Vietnam here? Are you unhappy here?"

And she said, "No, no, I'm just sad sometimes." I told her that she had to learn to control herself, and she nodded yes. We had that same discussion, say, three times during the summer. And finally she began to understand.

Still, tantrums were her chief mode of expressing her fear. She fiercely resisted her eye doctor, swatting him when he tried to examine her. The doctor feels that with an operation, Tam—who can register brightness when you turn on a light bulb—may have an opportunity to see in one eye again. But the procedure involves a certain amount of maturity. Tam would have to be responsible enough to keep the bandage on and to do certain other things to take care of herself, and until now she has not been up to it. So we will try again sometime in the future.

Going to the dentist was also an ordeal. I don't think Tam had ever been to one before in her life when we took her for her first visit. Satchel and Dylan also came along for their regular cleanings. And since the dentist, Glenn Wilson, is a friend of mine, the kids would run around the house beforehand, chanting, "Kristi loves Dr. Teeth, Kristi loves Dr. Teeth." Once we got to Dr. Teeth, Mia needed to show Tam what the dentist was all about. So she slipped into the dental chair and sat Tam on her lap. As the doctor cleaned Mia's teeth, Mia brought Tam's hands to her mouth and held it there, letting the little girl feel the dentist and the cleaning instruments as he used them.

Over the course of her first year in Mia's care, Tam's tantrums happily eased up, and she began to develop into a child with a surprisingly strong sense of humor. Every time she sees me, she says in her booming voice, "Hello, Kristi, you big chicken." And I cluck and make chicken sounds in return.

As soon as Tam learned enough English, Mia enrolled her at P.S. 6 in Manhattan, where there is a fine program for learning-disabled children. There she has a braille teacher; at home she has a special braille typewriter on which to do her homework. Before she arrived here, Tam knew Vietnamese braille and has subsequently learned English braille. Recently, after teaching Matthew some of the braille basics, she confided to me proudly and loudly in her broken English, "Kristi, Matthew very braille."

Tam sometimes has a problem modulating her voice. She wants to make sure that everyone hears what she says, and because she can't see if you're looking at her, she talks very, *very* loudly. After school she used to come home and go into Mia's room and jump on her bed. And sometimes she would grab Mia with her arms and legs, and start chattering to her, and Mia would say softly, "Inside voice, Tam. Inside voice," which meant that she should speak more quietly. Tam is getting big now and Mia is so small, and Mia often wondered aloud whether Tam would be curling around her in the same fashion when she's, oh, thirty.

She may be physically clingy, but Tam is also stubborn and insistent on doing things her own way. For example, if left to her own devices, she will change her outfits four times a day and leave all her dirty clothes in a pile on the floor. "I sweat, I don't want to smell," she insists. But the truth is, Tam wants to be a fashion plate. Feeling her way with her cane, she would come into my room every morning and say, "Kristi, this okay? Does it match?" She always wore a skirt or dress, never pants; she loves her clothes, because in Vietnam she had nothing. Now, with so many new outfits and hand-me-downs from her sisters, Tam dresses up every day to go to school and switches outfits as often as possible, much to the exasperation of her normally unperturbable mother.

One night when Mia was out, Tam got into bed with me. I had a string of shiny black onyx rosary beads that John had given me before he went to Ireland, and I kept them by my bedside. I gave Tam the rosary beads to hold, and she couldn't stop fondling them. When she wanted to know what they were, I tried to explain the concept of God to her, and the fact that each bead signified a mystery of the faith or an event in the life of Jesus or the Virgin Mary. Tam thought for a moment, then she put her hands together as though in prayer, and she said, "Yes, the old ladies of Vietnam," which, thanks to the French colonials, was a Catholic country. I told her that saying the rosary was like asking the Virgin Mary for something, and that getting through it takes about forty-five minutes. She was fascinated. Afterward she called God "the Good Man," and she said, "The Good Man helps people like you and Mommy. Woody is a bad man, and the Good Man will never help him."

Woody deserved Tam's wrath. He would usually arrive at the house with bags full of toys for Satchel and Dylan, who were her constant playmates, and with zilch for Tam. He never said hello to her and rarely addressed her at all. Tam, prideful child that she is, started refusing to eat at the same table as Woody. After a while she refused—sometimes tearfully—to stay in the same room with him. Woody's hostile indifference scared her. "Woody no goody, Woody no goody," she used to say while she jumped on her bed.

That fall Mia began receiving boxes full of letters agreeing that Woody was no goody. Adoptive parents sent her notes of support. Sympathetic fans sent rabbits' feet, poetry, and strange

confessions, too. Some provided a few good laughs or sympathetic stories when we thought none were left. One note, for
instance, was written by a woman who left her husband because
he used to masturbate in front of her and her children. Someone
else sent index cards with hopeful sayings on them; Mia still has
them tacked to the fridge (One says, "Now that my house has
burned down, I can only see the forest more clearly"). Yet another supporter enclosed a religious medal which Mia wore
around her neck throughout the winter. We thought it might
bring good luck in the battles ahead.

Every week, as the autumn winds of 1992 turned frosty, Mia
would take Dylan up to Yale for her interviews. The pressures
on the family, and on Dylan in particular, continued. On November 12, Andre came to visit, and the next day Dylan announced
to the Yale–New Haven team, "Andre is my new daddy." Had
she been coached? Was she renouncing Woody as a way of pleas-
ing her mother? Or as a way of pushing all the Woody-associated
unpleasantness out of her life?

On Mia's many treks back and forth to New Haven, I would
send along a favorite Lindt chocolate bar for the hour-and-a-half
ride. Once I wrapped a handwritten copy of *Footprints*, a poem
that was a favorite of ours (good little Catholic schoolgirls that
we were), around the sweet, hoping it would bring comfort.

> *One night a man had a dream. He*
> *dreamed he was walking along the beach*
> *with the LORD. Across the sky flashed*
> *scenes from his life. For each scene,*
> *he noticed two sets of footprints in*
> *the sand: one belonging to him, and*
> *the other to the LORD.*
>
> *When the last scene of his life*
> *flashed before him, He looked back at*
> *the footprints in the sand. He noticed*
> *that many times along the path of his*
> *life, there was only one set of*
> *footprints. He also noticed that it*

*happened at the very lowest and
saddest times in his life.*

*This really bothered him, and he
questioned the LORD about it. "Lord,
you said that once I decided to follow
you, you'd walk with me all the way.
But I have noticed that during the
most troublesome times in my life,
there is only one set of footprints. I
don't understand why when I needed you
most, you would leave me."*

*The LORD replied, "My precious,
precious child, I love you and I would
never leave you. During your times of
trial and suffering, when you see only
one set of footprints, it was then that
I carried you."*

During this time Mia kept waiting—in vain, as it turned out—
for the Connecticut police to indict Woody. And Woody per-
sisted with his battle for custody of Satchel, Dylan, and Moses.
Clearly, there would be a trial in 1993.

So even the smallest comfort was a welcome one.

"My heart does not know from logic."
Gabe in Husbands and Wives

ELEVEN

She Said, He Said

66"The amount of nonagreement between them was so great," Satchel's psychiatrist, Dr. Susan Coates, observed of Woody and Mia in court, "that it led me to ask why they were together."

In twelve years what began as Mia and Woody's kooky New York fairy tale unraveled into a tragic fable whose larger issues touched on our most nightmarish fears. They were issues worthy of Greek drama—issues of deception, betrayal, and revenge. Themes such as mother-and-daughter jealousy, father-and-daughter boundaries, and mother-and-son boundaries. The Allen-Farrow custody battle also provoked lofty questions like what comprises a family in this day and age, and how shall we live in a moral way.

Yet I think of Mia's story mostly as the journey of a modern woman who loved not wisely, but too well. No matter what beauty, power, and intelligence Mia possessed, she was enslaved by her blind trust in Woody, and by her eagerness to overlook his faults. I guess you could say she was desperate to continue even though the relationship had become increasingly chilly. In court Mia testified about her commitment to Woody:

Well, at that point we were in our twelfth or thirteenth year of being together. We had a biological child to-

199

gether. I was in love with him. I intended to and expected to spend the rest of my life with him. I was
absolutely committed to him and had thought of no other
man or partner in those twelve years that we had been
together. We worked together. In fact, we were, in that
six months beginning in October [1991], beginning our
thirteenth movie together. We had a close and constant
and, I thought, continuing relationship.

Q. *Now, had you and Mr. Allen ever discussed marriage?*

A. From time to time over the years.

Q. And what would you say? What would he say?

A. He said that this was something that he just didn't believe in, just a piece of paper. He reassured me by saying, "Do I not behave as if we were married in every
way?" I wanted to be married, and there were times in
our relationship that I needed it, but I also tried to understand that it was something that he didn't want for
whatever reasons. He had been married twice before,
and he said that that was something he didn't want to
do, that it should not reflect on his lack of commitment
to me.

As for their sexual relationship during the six months prior to
her discovery of the affair, Mia admitted to the court that it was
virtually nonexistent. At that time, she claimed, Woody showered
her with a litany of excuses—his version of "Please, honey, I
have a headache." Except in his case the excuses were more
farfetched. In the fall he put Mia off, sometimes saying that he
had come down with a recurrence of his Lyme disease; other
times that it might be chronic fatigue syndrome; still others, he
was fearful that he had AIDS. "[He said] that he had been with
prostitutes thirteen years before, and he had just received some
data or read something where you could get AIDS even as long
as thirteen years after being exposed to it," claimed Mia. "He
had blood tests [finally], and in early December he told me
the results: he did *not* have AIDS, but he couldn't account for
his fatigue."

Mia traced the decline of their sexual relationship back to the birth of Satchel. "I thought about it a lot," she said, "and I thought that maybe I'd made a mistake having him in the room during my Cesarean." She also wondered if perhaps Woody's disinterest in sex was because he was getting older, or, yes, "Maybe this is what happens after twelve years together."

On their third family trip to Europe, specifically Ireland, in June 1991, Woody and Mia stayed in separate rooms. Woody, she said, needed his own bathroom and a quiet place to write. In New York, she explained, they would occasionally have sex in Woody's apartment or his screening room up until July, 1992, but never in her house.

Still, Mia was willing to put up with the ebb and flow of Woody's sexual appetite for her. She had had *her* moment of doubt about Woody during her pregnancy with Satchel and had resolved it in her head, and now she was in there for the long
   Tragic.
the ups and downs of their passion without seeking romance elsewhere, Woody clearly was not. I guess some might call this a difference between women's need for nesting and men's need for roving, but I'm sure that in this case it also has to do with their own individual natures.

Woody, for his part, seemed to be moved equally by the artist's notion of what the world owed him, by the psychoanalytical patient's self-centeredness, and by the nerdy guy's need to prove himself over and over with women. Add to this his history of distancing himself from conflict, which was once, perhaps, a childhood strategy to deal with his parents' constant screaming fights, and you have a man who appears to be a king of denial and a master of self-absorption.

Woody was so self-absorbed that, when questioned in court about the fact that Moses, Matthew, Fletcher, and Sascha shared a room, he answered, "That I couldn't tell you." Let me assure you, there are only four bedrooms in Mia's apartment (and a similar setup at Frog Hollow)—one for Mia, one for the babies, one for the older boys, and one for the older girls. You don't have to be a genius, or to have lived there, to figure out the arrangement. In the twelve years that he had been spending with Mia and her children, how could Woody not have known this?

Woody's behavior toward Mia during the last year of their relationship revealed incredible self-absorption and, worse, dishonesty. An ostrich when it came to confronting her with unpleasant news, Woody took on the role of a perennial pacifier. He would do and say anything to avoid her tears and her wrath. "I was always in a placating mood with Miss Farrow," he testified, claiming that he just *had* to "pacify" her in order to prevent her from suicide. As for their much-written-about discussions of marriage in the months after Mia discovered Woody's Polaroids, he gave a rambling, unfocused testimony in court:

> Miss Farrow said to me in the middle of a hysterical outburst, would I consider marrying her, and that was the only way that she could prevent me from seeing Soon-Yi. You know, the trick was control of the eruptions in front of the children. And so I did say to her that I was *not* going with Soon-Yi . . . because if I didn't say that, any time the slightest suspicion of that came up, there was an eruption in front of the children.

> There were threats of suicide and violence in front of the children, and so I did say very frequently that I am not going with Soon-Yi. And if she brought up marriage—I certainly didn't bring up marriage—I tried to walk a middle line. Certainly, I wasn't going to marry her and didn't want to. . . . And it's laughable when you think she said, "to prevent you from being with Soon-Yi." But I tried never to take a harsh and extreme position on anything. I always tried to say, "Well, it's possible, we'll talk about that. We're going to work on a film, let's see what happens in the future." I always tried to soft-pedal things, and my hope was [that] with the passage of time, with some therapy, some drugs, maybe she would . . . not have these violent outbursts in front of the children all the time.

Woody also gave his version of their visits to the Carlyle Hotel during early 1992, visits that Mia had hoped would serve up romance and reconciliation:

Both times at the Carlyle were quite similar. Remember now, I had not had a romantic relationship with Miss Farrow for years. I was certainly not going to start [one] at the epicenter of this violence. I was placating her in all of these instances, on the advice of lawyers and doctors. I was trying to defuse the situation. I did not think . . . the rage would remain unabated. I thought that [it] would go on for a month, two, whatever, but I didn't think it would go on forever.

Therefore, when she said to me, "Let's check into a hotel and sleep together," I said fine. Just as I said fine to any offer of dinner, any offer for a walk, three-quarters of the things in our negotiating, anything I could do. "I won't see the kids here, I won't do this, I won't take them to my house—whatever you want." I was just as sweet as I could be. I just wanted to calm her down. She had possession of the children. I went to the Carlyle with her, she became totally hysterical, I thought she was going to jump out the window. Then I realized mercifully, at the Carlyle the windows are just glass walls, and there really were no windows. But it was an absolutely terrifying experience. I related that experience, I believe, to my doctor. . . . I was advised not to do it again.

I did do it one more time when she suggested it, and then, with the exact same situation. . . . And I never went again. She suggested it one more time, I did not do it.

The Great Pacifier even placated Soon-Yi at camp—at least that is the reason he came up with for telephoning her six to eight times a day. He also did not seem to give much thought to how important, or complicated, this union might be to her. Soon-Yi had never dated before; there's a good chance that she had never even *kissed* a man before. She mooned over Woody for at least a year before they actually got together, and now she was in the throes of her first affair—which just happened to be with her mother's lover and the father of her siblings. Yet in court Woody seemed casual about the relationship. Speaking about the days after their sexual relationship first began, he told the judge:

> I thought that she was going to go back to school very soon. And that I didn't know what was going to happen at that point. And the thing just exploded so quickly that, you know, I think we would have looked up a week or two weeks down the line, she would have been going back to school. And we would have said, "This is crazy, obviously we're not going to continue this." Or, "Let's go to Mia and say we want to go get married." I don't know. It just happened so fast.

And what of the possibility that he might not want to continue the relationship with Soon-Yi? Woody, astonishingly enough, dismissed such a thing, saying instead, "I thought maybe it would be the other way around."

He also never considered the possibility that *he* would want to dissolve the affair and *she* would want to continue it. Who, asked the judge, would be Soon-Yi's support system then? "Well, it was not something that I had entered into lightly," Woody replied. "Her support system at that time would have been me."

No, the court reminded him, it *wouldn't* have been if Soon-Yi wanted to stay and Woody wanted to walk. Then, he suggested, she could rely on her family.

No, the court reminded him again. Under the circumstances it would not have been something she could have discussed with her family. Luckily, Woody had his own solution. "She could have discussed it with her friends," he said, "or seen a therapist, who certainly would have helped with that."

Is this man out of touch, or what?

It wouldn't be fair for me to suggest that Woody is totally self-absorbed and Mia not self-absorbed at all. After all, she *is* an actress and a star. Like Woody, Mia also tends to avoid confrontations. Sometimes, as when her accountant wanted to lower my salary after Woody stopped paying it, she refused to deal with it herself, saying instead, "Speak to my accountant, Kristi."

She hides behind other people. I worked with the woman for two years, and I *never* had an argument with her. Contrary to Woody's descriptions of her hysteria, the Mia I know is sweet-tempered. However often she has been provoked by him to rage and tears over their relationship, I have rarely, if ever, heard her raise her voice to her kids.

If in the course of their twelve years together, Woody had learned to look aside, placating Mia rather than confronting the unpleasant dismantling of a family, so, too, had she. Woody's motive, it seemed, was to have his cake and eat it. But Mia's was fear of losing her man—and her work.

In so many areas, Mia and Woody saw the world differently. He preferred the city; she, the country. He was an agnostic and cynic whose philosophy of life boiled down to Alvy Singer's observation in *Annie Hall* that "life is divided up into the horrible and the miserable." Mia, in part because of her Catholic background, had a genuinely spiritual nature. During the trial Mia was asked about Hecuba, the wife of King Priam of Troy, in the play *The Trojan Women*. Apparently, during an emotional conversation with Dylan's psychiatrist, Dr. Schultz, Mia had referred to Hecuba's tragedy. But Mia claimed that the doctor had "misunderstood" why she had been drawn to the story. It wasn't, as the shrink had feared, because Hecuba had been violent. No, she said, "The interesting thing about Hecuba is her struggle to maintain her moral roots, and I felt during this period of time that that was an issue for me. . . . I explained to Dr. Schultz what the moral dilemma was, and that Hecuba had been unsuccessful. . . . And how it was important for all of us—all my children and myself—to make every decision with everything that's best in you rather than what might be dominant in you."

It's instructive that one of the things that disillusioned Mia about psychiatry has to do with what Dr. Schultz didn't seem to understand about the story of Hecuba—its moral component. Although Mia herself saw a shrink, and sent her children for help, she is highly skeptical of therapists. As she once told me: "When I went to talk to Woody's shrink, she said that shrinks weren't there to make moral judgments. And I thought to myself, 'What does this mean?' I don't believe in psychiatrists in part because they don't differentiate between right and wrong. Yeah"—she stopped, pausing for a moment, then added with uncharacteristic anger—"and he was screwing my daughter."

The passion of those words reflects her deep feelings about her kids; Mia had always been unusually close to them. While I worked for her, she couldn't stand being separated from them for even one night. In fact, although she began to date men including screenwriter William Goldman, in the spring of 1993, I can remember only one time in the two years I've been with her when she didn't sleep in her own bed. And that was the night during the summer of 1992 when she went up to Tanglewood to see her friend, the composer Johnny Williams, conduct. During the evening she was gone from us, she must have called six or seven times. Later she told me that she had been terrified, traveling alone. Booked into a fancy hotel for something like $500, a price she felt she couldn't afford, she found the whole experience—strange hotel and all that time away from the kids, surrounded by so much quiet—unsettling, and so she stayed up all night. The next morning, right after breakfast, she drove directly back to Connecticut.

Mia liked being close to home. Usually, even if she'd go out on a date for the evening, she would be back home by eleven. And she *hated* going downtown. The Upper West Side and Upper East Side were okay, but she would get nervous if a man wanted to take her, say, all the way down to SoHo. Usually, she simply refused to go. I always kidded Mia that wherever she went, she had to make sure she could throw a rock and hit her own building. In fact, even going out for a casual dinner, she didn't venture far from home, which is why she always liked Fishin Eddie's in our neighborhood.

Of course, needing to stick so close to home can really put a damper on one's sex life, especially if there are as many kids to worry about as Mia has. Yet sex has, by her own admission, not played an important part in Mia's life with Woody these past few years. And I wonder if it was ever really that important to her.

Woody, on the other hand, seems very sexual, which I'm sure comes as no surprise to anyone who watches his movies. The

Woody screen character is a lovable lecher who is always on the make (usually with nice, shy Gentile girls), and, interestingly enough, always joking about incest and sex. Sometimes they're silly, cheap jokes. In *Crimes and Misdemeanors,* when his sister observes "Once the sex goes, it all goes," Cliff (Woody) replies, "It's true. The last time I was inside a woman was when I visited the Statue of Liberty." Yet sometimes his observations about sex have dead-serious undertones. In *Annie Hall,* Wife Number 2, fending off his advances in the middle of a party she is giving, chastises Alvy: "Alvy, don't! You're using sex to express hostility." In *Husbands and Wives* Judy (Mia) tells Gabe (Woody) something very similar: "You always get sexual at the oddest times. You use sex to express every emotion except love."

Woody and his alter egos share much in common. His driver, Don, told me that he had numerous flings during the years he was with Mia. Which, of course, makes his affair with Soon-Yi even more curious—and, well, unnecessary.

Scratch the surface of Mia's naïveté and bewilderment, however, and you get a woman who knows what's happening. In August, 1993, columnist Cindy Adams reported the contents of a telephone conversation between Woody and Mia that was made by Woody at some point after the alleged molestation of Dylan. In it, Mia told Woody, "You changed. You're old now. Now you want little girls to turn you on because you can't get a – – – – – – with me anymore. That's all it is." Mia then charged headlong into the reasons why men edging up toward sixty choose "little girls": "To get sexual stimulation," she said bluntly. "Something new. Something forbidden. More erotic." As for Soon-Yi, she warned Woody, "She's not the easiest child, as you'll find out—but I loved her with all my heart."

Yet Mia has fueled their fight by refusing to settle the custody case out of court. Woody wanted to, she didn't. She tells me, however, that Woody was making absurd, impossible demands, asking for custody of Dylan on weekends. "I can't do that. I have to represent Dylan's interest," she said. Maybe that's Mia exercising her control. For, by going forward with these child-abuse allegations, she has created a situation in which, for perhaps the only time in their relationship, she has power. Of course, it is not only the power to make Woody heel, but, inadvertently, to pull him down, and her whole family as well, into the hideous muck of public revelation.

One day this May I finally collected my courage and asked Mia the crusher: Why, after so much humiliation, after the years of insults and put-downs, after the alleged Steffi affair, even after Soon-Yi—why did she stay with Woody? And she just shrugged her shoulders and, sounding less a child of Hollywood and consort of celebrities than a star-struck teenager, said, "I felt he was really *neat*, and great, and I really admired him." She then paused for a moment before adding, "I loved him. I honestly loved him."

Tragic.

"What my ex-husband doesn't say is that for the last two years of our marriage, he was impotent. I couldn't take the fact that he's unromantic in every way. He's the kind of guy who gives you an appliance for your birthday."

Judy Roth (Mia) in Husbands and Wives

TWELVE

Cold Winter Light

"Hey, Kristi, what if I hid a mike on ya?" I looked at Chris Rush, Mia's friendly electronics specialist, as if he were a madman. A stocky blond in his mid-thirties, he spoke with a thick Brooklyn accent whose cadences enhanced his already-well-developed sense of humor.

This time, I hoped he was being funny. "What do you mean?" I asked lightly. "You want me to play Nancy Drew?"

He nodded. It was December, and Satchel's visitations with his father would soon begin. Chris went on to explain that it might be a good idea for me to wear a wire during this time—if not with Woody, then at least with Woody's driver, Don Harris, who had a very loose tongue. I hesitated. What could I say? I didn't want to be a coward, and I didn't want to desert Mia. But it struck me as deceptive. "Don't worry, it's not illegal," he told me. I stalled, telling him that I had to think about it for a while.

Later that evening, when Mia and I were sitting on the chest at the end of her bed and having one of our heart-to-hearts, I mentioned this proposition. We both laughed at the notion. It sounded like something out of "Charlie's Angels." The prospect of being a bonafide adventuress, I confess, appealed to my dramatic instincts. Still, I was glad when Chris dropped the idea.

As the new year dawned, I thought, Good riddance to 1992, twelve months that had brought nothing but the worst kind of grief. Still, it was difficult to summon up much optimism about what lay ahead. For one, the defection of Soon-Yi was still an open wound for Mia. An entry in my journal on January 10, 1993, read:

Tonight after Mia went out, Moses, Lark, Jesse, Fletcher, and I pulled out old family videos and watched them. When Mia came in later on, she sat down with us and got caught up in the images on the TV. There were Daisy and Fletcher as little kids, swimming. And Larky and Mike Nichols's daughter, Jenny, playing ball on the lawn. And, of course, there was Soon-Yi, age eleven, sitting on the grass and looking so solemn and frail as she sewed her needlepoint (a piece which, Mia later said, she had worked on for years). Mia watched the tape for a moment and then began to cry. I felt so bad for her, she looked like her heart might break. After she regained control of herself, she said that someday, and in some way, Woody would pay for what he has done to this family. He will pay, I agree, but I don't think it will be in this lifetime.

Mia spent most of her time in December, 1992, and January, 1993, preparing her court case against Woody. The two met for the first time in months at Yale on Friday, January 15. For the week leading up to this encounter, Mia was withdrawn but resolved. On Thursday morning we had a conversation that seemed straight out of Catholic school. Later on, I scribbled in my diary:

Mia looked like a schoolgirl in her pleated skirt and blouse [which she had slipped into to wear to Eleanor's office that day]. "Kristi," she said, "this has been incredibly difficult and trying, but I will take with happiness anything that God hands me in order to be a better and more moral person." She also said that she thought I had grown so much as a person since John's death, and that I have been able to help her through her pain because of this. I was very moved by what she said. I wish I could be as self-sacrificing as she is. I think it's tragic that misery is what makes us more understanding as people. On a brighter note: Mia's mother, Maureen, and her husband Jim Cushing sent me a lovely Happy New Year's card with $100 in it. I hope I'm capable of loving again, even if it hurts. I miss John.

Around this time we received information from Eleanor confirming what we had suspected—that Monica had definitely been spying for Woody. In an affidavit that she had given to Woody's attorneys in December, Monica claimed that Mia "has suffered dramatic mood swings and had screaming fits about Mr. Allen." She went on to claim that "Ms. Farrow . . . not only gives her natural children more material gifts and possessions, but more physical love as well." Finally, and most damning, were Monica's remarks about Dylan's videotape. "I know that tape was made over the course of at least two, and perhaps three days," she said. "I was present when Ms. Farrow made a portion of that tape outdoors. I recall Ms. Farrow saying to Dylan at that time, 'Dylan, what did Daddy do, did he tell you to take your underwear off?' " (Mia, by the way, denies ever asking her daughter such leading questions.)

When Monica left by mutual agreement on January 19, I had to bite my lip not to say to Mia, *I told you so*. I knew Monica, with her fat salary, courtesy of Woody—and her "severance of some sort," according to Woody's publicist, Leslee Dart—was a bomb waiting to go off.

The chief thing that sparked Mia during this period was the prospect of appearing opposite Jack Nicholson in the movie, *Wolf*, a modern werewolf tale, and early in February we gathered up Isaiah and Satchel and flew to Los Angeles for a cast reading—and a welcome holiday from the daily grind of court preparations. I had not been to Los Angeles in five years, and I hadn't traveled in the States since I had been on the National Collegiate Athletic Association Student Advisory Board in 1989 and 1990, when I was sent to meetings at least once a month. So this trip was a treat for me.

It was also an example of the contradictions in Mia's life: On one hand, she enjoyed such extraordinary privileges; and on the other, she lived such a routine, ordinary life. We began our adventures in Movieland by jumping into a fancy limo that Columbia Pictures sent to take us to LaGuardia Airport. Both Mia and I looked like a mess. We dressed, unintentionally, as twins, with our black jeans, black T-shirts, and black blazers splattered with baby food. On our feet we wore Doc Martens; on our backs, backpacks; in our hands, children. Nevertheless, American Airlines personnel treated us like visiting royalty, escorting us into an elegant waiting room to shield us from the press, and then directly into the first row of the first-class section of the plane. Lucille Ball's daughter, Lucie Arnaz, was on the same flight and came up to Mia to express her support.

Then, after landing in L.A., another small army of security personnel led us through the airport. I don't understand how the press knew it, but when we arrived, hundreds of flashbulbs popped in our faces. Mia has learned how to look the other way, how to not notice the photographers, but they still rattled me. Finally, we took refuge in yet another limo which had tinted windows to protect our privacy. This one sped away and headed up La Cienega Boulevard toward the heavenly Bel-Air Hotel.

On the way, I received the Mia Farrow tour of L.A. She would say, "Oh, here is the first Catholic school I attended." "Here is where I had my first sleepover with friends." Or, "Here is the driveway of the house where Frank and I first lived [in Bel Air]." I was extremely impressed—and might have gotten intimidated had Mia not confided in me during a dark moment along the road: "Kristi, I'm not good at being alone."

That made sense, since she hadn't had much practice. Right after she broke up with Sinatra in 1968 and returned from her meditation in India, she met Andre Previn. That was 1969. Ten years later she left him, moved to New York, and met Woody Allen. Early in 1980 they became lovers and were inseparable for a dozen years. Mia has spent powerful little of her time alone. Why on earth, then, should she actually be good at it?

And if she felt awkward or lonely without a famous man to protect and amuse her, the luxurious Bel-Air Hotel may have helped subdue her qualms. Who could gripe too loudly when ensconced in a gorgeous pink stucco bungalow set in the loveliest landscaped gardens I have ever seen? When the bungalow includes a living room decorated with gorgeous antiques and a fireplace, and two large bedrooms, each with its own bathroom and entrance? Mia also found time for a dinner together with her ex-stepdaughter, Nancy Sinatra, and her old friend Maria Roach. The next morning we all had breakfast with her "Uncle" Lenne Gersh, a playwright. Then the kids and I spent the day with him while she was at her reading.

Yet her business at hand did not proceed smoothly. On the evening of our arrival, Mia's agent phoned to deliver some devastating news. He told her confidentially that the producers and executives on *Wolf* had not wanted to give Mia the role and were trying to get her to back out of it. "The Woody thing is too controversial for everyone," he explained. But Mia's old friend and one-time boyfriend, Mike Nichols, who was directing the picture, fought bravely to hire her. Mia went to that reading the next day knowing that Mike was her sole champion. She said that she was so humbled and scared by it. Even afterward, the producers gave her a hard time. They wanted her to take a cut in the salary that they had originally offered her. They were even refusing to include her name in advertisements for the picture. What they didn't understand was that Mia was a formidable adversary. She was ready to do whatever she had to do to remain in the movie. And a "no-frills" contract didn't bother her. She was used to it with Woody.

We returned to New York, grateful for the break from legal matters, but sobered by the chilly Hollywood climate. Mia promptly became ill with another bout of flu. However, she was cheered by flowers from Liza Minnelli, who had been Mia's best childhood friend. Sinatra, Carly Simon, and Barbara Walters (who was trying to get Mia to be a guest on her show) would also from time to time show their support by writing a note or sending a bouquet.

In February Mia toyed with adopting a six-year-old MS child who would most certainly die at an early age. She said the adoption agency had been looking for a home for the boy since he was two, and she didn't want him to die alone. "No one will understand, Kristi, but it doesn't matter," she explained to me in a voice that sounded very sure. "What's right is right."

That may have been so, but I didn't want her to take one more emotionally draining responsibility into her life. Mia said that she could handle this child because she had been through so much tragedy herself. I, however, thought it would be too hard on her kids. They were already suffering. Happily, the red tape to adopt this boy became too complicated—and Mia eventually abandoned the idea.

The children she had were demanding enough. There was the time, for instance, when Mia took Satchel to the dentist for a fluoride treatment. Although he was told not to eat afterward, he did, and was then stricken with worry. Driving home in Big Red, he asked Mia about twenty-five times: "Mom, do I have to go back to the dentist?" "Mom, do you think what I did is bad? Are you sure I don't have to go back to the dentist?" Ten seconds later: "Mom, I *hate* the dentist. What if I have to go back?" *I* was ruffled at his persistence, but Mia remained calm. Finally, when he had asked for reassurance beyond all reason, she said in her small, soft voice, "Harmon (the new name that Satchel chose for himself), I don't want to discuss it anymore. I'll call the dentist when I get home." That was about as temperamental as she ever got.

It was early during that winter of 1993 that Dylan and Satchel decided to change their names—a decision that infuriated Woody. Dylan took the name Eliza because she was so charmed by Audrey Hepburn's performance as Eliza Doolittle in the movie *My Fair Lady*), and Satchel chose Harmon, from a list of male and female names that Mia keeps in the rear of her Filofax for new adoptions. Both children had expressed interest in this. Maybe, I thought, they wanted to reclaim themselves from the reporters and photographers who hounded them at every turn of the corner. Mia consulted with the kids' therapists, who felt that these changes might help them put the bad times behind them, and so she encouraged them as well.   ·

On February 26, the twins' birthday, we put together a birthday breakfast for Matthew and Sascha which, not surprisingly, was weighted down by the events of the past year. I had awakened at six to blow up balloons, hang streamers, and defrost bagels to serve with lox (we may have been Catholic, but we are, after all, New Yorkers!). Somehow, despite the decorations, there was nothing festive about the atmosphere—or our moods. Mia was rushed because she had to prepare for court; Matthew had to dash off to work as a paralegal at a law firm (where he was trying to clock in some experience in order to get accepted at law school); and Sascha was hurrying off to business classes at Fordham. Naturally, the little kids had to get to school too. Everyone was looking at the clock. It was more like Grand Central Station than party time.

One of my jobs during this period was to escort Satchel back and forth from his court-appointed visits with his dad. On these visits, which had begun in December, I felt the impact of the Woody charisma—and the Woody quirks. This is a man who can cut you dead if he is not interested in you. Says Casey Pascal, who got used to the cold treatment from Woody: "He rarely interacted with me or my husband Jack when we were at Mia's. He was in another world. He would occasionally talk, but he certainly wouldn't sit down and have a glass of wine. He's very selective, I think. He was always nice to my children. But he didn't talk to anybody, so we didn't talk to him. I thought he was weird, and I knew he was fiercely neurotic, so I didn't want to upset him by imposing any kind of conversation on him."

Yet if Woody wants to, he can turn the charm on full force, and it's almost impossible to resist. I loved to sit around the kitchen table with him, Satchel, and Dylan, and listen while he told them stories. The children, and Dylan especially, would watch him, mesmerized. Sometimes he would talk about how as a kid he hated school and so used to put cheese inside his teacher's hat. Then the teacher would put her hat on her head, and everyone else would be walking around wondering, "Pee-youw, what's that disgusting smell?" Well, the kids would go crazy laughing. "Pee-youw!" Satchel, the great giggler, would echo his dad, holding his nose and then—as he dissolved into laughter—his belly.

In another yarn about school, Woody the kid fell asleep at his desk and when the teacher called on him, he woke up, shaking all over. Woody, the grown-up, would really give a performance, shaking from tip to toe, and, in response, the kids would shriek with joy.

One of my favorites was the story of how Woody found shrinking dust, sprinkled it all over himself, and got really tiny. Then he crawled inside his teacher's mouth, then into her brain, and was able to listen to her conversations with herself. All his stories were like this one: amazing and imaginative. It is little wonder that the children themselves have developed terrific imaginations.

Woody was less effective at trying to meet the physical demands of playtime. One day we had to put together Satchel's Creepy Crawlers, a machine into which you pour rubber, which then cooks and congeals to form different kinds of spiders. This required hooking up a light bulb to some wires. The kids waited with unbelievable patience as Woody tried and tried, but couldn't quite get the knack of it. So I took over. And he said, "Look, kids, isn't that great? Kristi hooked up the Creepy Crawlers." At that, they both applauded. I, of course, flashed back to the time when Woody couldn't pick the bathroom lock. The guy doesn't have great manual dexterity.

Every so often that winter, Satchel's visitations created unforeseen emotional hazards. Once, in an effort at a playtime collaboration with his son, Woody drew a heart and inside it a picture of Satchel, Dylan, Moses, Mommy, and Daddy. As he told the court a few weeks later: "My practice was always to try and promulgate for Satchel some kind of warmth and respect for his mother and for Dylan and Moses." Yet after examining the heart, Satchel blackened out Woody's face and drew a black line through the word *daddy*. Then, according to Woody, Satchel "drew his own heart with a line through it, a forbidden line, and wrote the word *no* and crossed out my name." Revealing of Satchel's own mixed feelings, yes. But not exactly the kind of family portrait to give Dad a warm-all-over feeling.

When I brought Satchel to Woody's Fifth Avenue penthouse for their first playtime together, I remember how nervous Satchel was as we stepped into the elevator taking us up to Woody's duplex apartment. Clutching my hand tightly in his, Satchel begged me, "Kristi, please don't leave me." He always seemed indifferent and anxious when arriving for a visit with his father, and unwilling to be alone with him; yet by the time I picked Satchel up, he was bursting with enthusiasm about what movie they had seen together in the screening room, or about the improbable seven layer cake they had baked. He would always carry under his arm a little shoebox filled with his handiwork, whether it was a drawing, a clay model, or a dozen cookies. At home Mia would regard its contents with disdain and tell me to put them away.

I admit that I, too, at first felt hostile when I took Satchel to visit his father. We would enter Woody's vestibule, where the first thing you see is an elegant mahogany table that holds big portraits of Satchel and Dylan (there is none of Moses). Then I would take a deep breath and knock on the apartment door, and Woody would usually open it up and whisk Satchel inside. Once, he started to close the door, but inadvertently slammed it on my arm as I said, "Wait a minute, Woody, is the court-appointed matron here?" I admit I was playing the hardnose, but I, like Mia, was angry at him, and now, I guess, I was letting it spill over. In a neutral voice Woody replied, "Yes, she's in here." And he opened the door just wide enough for me to shake her hand, which I did. Then he closed the door on my arm.

Two hours later I came back for Satchel, and Woody seemed contrite. "Kristi, come in," he said, gently touching my arm. A jolt of electricity shot through me. "I'm sorry about the way I acted before, about your arm. But everything has been so difficult, so heightened, lately." His eyes gazed at me intently. For a moment I was confused. I thought, *What is he doing?* Flirting? Just like Mia said? I glanced down at the floor and said, "Come on, Satchel, let's go." After that I made an effort to avoid eye contact with Woody.

One evening I showed up with Satchel—we were always driven over to Woody's apartment by his driver, Don—and the court-appointed matron had not yet arrived. "Kristi, can you do me a favor?" Woody asked, his voice pleasant and nothing more. "The matron is late, so can you come in and stay with us until she gets here?" Sure, I said, and I went inside. It is a breathtaking space dominated by a big, square living room with a vast semicircle of huge windows opening up to a view of all Central Park. We were so high up that we could even see the mist hanging over the park. Outside, as I would see later, there was a huge double-tiered terrace which surely sports the only penthouse basketball court in Manhattan. There was a garden as well, a barbecue, a table, and chairs.

What was so strange to me was how much Woody's apartment resembled Mia's. Sure, it was bigger and grander. Still, the living room seemed to be decorated like Mia's, with plump, inviting, lived-in couches, although his were covered in beige fabrics and hers in florals. A small office-library held pictures of him, Mia, and the kids. One room had been converted into a gym; another into a kids' playroom, complete with a plastic tarp on the floor. Here Woody was in the midst of doing arts and crafts with his son. "Satchel, show Kristi what you made," he said as I entered the room. Satchel held up a plaster-of-paris flower. Then Woody showed me what looked like a mangled ball of dough and announced, "This is my turtle." Oh.

"You're no Michelangelo," I couldn't help observing. We both laughed.

Playtime finished, Woody escorted Satchel and me through the doorway, through his study, where I saw that there were several biographies of him on its shelves, and into the living room and kitchen. Here he invited me to sit down while he served Satchel his favorite dish, chicken and broccoli, which the maid had left on the stove. As Satchel picked at his food, he looked out the window onto the terrace and asked his dad what had happened to the birdfeeders that Woody had—uncharacteristically, I might add—put on the terrace for the kids. Woody replied that the neighbors had begun to complain about the chirping and cooing. "Also," he pointed out, "there was bird doo everywhere." So the birdfeeders, and, of course, the birds, had to go.

Then Woody began to turn up the charm. Scrutinizing me from behind his black-rimmed glasses, he asked, "Kristi, what are you going to do in the future?"

And I replied that I was thinking of going to graduate school to study physical therapy and holistic medicine. He lit up, and we talked about that for a few moments. Yet I felt slightly self-conscious. I could feel his penetrating glance. Was he coming on to me? Or was he just intense? Was it one-sided? Could I be imagining this? Damned if I knew.

Surely, Mia had fed this fear. If Woody was at all attentive to me on the phone, she would say slyly, "Remember my words, Kristi, I know him. You're next." In fact, I couldn't help wondering, Was Woody merely being pleasant? Seductive? Or was he just trying to lure me over to his legal camp. Whatever his motives, I clearly felt flattered. In March, I wrote in my journal:

Last night I dropped Satchel off at Woody's. Satchel had grabbed my nose on the way up in the elevator and made honking sounds, so Woody got into the elevator with us, and I said, "Why don't you honk your father's nose too?" And so he did it, rather aggressively. First Woody's, and Satchel said, "Honk!" Then mine. "Honk." Then Woody's. "Honk. Honk." Mine. "Honk. Honk." Woody looked at me as if to say, Why in hell did you do that? I started laughing and said, "I'm sorry." Then we stood close together, and Satchel honked both of our noses in a song pattern. As we all walked out of the building together, Woody pointed at his Mercedes and said, "Why don't you let my driver drop you off, and Satchel and I will take the station wagon." After we parted, Satchel called me back for a kiss. Then, I slipped into the luxurious backseat of the Mercedes, and I remembered that while we were honking, Woody was staring at me in the elevator, smiling. It makes me shy and nervous to contemplate. And wary.

Maybe that's why, when Chris Rush, our electronics Einstein, once again brought up the idea of my wearing a wire during my limo rides with Woody's gossipy driver Don, I reluctantly agreed. So in early March, when Don once again droned on and on about how Woody had had plenty of affairs during his twelve years with Mia, I got it all on tape. I have to admit, I was so nervous that he might notice the wire, I could barely listen to his juicy tidbits. Although he never mentioned names, Don claimed that Woody was seeing other women, including an ex-girlfriend of singer Paul Simon's, whom he would squire to restaurants all over the city. "Everyone else knew," he told me. "How could Mia not have known?" It was fortunate that the tape was turned over as evidence, and Mia never had to listen to it. Although Don insisted that she *had* to know about Woody's infidelities, *I* knew she hadn't had an inkling.

One afternoon, just as Mia and I were to take the kids out to the park, the telephone rang. I could hear Mia chatting animatedly with the party at the other end, but the only part of the conversation I could really make out was right at the end, when she gave the caller Woody's address. Then she hung up, and as we left the house, she announced with a little laugh, "That was Frank." I couldn't help wondering what Ol' Blue Eyes would have wanted with Woody's address. For sure, he wasn't going to send him flowers.

All winter we waited in limbo for the date of the custody hearings to be set. At the end of February, I began what is known as witness preparation, or coaching. Nine months after the alleged molestation, I was already doubting my own memory of things. Luckily there were mountains of police reports, and I was comforted by the knowledge that I had told the same story several times after the fact. The truth is, as I said then and now, those 1992 summer days were always approximately the same. Every day I would spend some time looking for the children, and every day there were periods of five or ten minutes when I could not locate them. It usually had nothing to do with guarding them against Woody. I wanted to make sure that the children weren't playing unsupervised by the lake and didn't have their heads in the toilet bowl or their fingers in an electrical socket.

On the evening of St. Patrick's Day, March 17, Mia's case received a huge blow when the Connecticut police telephoned Mia to inform her of the Yale report's findings. Basically, they told her, the Yale team had concluded that Dylan had been making up the molestation story. On March 18 I wrote in my diary:

Is this true? Has the prestigious Yale–New Haven team been swayed by Woody's reputation and power as a filmmaker? I'm so utterly confused and upset for Mia. While she went to court this morning, I got up and took Eliza in the limo to New Jersey to see a court-appointed psychiatrist named Dr. Brodzinsky. Leaving the apartment building today was a nightmare. Channel 7 reporters, as well as about fifteen photographers, were outside waiting for us. So I picked Eliza up and carried her to the car, her hood pulled down on her head, her face buried in my neck. Throughout the ride, she sat on my lap, holding me close.

Despite the Yale report, the Connecticut police still believe Eliza. They say they don't understand Yale's decision. Could Dylan have possibly made this story up out of fear that her father would take her away, too? Mia called me on the car phone as we drove to the doctor's office and said, "All hope is lost." I didn't know what to say. I told her to pray and be strong.

After the Yale report was released, it was clear that, between the lines, every paper in New York was supporting Woody. "MAMA MIA WAS ROYAL MEANIE, SEZ EX-MAID," (*Daily News*), "FORMER NANNY TESTIFIES MIA SLAPPED SON," (*The New York Times*) "MIA: 'MY EX-HUBBY JOKED THAT HE'D BREAK WOODY'S LEGS," (*New York Post*) "WOODY'S SIS: MIA HASSLED OUR FOLKS" (*USA Today*). Moreover, we had to deal not only with the biased press, but with the annoying cameras that followed us down the street every day. Whenever I would spot the photographers waiting in front of Mia's building, my heart raced, my body vibrated with anxiety. This has been such a tragedy for all of us.

Sascha seemed especially overwhelmed by the new round of attention. One morning when we brought Eliza down to the car, he told me, his eyes brimming with tears, "I'm so sick of this whole thing. I wish it would just end."

As a result of the Yale–New Haven report and its strong claim that Woody was innocent, Mia and Woody were rushed into their custody hearing the very next day. For Mia, the timing was terrible. She had been scheduled to go to California the following week to film *Wolf*; now she had to bow out of the picture that she had struggled so hard to hold on to. On March 19 I wrote:

> Mia is devastated. She thinks *Wolf* was her last shot at an independent movie career. Things have been so difficult the last few days, and Mia seemed so frazzled. We all sat on the couch last night after the Yale meeting, and she just cried and cried. She said she has hit rock bottom now—no money, no work, and her reputation is ruined. She says Woody has taken everything, including one of her daughters, and now he's going after the last thing he can: her remaining children.
>
> I haven't been too well, either. All the stress is taking a toll on me, and I feel that I can't take care of myself properly anymore. I'm not eating much, and my stomach lining is so irritated that I would rather skip a meal than bear the pain in my belly when I do eat. I'm also not sleeping. When I manage to fall alseep, I have frightening dreams. John's mother and father sent a St. Patrick's Day card to me. They said that they hope I'm getting on with my life and that I find someone else to love. I go in and out of mini-depressions every day. None of the guys who are calling interest me. If only I could go back in time.

Although she had to concentrate her attention on the court battle ahead, Mia was disconsolate about *Wolf*. She felt that, with the lawyers' fees piling up, she needed work desperately. Not even the recent sale of her as-yet-unwritten autobiography for the whopping sum of three million dollars (most of the money is paid only after the manuscript is written, delivered, and accepted by the publisher) could offer comfort. She was and is so hard on herself all the time. Living in fear that her book would provide the last dollar she would ever earn was one more way to keep herself on the edge of hysteria.

Of course, her expenses, now that Woody was no longer paying the bills, were exorbitant. The monthly budget that follows provides an idea of what it's like to run a Manhattan household with eleven children:

Mia's Average Monthly Budget

Rent for Central Park West apartment ....2800.
Connecticut home (mortgage & taxes) ....600.
Monthly phone bills (approx.)..200.
Gas and electricity..100.
Therapy for Satchel, Moses, and Dylan
    (based on a twice-weekly schedule) ....3000.
Baby-sitting..1600.
Housekeeper ....1500.
Manhattan parking garage rental.....................................300.
Security maintenance ....1500.
Groceries ....1200.
City taxis...500.
Private elementary schools: For Satchel, Dylan, and Moses..........1000.
College tuition (1/2) + college expenses for Lark,
    Daisy, Matthew..3000
Monthly spending money for Moses, Lark, Daisy,
    Matthew, and Fletcher (Sascha is independent) ....1000.
Clothing and shoes for eleven children.............................1100.
Tutors (approximately three per week at $25 an hour)...................300.
Piano lessons (two a week at $25 an hour)................................200.
TOTAL ....$19,900.

Almost twenty thousand dollars! That's quite a monthly nut to
crack. No wonder that those secret worries about not finding
work as a movie actress were what also led Mia, during the
summer of 1992 and the last pathetic days of her relationship
with Woody, to lobby to keep her job as his number one leading
lady. Woody had written *Manhattan Murder Mystery* for her to
star in, and she was dashed when he let her know in no uncertain
terms that she was out of the picture and Diane Keaton was in.

I always thought that there was something disconnected about
her expectations. She had just accused her lover in public of
molesting their daughter, and she expected that he would overlook this while they made a movie together. Get real, Mia.

That disconnected way of thinking about the big picture also
showed up that August when Mia learned that Soon-Yi had been
fired from camp and Woody was continuing to see her. Mia

called Susan Coates and began their conversation by begging the doctor to "find a way to stop him." Moments later, she admitted that she and Woody had been talking about getting married, and she even went so far as to ask the psychiatrist, "Do you think I should marry him?" "I said, 'Are you serious?' " Dr. Coates testified in court, adding, "[Mia] heard my reaction to it and realized there was something absurd about it." She did, indeed. Nevertheless, like any woman who couldn't shake off her deepest fantasies, she was still tempted.

Of course, for full-blown disconnection, nothing in the couple's entire history beats Woody saying, "I am not Soon-Yi's father or stepfather. I've never even lived with Mia. . . . There's no down side to it. The only thing unusual is that she's Mia's daughter. But she's an *adopted* daughter and a grown woman. I could have met her at a party or something." When I read that interview in *Newsweek* to my parents, we were astounded.

As the trial took shape and form, with the world examining every sorry twist and turn of Mia and Woody's private lives, once again tension grew at home. On March 22, Mia tiptoed into my room at six-thirty A.M. She sat on the end of my bed, wearing her shorts and T-shirt, and as I rubbed the sleep out of my eyes, she asked me if she thought it all might be a sinister plan—that Woody and Soon-Yi planted the nude photos on Woody's mantel specifically for her to find. "Maybe," she wondered aloud, "they did it to make me go crazy?"

What a goofy idea! How, I wondered once again, could Mia even imagine that the court would award custody of the children to Woody, a man who had seduced her daughter? It just proved that she was still seeing the world through *his* eyes and not her own. Besides, wasn't this a common ploy of powerful men who were used to making rational, logical, and persuasive arguments? How easy it was to dismiss the intuitive intelligence of their women by saying, "You're hysterical" or "You're crazy." And women as bright as Mia believed them.

Yet so, it seems, did everyone else. Reminders of the public's affection for Woody were everywhere. I wrote in my journal on March 22:

Daisy, Dylan, and I went to lunch at Diane's Restaurant. An older couple came in an sat right behind us and decided to analyze the whole Woody-Mia imbroglio. One of them said, "I wish that woman would just drop her court case and leave him alone. She's a kook!" If only they knew who their table neighbors were! At first I was angry, my hands shook and my face was all red. Then Daisy said, "Calm down." I am glad someone in this family is mature.

During her phone conversation with her attorney tonight, Mia gasped with delight, giving me a thumbs-up sign. She told me that the police had concluded that the Yale team had been sloppy, stupid, and possibly venal, and that the police would be coming down to testify for Mia in court [which they were eventually prohibited from doing, since it was deemed a conflict of interest]. Fletcher and Andre called from Germany. Mia talked to Andre about testifying on her behalf. He seemed unwilling—maybe he doesn't want to be part of the tabloid circus—and she broke down during their conversation.

Even Tam was subject to Woody fallout. At the end of March she tearfully confided to me that her bus driver had been taunting her by calling her "Woody" or "Woody girl." So I asked Mia for permission to pay a visit to P.S. 6 to speak to the child's principal.

Mia always called me the German inspector because I would put on a thick German accent for the children and tell them, "The German inspector is coming to your room to do a white glove test, and if your room has one itty-bitty speck of dust, I vill cook you in my soup tonight." And they would give me a mock scream, then run upstairs to put away their toys. Anyway, in *her* mock-German accent, Mia said, "You go into school tomorrow, Kristi, and give them hell." Which I did. And shortly after my visit, Tam's bus was changed, and with it her bus driver.

Mia had to protect her children and deal with her own state of mind on a daily basis. Once, at dinner, I remarked that I could not imagine sitting on the witness stand and being grilled, day in and day out. Without hesitating, Mia conjured up the most dramatic image: "Kristi, you know what it's like?" she asked, tears welling in her eyes. "It's like a tornado swirling around me and ripping my skin and my limbs off."

When Mia once again began to talk of adopting, I figured that her emotional state was pretty delicate. Even though we shared a devout Catholic background, I couldn't understand this need. Was it a way of distracting herself during hard times or even dull times? Or was it a real drive to do good in the world, to help others, as she claimed? I decided to have faith, for a change, and believe the latter.

March 30.

This morning we sat on the edge of Mia's big tub eating our raisin bran while she was getting ready to go to court. She was describing her needs and what fulfills her. She admits that it is in part a selfish need she has to adopt all these children. But as she ate her cereal, she explained to me that everyone must find a way to give in God's eyes, and this was her way.

I wondered about the way my own life had been taken over by Mia's reality and Mia's family. While I loved them all, I was concerned for myself. Working for Mia had been a temporary thing, a stop-gap measure for me. I had simply gotten caught up in the terrible events that had washed over the Farrow household. Now, like them, I was exhausted all the time. I had not a moment for a personal or a social life. I wasn't being overpaid ($275 a week plus room and board). I suffered from bad dreams and a bad stomach. What, I asked myself, would give my life meaning? Did I want to return to school? To competitive running? I didn't know. Yet I felt that the first step was to reclaim my space and my time. I decided that when the trial ended, I would leave Mia's household. I had to find a way to break the news to her. And yet the moment I flirted with the notion of separation, I began to panic. I jotted these questions down in my journal at the end of March:

How am I ever going to leave Mia and the kids? How did
Monica feel when she left? Did she miss them, as I know
I will? It's almost as if I'll mourn them. Once again, mourn-
ing is a theme of my life—something I've become a pro at.

On March 31 Mia called me into her room right before she
left for court to testify. She looked demure in her black skirt
and jacket, and yet I saw the fear in her eyes. We knelt on the
floor at the foot of her bed, where she stored what she called
her "chest of memories"—literally, a wooden chest full of me-
mentos—and I suggested that she say the rosary over and over
again if things got rough in court. She opened up the chest and
took out her father's rosary, bleached wooden beads with a heavy
silver cross. Inside it there was also a thick braid of Larky's hair
from her first haircut, and the rosary beads that had belonged
to Mia's brother, Michael. Before putting her father's beads in
her bag, Mia closed her eyes and kissed them. It was such a
sad sight.

I knew that I, too, would soon be called to testify. When I
thought about it, my stomach, which had been irritated all winter, began to flutter. I didn't want to let Mia down. Yet I understood how serious the charges against Woody were, and I was
reluctant to say anything that would accidentally or inadvertently
incriminate him.

Meanwhile, I was deluged with offers from the tabloids and
TV news shows. On April 10, Patty Vine called me from *A Current Affair* and told me to name my price to come on her show.
She suggested somewhere between five and eight thousand dollars, but I decided that I couldn't go through with it. This wasn't
the first tempting offer that would have made a difference to
my pathetic financial situation. An English tabloid, *The Sunday
Mirror,* offered me $20,000 for an interview, and when I de-
clined, the editor said he would go higher. I had never had
so much money, but I couldn't do it. Another English tabloid
representative promised $500 for any single photograph I
brought out of the house. I despised that request; I would never
lower myself to such a standard. I later spotted this rep and
another guy—probably a coworker—stealing garbage from Mia's

Bridgewater house. After that, we kept the trash inside the house until the sanitation truck arrived; and Mia began using a paper shredder for her important documents. Maury Povich sent me flowers, and every talk show, with the exception of *Donahue* and *Oprah,* called to request me as a guest. Each time an offer was made, I told Mia about it, but she asked me to wait until the custody hearing was finished. And I chose to honor her request. I may not be rich, but I know I can (sometimes) sleep at night, and that's worth everything.

As the trial progressed, I had a sense that Mia was coming out of her depression. Maybe it was simply facing the monster that relieved her.

April 14.

Mia and I spent a few hours together early this morning organizing her room. We talked, and she said she has been dating two men [one was screenwriter Bill Goldman whom she saw last night—he wrote *Butch Cassidy and the Sundance Kid* and *The Princess Bride*]. She kind of threw her hands in the air, a gesture of surrender, and we laughed. She listened to classical music for the first time in about a year. We then took Isaiah out for a walk and a muffin. I had pain again in my chest today. Stress-related, I'm sure. Dylan—I can't bring myself to call her Eliza despite her insistence—said, "I love you" as we left school today. Then she wrapped her arms and legs around me on the corner as we got into the car.

On April 10 I took the stand. I had been such a bundle of nerves but the session went better than I had anticipated. Mia's attorney, Eleanor Alter, and Woody's lawyer, Elkan Abramowitz, both quizzed me endlessly about the events of August 4 and those twenty minutes that had never been accounted for.

After I left the courthouse, I returned to Central Park West and waited for Mia to get home. I was concerned about the time, since I planned to go to Connecticut to see my parents that afternoon. Finally, Mia arrived at the apartment. "What took you so long to get back?" I asked, and she replied, "Oh, Eleanor, a couple of the lawyers, and I went to the Central Park boathouse to have a few drinks. You should have come." Before I could answer that I might have if I had known about it, she looked at me and smiled, adding with a light touch that was rare these days, "I had a hard time making the transition from the courthouse to the boathouse, but I did." I couldn't help laughing.

A few days later, Mia received good news. The Connecticut police determined that the original tape of Dylan had not, as Woody had insisted, been doctored. Mia seemed to be in such great spirits that I mentioned leaving. However, I did it in such a roundabout way that I didn't think she took me seriously.

Meanwhile, the Soon-Yi drama continued, out of court and on the stand.

April 16.

Mia told me that in court Soon-Yi was reprimanded by the judge for possible perjury. Mia felt that Soon-Yi had been coached not only by Elkan, but by Woody, and so she misled the judge when she described, under oath, the family's home life. After Judge Wilk listened to the other children's (sealed) testimony, he took her aside—and took her to task.

This morning, as I was taking Satchel to school, I saw Soon-Yi's green Gap bag in the front seat of Woody's Mercedes. The zipper was open, and her little makeup case and some other belongings were visible. I thought of slipping a note into the bag, reading, "Daisy misses you." A few days ago Daisy acknowledged that she *does* miss Soon-Yi, but she hates the way that Soon-Yi has been saying such horrible things about the family to reporters.

On April 20 Mia burst into the girls' room to share some small victory that she had won in court that day. Her face was flushed and she appeared really delighted. But her joy fell on deaf ears. After Mia left, Daisy turned to me, exasperated, and said that she wasn't interested. "I can't stand it," she practically shouted. "I don't want to hear about this trial anymore. That is why I

spend so much time out of the house. It's why I hang out with
my friends so much. I am really fed up." She has had her fill
of the upheaval, the tears, the depression, the headlines, the
humiliation, the whole Woody-Mia affair. "My poor favorite little
sister," I said jokingly to her, using a sisterly term of affection
we occasionally shared in the hope that it would put her in a
better mood. "Your only little sister," she retorted with a half-
smile, playing on the fact that in *my* family I am the baby.

In the end, Mia took heart from what she considered Woody's
inept performance in court. He seemed arrogant and indifferent,
she said. He was unable to tell the judge the simplest things
about his children's lives—the names of their friends, their doctors, their teachers, their classes. He admitted that he never
bathed or dressed the children, took them for haircuts, and that
he didn't recall what grades Moses, his "son," got at school. On
their family trips to Europe, he said, "The purpose of my going
was to be with my three children. The other children did not
interest me. I did not speak with them. I played with my own
children and primarily worked on my film scripts."

When the judge asked Woody why he wanted custody of his
children, he rambled on about his "joyless, sexless relationship"
with Mia and about falling in love with Soon-Yi. He dismissed
Mia's household and raged on because she had told the kids
about his betrayal. "The children were used by Mia in the most
shameless, degrading way as pawns right from the start," he said,
adding, "I would have hoped and assumed that the little children
would be spared this." As if he had had nothing to do with the
events that unspooled.

After talking aimlessly for five minutes, Woody admitted, "I'm
not saying my selection of Soon-Yi was a brilliant selection, a
wise selection." Then he went on to answer the judge's question—after a fashion. He explained that, if granted custody, he
would provide his kids with a comfortable home, a fine education, all the comforts they wanted. "I would tell them to love
their mother," he said, adding that he had no problem with them
seeing Mia fifty percent of the time. As a crowning gesture, and
one so typically Woody, he claimed, dead serious, "Their day-

to-day behavior will be done in consultation with their therapist. The therapist can be chosen responsibly by the court." He then drifted out of his tirade, concluding lamely, "I just want a good life for them. And I feel that I can better provide that. . . . I want what's right for the children. That's all I can say."

Of course, Woody's words seemed especially hollow to me. Am I dreaming, or isn't his affair with his children's sister (and his lover's daughter) how this all began?

As the hearings drew to a close, I decided to square up with Mia. I felt she was less tense and less needy. She was also beginning to build a brand-new social life and would go out on dates a few nights a week. So I took Mia to lunch at Diane's and discussed quitting. As we sat down to omelettes and bacon, she came right to the point. "So what's the story?" she asked. "Are you leaving me?"

I nodded. "Yes," I answered, "I have to leave."

Then she said, "Well, if it's about money, Kristi—I can raise you back up to what you were making before."

When Woody was paying the bills, I had been earning ten dollars an hour, but after Mia took over paying my salary, she told me she had to cut it to seven dollars an hour. I had not been happy about this decision but had decided to live with it. Now I said, "Mia, at this point the money isn't even the issue. It's the stress. For a year and a half I have been under so much stress, and it has affected my health. I have to start living my own life."

A few weeks later we would have this conversation again. I would sit on the edge of her bed and, when she offered to give me a raise, I would tell her once more that it wasn't a matter of money. That I had to leave her household in order to rediscover my own life. Still, I said, "I want to help you, I love you."

She smiled and hugged me. "I love you too," she replied.

But in my heart I believed that she was missing the meaning of my words. She couldn't grasp them, I thought, because of the constant stream of men, specifically, and people, in general, who were always running after her and trying to do her bidding. It was the Star Trap. The Star Trap is part of the reason Mia left it to Woody's attorneys to prepare Dylan's and Moses's adoption papers, *never even bothering to read them* ("I just asked the lawyer, 'I'm not surrendering any of my rights or custody or anything, am I?'" she reported in court. "He said no, not at all"). The Star Trap had made her helpless and isolated, blurring the difference for her between her butt-lickers and her friends. After the past year we had spent together, supporting and soothing each other, laughing and crying together, how could she possibly misunderstand my commitment and affection?

Breaking the news to Mia about my intention to leave had been awkward, and I was grateful when she said she would support me with whatever I decided to do. On our way home from that initial lunch at Diane's, we took a moment to linger in front of a Seventy-second Street pet shop. Instantly, we fell in love with a little beagle puppy who was wagging its tail in the window. Impetuously, we went inside and bought the dog for Moses, who had been pretty low all spring. We hoped the pup would cheer him up, and as we walked along West Seventy-second Street, foolishly excited, we tried to think of puppy names. After trying out a few, Mia joked, "We'll just call it Custody."

Appropriate, perhaps. But the kids had their own ideas. Satchel wanted to call the beagle Pete, and Dylan sat in the closet and cried for the whole afternoon because she wanted to name him Sparky. For a while we referred to the pup as "Jim Pete Bob Joe." In the end Moses made the decision. He named his new best friend Joe. He said it would be his buddy "Joe."

Life, I thought hopefully, was definitely getting back to normal in the Farrow home.

"What the hell am I doing with the 'midlife-crisis set'? I mean, they're all wonderful, rather accomplished men, but in the end I felt that I was some sort of symbol of lost youth and unfulfilled dreams. Am I right?"

Rain (Juliette Lewis)
in Husbands and Wives

THIRTEEN

The Verdict

66 "Yippeeee!" Mia's whoop of joy broke the mid-morning silence.

It was Monday, June 7—truly a day of victory. Although I was no longer working at Mia's—my last day had been May 10—I had spent the previous night there. On Monday morning at eleven the phone rang, and suddenly I heard a burst of footsteps in the hall. That was followed by Mia shouting and calling out Fletcher's name in a voice at once frantic and elated. I immediately ran into the hall and headed for Fletcher's room behind her. Fletcher stood there smiling, saying over and over, "That's great, Mom." Mia, seeing me, hugged me and jumped up and down like a schoolgirl. Then she told us that she had been granted custody of Dylan; Woody was given visitation with Satchel only, and he had to pay all legal fees. Spinning around the room, she asked us both to come down to Eleanor Alter's office with her. Declining, Fletcher said he had to go off to Collegiate, his high school on West End and Seventy-eighth Street—only a few days were left before graduation, he apologized—but I agreed to accompany her. Somebody needed to anchor her to the planet.

Mia hurried into her room, quickly peeling off her shorts and jumping into jeans and boots, calling her mother as she did so. Then we ran downstairs and hailed a cab. During the taxi ride we didn't even speak, we just sat there, savoring the victory.

237

Eleanor wasn't in her office when we arrived at the swanky law offices of Rosenman and Colin, so we ran back into the street to buy children's books from a local vendor while we still had time. We loaded up—Mia picked up fifteen books for the kids, she clearly wanted to share her happiness.

Back upstairs, we sat down with Eleanor to read the judgment together. It was astounding, so supportive of Mia and so damning of Woody. Then we went down to the cafeteria in Eleanor's building and brought back poached salmon, avocado salads, and rice. But I couldn't eat. I was too excited.

After lunch, when we returned upstairs to Eleanor's office, Roseanna Scotto from Fox-5 News, and Carol Agis from *Newsday* were already there, waiting for a press conference—something Mia had not thought much about. I suggested that she might want to change her clothes for it, and when she agreed, I ran home to grab a shirt, a blazer, and some makeup for her. By two P.M. the conference room of Rosenman and Colin was packed while Mia made her victory statement.

That evening Mia, all dolled up in a black Betsy Johnson hook-front baby-doll dress, went out to celebrate with Bill Goldman. While Isaiah threw toys into the toilet and Dylan and Satchel watched television, Daisy, Moses, and I pored through Fletcher's senior yearbook. On one hand, it was just another evening at home; on the other, there was a sense of well-being, the sort of well-being that used to be common before this mess began. The following morning Mia and I sat around the kitchen table eating toast and cereal and reading newspapers that one of the neighbors in the building had gone out to buy for her. It was the first time in well over a year that Mia seemed able to relax.

Two weeks later, on June 22, we formally celebrated our triumph at a party thrown by Bill Goldman's brother, Jim, the author of the play *The Lion in Winter* and the movie *Robin and Marian,* and his wife Bobby. The evening was like one long, sweet scene from a sophisticated New York movie. In fact, like a scene from a Woody Allen movie. At about seven on this Tuesday evening, Mia, Fletcher, Daisy, and I arrived at the Goldmans' and we stepped off the elevator into the hallway that led into a wrap-around living room with a 180-degree view of the city. Decorated in earthy colors, it had beautiful moldings and criss-cross diagonal shapes painted onto the ceiling in shades of green and beige. A huge fireplace was off to the right. In the dining room a staff of waiters in black and white uniforms were serving the most tender filet mignon I ever tasted, as well as potato and string bean salads. There was even a high-backed tray holding an array of ten different kinds of foreign cigarettes, Gitanes, Gauloise, and brands I'd never heard of.

A group of us—Sophie Bergé, the French tutor, Eleanor Alter's associate, Marty Jubileer, and I—climbed a flight of stairs into a workroom, and then headed out to the terrace. And what a sight! From this fantastic set-back terrace, wrapping 360 degrees around the entire apartment, the setting sun glowed like an orange jack-o'-lantern in the purple sky. It seemed we were at the absolute pinnacle of the city. I've never been at a higher point. It was even higher than Woody's penthouse.

Mia just glowed with pleasure that night. She was underdressed, as usual, in a black thermal shirt with a little bow (the kind you see at The Gap), black Edwin jeans (which she buys by the dozen), and funky black platform sandals from 9 West. Around her neck was her simple gold chain with a tiny gold heart dangling from it (Dylan and Tam both have the same one). Despite the simplicity of her outfit, she looked so pretty. She walked among her guests, fumbling a cigarette in her hand, and toasting almost anyone who rose to drink to her. She had a great time. It was her celebration.

Mia had also made sure to invite to the party members of the press and other people who had gone out of their way for her during the past year. Roseanna Scotto was one. Carol Agis was another. And Paul Williams, the New York State Department of Social Services social worker who is now suing the city (He says the Farrow-Allen case was pulled out from under him after he complained that important case papers were missing and Woody was being let off the hook.). Even attorney Alan Dershowitz, who had briefly represented Mia, showed up for about an hour. Only Bill Goldman, Mia's boyfriend, was absent, and that was because he and Jim don't get along. This was decidedly odd.

As for Mia's kids, Lark, Daisy, Matthew, Priscilla, Moses, and I all chose a corner by the air-conditioner, where we told jokes to each other and laughed. It was a happy night for everyone. Fletcher and I left at around ten and went to an HMV store. He was flying to Greece the next day and wanted to do last-minute shopping. In a matter of moments he loaded up on Peter Gabriel and Erasure, among other groups.

Mia came into the house at about ten-thirty and called Bill Goldman. We stood over the stove and picked at leftover chicken. As we relived the high notes of the evening, Isaiah let out a cry, and I brought him in a bottle. I must be ready for motherhood, I figured. After all, I can change a diaper in the pitch dark and not wake a soul, as I demonstrated on the spot.

I spent the next day visiting with Mia's children. That evening I had my first date with my new beau, Dan, whom I had met at a family wedding. I was excited. At the same time, Mia had a blind date with a friend of a friend. Like two college girls, we went down to the lobby together to wait, and she mused about her date, who was an Irishman. "Oh, he's probably the kind of man I should be seeing, but I think I'm doomed to impossible Jewish men."

Mia's date showed up early, while mine, who was a half hour late, still hadn't arrived. As she skipped down the steps of the building toward his little red sports car, Mia turned to me and said jokingly, "Punctuality is everything. I'm going to have to have a talk with your guy." And she was gone into the summer night.

"You can't stay together out of fear because you know then what you become? My mother and father."

Sally (Judy Davis)
in Husbands and Wives

FOURTEEN

Truth and Consequences

It has been two years since Mia first discovered her daughter's nude pictures on her lover's mantel. And, almost despite herself, the healing process has begun.

Last October she had an operation to repair her tear ducts which had been blocked from two years of constant crying. But, of course, that's the easy, cosmetic stuff. The more difficult healing is the emotional kind. For Mia, it was a definite sign of recuperation, and of her faith in the future, that in January 1994 she received another new child from Vietnam.

Shay was her name. She was two and, like Tam, blind. Mia had been awaiting her arrival for almost a year. Yet, Mia had the baby at home for less than six hours when she realized—as she had with Sanjay the year before—that the child was severely retarded. Shay had an impaired sucking reflex, was unable to sit up in the crib, and her eyes were misshapen. Mia immediately brought her to the hospital for tests and began to fret about how difficult it would be to enfold a child like that into her family. Blindness was fine; mild retardation, fine; but with a brood as large, diverse, and needy as the Farrows, Mia quickly decided to give Shay up. (Another couple immediately adopted her.).

What a thing to happen again! I remember how difficult it was for Mia when she told Tam last November that she might have to be gone for a few weeks to bring home her new little sister. (This, in fact, was *not* the case; the child was brought to New York by the adoption agents.). Tam, sitting on Mia's bed with us, whined, "Why do you have to go to Vietnam? I don't want you to leave me."

Mia, in her patient and deliberate Bambi-style, soothed her daughter. "Tam, I had to go to Vietnam to get you," she said. "And I had to leave your brothers and sisters here when I did. So you must understand and make room for your new little sister, just like *they* did for you." What could Tam say? She laughed nervously and agreed to do just that.

She will have to make room again, it seems. When I spoke to Mia in late January, shortly after she had given the baby up, she was saddened but resolved to adopt soon again. "I have a hole inside of me," she told me. "I couldn't bear to give Shay up, but I couldn't keep her." To fill her emptiness, Mia has already applied for another African-American crack infant, a little girl who will be a companion and playmate for Isaiah. She has already chosen a name from her Filofax list: Bailey.

The older kids have begun to reclaim their lives too. Perhaps they've had an easier time of it since they were less involved in the daily drama. Still, they were deeply affected by the two years of mud slinging and misery that Mia went through. Fletcher was the first to bail out. He fled the whole mess, heading for a German prep school somewhere near Hamburg. He is, as always, happy.

Both Sascha and Carrie quit their jobs and moved out to Colorado last October. Mia was supportive. I think it pained her to see them fly so far away, but she realized that Sascha needed a change. All that public airing of her and Woody's dirtiest laundry just mortified him. I mean, even Beavis and Butthead joked about the situation, with one of them referring to his sexual organ as "my Woody Allen." Sascha is a highly emotional person, and such slimy aspects of this soap opera took a big toll on him.

Matthew and Priscilla managed to stay together, trying to will away their pain by focusing on each other, and on their emerging lives together. He is still at Georgetown, happily immersed in the demands of first-year law school; she is still at Yale.

Lark left thoughts of a nursing career behind her and switched to a major in psychology instead. As a result of the Soon-Yi affair? Why not? I guess she wants to figure out why we all do the crazy things we do. For a while she was pretty low because her long-time beau Jesse broke up with her, but she is as sunny and strong as ever.

Daisy claims to have sailed through the breakup and the trial, yet by June, 1993 she, too, had had enough of the tension at home. Last summer, when Mia went to Ireland to shoot the movie, *Widow's Peak,* Daisy was thrilled to have the apartment all to herself.

Because of her movie commitment, Mia was not around to help Daisy get ready for her freshman year at Wheaton College, which she was to begin in September. So I did my best for her. For a few days I stayed over at Mia's apartment. In the morning Daisy and I would select the clothes she was to take, pack her suitcases, and then we would take turns exercising on the tread-mill in Mia's bedroom. While I would run, she would do situps, and vice versa. Then, when it was time for Daisy to leave for school, her dad Andre drove her up to Norton, Massachusetts.

Too bad that by the end of the first semester this past December, she discovered that she doesn't much like Wheaton. It's too isolated, too small-town for her. Daisy yearns for New York—and for her boyfriend James, who just happens to be studying at Columbia University.

In September Mia herself returned from Ballyknockan, Ireland, where she had shot the movie, *Widow's Peak*, all summer, and she seemed relaxed and radiant. For one, she had had a romance with the set designer on location. She had also adored working for British director John Irvin, who had made *Dogs of War. Widow's Peak,* she explained, was an Irish comedy set in the 1920s, and in it Mia plays a mousy woman named Miss O'Hare whom, she has said, she admired for the "steel in her bones." Sort of like Mia herself.

The movie clearly lifted Mia's confidence. "I can't believe that I thought I wouldn't be able to get work without Woody," she recently said to me. "It wasn't just that *Widow's Peak* was something of my own, something that I did without Woody. It was also a good script. And I love Ireland, where my mother was born and where I have relatives. I made new friends. And John Irvin was a *very* good director. It was a wonderful experience for me." In addition, *Widow's Peak* had sentimental value of sorts. It was a script that playwright Hugh Leonard had, coincidentally, written for Mia's mother ten years ago; Mia was to have played a lesser role.

The younger kids, who traveled with her, also seemed renewed. Tam, especially, was brimming with stories about "Auntie Joan"—that is, her costar Joan Plowright—and Natasha Richardson, who, she said, "bought candy for us every day on the set. She's so nice. And Natasha's boyfriend [Liam Neeson] was there every day. Oh, he doesn't have a job, he just goes to work with her. And the boss [Irvin], he was sooo nice."

One weekend afternoon this past fall, I took the younger kids to a movie and then to a local McDonald's—the kind of kiddie afternoon you could have anywhere. Tam showed me a set of rosary beads made from clay, and I had this exchange with her, Dylan, and Satchel:

TAM: The W man gave this modeling clay to me. Well, he's a bad man. (She laughs.)
KRISTI: Don't say that about Satchel's daddy.
SATCHEL: He's not my father. He's not part of this family.
DYLAN: He doesn't deserve a family.

When the 1993 holiday season rolled around, Dylan begged me to tell her the story of the magic Christmas cake, a variation on our story, "The Magic Birthday Cake." Here we pour magic powder into our cake mix, bake and eat the cake, and then become invisible. In this state we play tricks on people. "So what are you going to do?" I asked her. For her first trick, Dylan replied, she would like to go to her ex-shrink Nancy Schultz's bedroom to sprinkle flour all over her head. "Then when Nancy Schultz wakes up in the morning, she'll think that somebody dyed her hair blond," she told me gleefully. "And she'll go to work, and everyone will make fun of her."

Next, said Dylan, giggling mischievously, "I want to go to Woody Allen's house. And I'm going to take banana peels and put them on all the stairs, so that when he comes down in the morning, he'll fall on his bum and slide down the stairs."

The kids keenly feel the impact of their parents' split. Their sister Soon-Yi is lost to them. Their mother is just pulling out of a two-year depression. And Woody has emerged the Big Bad Wolf. In school, when asked about her father, Dylan completely turns her back on Woody, insisting, "I don't have a daddy." When she asks Satchel about *his* visits with Woody, Satchel repeats over and over, like a little song, "He buys me toys, he buys me toys, he buys me toys."

Still, now that the trial is over and the press has stopped stalking us, the children are much calmer and happier than they were even last summer. Dylan, especially, is thriving like a little flower. "She has friends now," says Mia. "She is outgoing and exuberant. Even her teachers have commented that she is doing much better socially. She is simply a different kid now."

Mia is determined to restore their normal childhood. This past Halloween, as if to celebrate the end to sadness, she went all out, carving six pumpkins, lighting electric "witch" candles, and icing a cake that Lark had baked earlier in the day. She also made costumes for the kids—Tam and Dylan were done up as matching black cats in bodysuits, tights, little black ears and tails; and Satchel was their enemy, the mouse, wearing a gray velour mouse costume with a hood, pink ears, and baggy legs. Even the baby Isaiah, who is now two, wore a little bumblebee suit. Finally learning how to talk, he ran up to me and laughed, "Twick or tweet. Twick or tweet." After their party, Mia took them all trick-or-treating in her building.

On another afternoon, as I sat in the kitchen with Mia, she confided to me her worries about Tam. Tam, she felt, was extremely immature for a girl on the verge of thirteen. A little while later, when Tam came into the kitchen, Mia summoned her most thoughtful voice in order to explain to her daughter that she would have to start working harder at school. "I think you've adjusted well," Mia softly told her little blind girl, "but you're not seven or eight anymore. You're a young lady. You have to start reading, doing your homework, and practicing your math." Otherwise, she said, when they moved to Bridgewater, Tam might be left back.

Mia promised her daughter that the two of them would do the times tables together every day until Tam raised her math skills from their fourth-grade level. "I love you," Mia added, "which is why I'm telling you this. Mommies who don't love their children let them run around all day and don't care what they do. But I want you to go to college someday. You will need a job and a [Seeing Eye] dog. And you'll have to be able to get back and forth by yourself. Mommy will always be here for you, but you'll have to start taking care of yourself." Tam just sat there, and she didn't say a word the whole time. Then, without speaking, she got up and left.

Mia and I just looked at each other, bewildered. "What happened?" I asked. "I thought she was supposed to move into the girls' room this year." Tam had been sharing a room with the little kids, and, as it turned out, spending too much time with them. "Don't you think," I asked Mia, "that she is old enough to have a bedtime like Moses, not like Dylan and Satchel?"

I felt guilty. We had all hampered Tam's emotional growth during the past year. True, coming to America had been a big adjustment for her. But with the physical and emotional drain of the trial, Mia simply didn't have much energy left over. It was easier to take care of Tam's special needs by lumping her with the younger children.

Unfortunately, Tam rebelled against sleeping in the older girls' room, especially since all the others were out of the house, and she was alone in it. Mia hopes that when the family moves up to Bridgewater full-time, she will adapt more easily to a room of her own.

Mia has big plans for her move. She wants to fix up her two little cottages on the far side of the lake so that the older kids will have privacy when they come up with various girl- and boy-friends. She will also expand the design of the farmhouse, building a huge kitchen, computer room, and chicken coop out back for fresh eggs. She intends to buy a pony for the kids, whose menagerie now includes Tipperary, a mutt picked up last summer at an ASPCA in Ireland. Last fall, however, just as renova-

tions were about to begin, Mia discovered rats running wild
under the house, and she spent thousands of dollars tearing up
the floorboards and digging a new foundation.

Good thing, then, that she got another movie, *Miami*, costar-
ring Sarah Jessica Parker and Antonio Banderas, and shot in
Florida last December, to help pay for it. In it, Mia plays a
wealthy mother and wife who is having an affair. At her request,
I accompanied her and the children to Miami during the location shoot.

Here are some notes from my journal during that trip:

Dec. 10.

This morning, just after we got settled into our fancy hotel
rooms at the luxurious Mayfair House, Mia gave me a shopping list, and I went to the local grocery store by cab. I
think we were the only people staying there who brought
in our own groceries. When I returned, two porters carried
up ten bags of food. After all, Mia was on a *per diem* allowance and had so many mouths to feed. Satchel, Dylan,
Isaiah, the new nanny, Geraldine, nicknamed Delaney, and
I were all part of her contingent; and the going rate for
a room-service dinner for two, including wine, was $200
a pop.

In the afternoon we took the children to the mall for
lemonade. Later on, while Geraldine made dinner for the
kids, Mia and I feasted on chocolate Slim-Fast. Both of us
had been complaining about those nagging ten pounds, but
we consoled ourselves by drinking the thick, sweet liquid
together.

Dec. 11.

We went shopping this afternoon. Mia, searching for a new
look, bought three snug-fitting bodysuits from a boutique at
the mall. Then we headed over to Easy Rider, a leather
shop, where she modeled a leather jacket. Insisting that she
looked like Cher in it, Mia danced around the store and

sang, "I Got You, Babe." I had never seen such a playful side to her before. On our way back to the hotel, a pregnant woman chased us down the street for an autograph. As usual, Mia pleasantly obliged.

Dec. 12.

I listened tonight to Mia's soothing voice as she read *The Secret Garden* to the children. They lay there, dreamily listening. When she finished, Satchel begged for more. "It's so much nicer imagining I'm there in my mind," he told her. "It's so much better than TV." Mia hugged him, touched, and said, "You're such a little brilliant star." He is a really neat kid and as close to an intellectual as a six-year-old can get.

One evening after Mia returned from the set, she sat quietly on the couch and told me that she wanted Satchel to be in the next movie she is in, which calls for a six-year-old boy. She had just finished Shirley Temple Black's autobiography and we began to talk about show business and whether or not it was good for children. "Some people just can't handle it," Mia said. I asked her what she would do if she could go back and choose another career instead? "It's not that," she said. "That's done. It's Woody. I would have changed that part of my life. I never would have met him. But I feel that acting has given me a good life with the kids."

Yet so much of it, I observed, seemed so stressful. Mia agreed. "You never know if someone is using you or trying to get close to gain something," she said. When I mentioned that I wasn't nearly as impressed with celebrities now that I knew her, Mia laughed and said that she had been impressed the week before by her meeting with Al Pacino. Pacino wanted her to star in a movie to be directed by his girlfriend, Lyndall Hobbs, and Mia was considering the project. I don't know if Pacino himself planned to be in the movie, but I actually thought they would make a great screen team.

But the actor she really seemed keen on was Daniel Day-

Lewis, the Britisher who won an Oscar for *My Left Foot* and recently starred in *The Age of Innocence*. One afternoon in Miami, while we were lunching at Johnny Rocket, she told me: "A few days before we came down here, I had such a wonderful time hanging around with Daniel Day-Lewis. He is so terrific."

"You're kidding me," I responded. I, too, was impressed. Day-Lewis, whom she had met in Ireland, in fact invited Mia to the premiere of his movie, *In the Name of the Father,* but she declined for fear of the mob of reporters that they would have to contend with. Still, she said, they were great, great friends, whatever that means, and were thinking of doing a film together. "Kristi," she told me, "I think he is too young for me, but he is such a good catch. After all, he's handsome and is a wonderful actor." She went on and on, like a heartstruck teenager. And I listened, like a jealous one.

The following evening, when Mia came back to the hotel after filming, I told her that there was a present for her in the bathroom. She headed inside to find a little photograph of Day-Lewis, which I had cut out of a magazine and propped up on the vanity. "Oh, Daniel!" she gasped. "He's so handsome."

Unfortunately, there were far too few silly moments like this. On the whole, I found our Miami trip to be disappointing. I had originally allowed Mia to persuade me to go south on the assumption that I would be tutoring the kids three hours a day, and that I would have time to spend shopping with her, going out at night, and playing. But somehow it all began wrong. I found out when I landed that I would not be tutoring at all. Mia said that she would have to find a certified tutor from the set, or Woody's lawyers would raise hell. If that were the case, I wondered what I was doing there at all. I felt like a second-string baby-sitter. Similarly, the new nanny, Geraldine, was totally insulted that I had come down in the first place. "What am I, not capable of doing my job? *You* have to be here?" she confronted me angrily on my first night in Miami. I thought it was a triumph of sorts when, by the week's end, we had become friends.

During our free hours Mia and I did do our Christmas shopping, and I played with the children and read. But Mia was tense and upset for a good part of the time. She anguished over whether or not the adoptions of Dylan and Moses would be overturned, and as she waited for a verdict—to be handed down sometime in after May—she became increasingly disheartened.

It was odd. As Mia grew miserable, I in turn grew miserable. I promised myself: No more. I didn't want misery around me anymore. My life, I felt, was different now. I had found a wonderful job working with kindergarten children at a local grammar school. I had fallen in love with a wonderful man, Dan Guadagnoli, an aerospace engineer. And I was finally happy. So why was I depressed? And with an overwhelming sense of obligation? Why was I again beginning to feel responsible for Mia's feelings and for her children?

Although Mia wanted me to stay with her in Miami for another week, I found myself counting the days. The Friday before Christmas couldn't have arrived soon enough. When I landed at Newark in New Jersey, I was so surprised to see my boyfriend, Dan. He stood, straight and slim and dark-haired, at the bottom of the escalator among an assortment of overweight, balding chauffeurs, holding up a sign that said GROTEKE. And I was never so happy in my life. On New Year's Day Dan and I went to Mass. And I realized that I was no longer praying for John's soul or Mia's peace of mind. Now I was saying prayers for my sister Kelly's health and for my family. It gradually dawned on me in church that my life wasn't about movie stars, scandals, and flashbulbs anymore. It's about my mother and father, who carry me through the bad times, and about my sister, who has been battling Lyme disease for eighteen months now. And it's about my relationship with Daniel. I felt hopeful and peaceful. My life is simple, but it's awesomely happy.

Mia is not so lucky. As long as the adoptions of Dylan and Moses are still pending, she remains tense. It means that the Woody chapter in her life is still wide open.

In the fall Eleanor Alter sent a letter to Judge Renee Roth, who is presiding over the new court case in which Mia is trying to overturn Woody's adoptions. Here, Eleanor quoted Dylan's new psychiatrist, Dr. Hektor Byrd, who wrote that, in his opinion, it would *not* be advisable for Dylan to visit Woody right now. Byrd explained that Dylan had told him that she was afraid of Woody and afraid, too, to be taken away from Mia and forced to live with him.

Dr. Byrd, in his letter, further noted that on several occasions Dylan had told him: "Woody Allen touches my privates." She once again referred to "the incident of the ladder," in which he had allegedly touched her in the genital area while she was climbing to the top of a bunk bed. If Dylan were to visit with Woody right now, claimed Dr. Byrd, she could be set back to the emotional equivalent of the fetal position. That's a pretty strong statement, if you ask me.

Dr. Byrd asked for a two-month grace period in which Dylan might continue her therapy without beginning visitations with Woody. This request was granted. In March, 1994, another review and recommendation was made. Dr. Byrd once again recommended against Woody's visitations. When Woody did not greet this news lightly, an independent, court-appointed psychiatrist took the case on. It is still pending.

It's odd, and sad. Just a few years ago Mia went out of her way to help repeal a federal law prohibiting unmarried couples from adopting children together. Now she is trying to undo the very adoptions that took so much effort. Judge Roth, she worries, is unsympathetic to her, so Mia is not optimistic about the outcome. Nor is she pleased about it. "Woody was Dylan's father for only two weeks before I found the pictures," she told me. "I was tricked, and Moses was tricked. If he had known what was going on, he would never have wanted Woody Allen to be his father. In New York if you can prove fraud, you can overturn an adoption. If this isn't fraud, what is?"

Woody, for his part, made another attempt at closing the adoption case, offering a huge settlement if Mia withdrew her suit and agreed *not* to undo his adoptions. "No way," she told Eleanor. Neither her money problems nor the perks that Woody could provide the kids mattered. "My children are not for sale."

On September 24, 1993, the state of Connecticut dismissed child-abuse charges against Woody. However, Litchfield County prosecutor Frank Maco, speaking for the state's Criminal Justice

Commission, remarked that while he had actually drawn up an arrest warrant and found "probable cause" to believe Dylan, he had chosen not to prosecute to spare her the grief of a trial. Claiming that Mia had agreed with this decision to drop the charges, he replied, when asked if he had enough evidence for a guilty verdict from a jury, "Arguably, I do."

Maco's statement to the press enraged Woody. He called it "McCarthyism," immediately filing a complaint against Maco and calling a press conference. Here he delivered an impassioned tirade against Maco and Mia. His children, he said, had "been made to suffer unbearably by the unwholesome alliance between a vindictive mother and a cowardly, dishonest, irresponsible state's attorney and its police. Even today as they squirm, lie, sweat, and tap-dance, pathetically trying to save face and justify their moral squalor by declaring that the investigation is being terminated because he and the mother suddenly do not want to put my daughter through any more, their cheap scheming reeks of sleaze and deception."

As he concluded his diatribe, Woody addressed a few sentimental words to "my little girl," promising Dylan that "I will never abandon you to the Frank Macos of the world." Then he beseeched Mia to make peace with him, insisting that, "if the Arabs and Israel can do it, we can."

Two weeks later, in a letter dated October 7, the New York State Department of Social Services sent Woody a letter informing him that it, too, had closed its fourteen-month-old investigation. "No credible evidence was found that the child named in this report has been abused or maltreated," the letter advised. "This report has, therefore, been considered unfounded."

The Department of Social Services letter did not offer any support for its conclusions, however. In fact, Deborah B. Adler, speaking for the department, said, according to *The New York Times*, that "she could not confirm even that there had been an investigation, let alone any details of it."

Woody's complaint against Connecticut prosecutor Frank Maco was dropped in November after a four-hour criminal justice panel review. The Connecticut Criminal Justice Committee unanimously found that there was no evidence that Maco had violated any ethical rule for attorneys. While one panel member, Superior Court Judge William Mottolese, characterized Maco's remarks as "insensitive and inappropriate," another, Ralph Elliott, remarked, "One can see a state's attorney who was attempting to let the public know and understand the bases on which he chose to exercise" his choice not to prosecute.

Yet Woody is someone to tangle with at your own risk. He filed a second complaint against Maco with the Connecticut state bar counsel, which has the power to disbar lawyers, and it is still pending. He is also appealing Judge Wilk's verdict in their child custody battle.

During the winter of 1993, between lawsuits, appeals, and complaints, Woody finished his new movie, titled, for the time being, *Bullets over Broadway*. It features familiar Allen actors like Dianne Wiest and Jack Warden, and some new ones like John Cusack, Mary Louise Parker, and Tracey Ullmann.

And, yes, he was still seeing Soon-Yi. These days Soon-Yi studies at Drew during the week. On weekends she and Woody have been seen together on the Upper East Side, dining out or driving around in his fancy black Mercedes with its soft gray leather interiors, fancy stereo system, and his-and-hers cellular phones. This Christmas they went to Venice, and in December, 1992, they toured New Orleans. It must be impossible for them to stay in New York during the holidays, knowing that across the park their former family would be gathering together.

Although Mia insists that there will always be a place in her heart for her daughter, that she would welcome Soon-Yi back into the fold if the girl left Woody, I believe that that would be a real test of her principles. For Mia's bitterness toward her daughter has not evaporated. "She doesn't love Woody. She's not capable of loving," Mia has told me, her words reflecting her sense of deep betrayal. She needs to believe that Soon-Yi is with Woody merely because he is rich and powerful. And the truth is that even in court Soon-Yi has said about their relationship, with an eerie toughness beyond her years and experience: "Don't romanticize it."

As you might imagine, after two years of painful betrayals,

hideous revelations, and expensive lawsuits, Mia doesn't have kind words for her ex-lover and creative partner. "He treated everyone like crap," she says. "Everyone else was insignificant to him. That is why he had no regard for Soon-Yi and no regard for me, and that is why he couldn't have cared less if his cleaning lady had seen the nude photos. All he cared about was himself."

Once again I discussed with Mia a question that had so often been on my mind. Why had she fallen for this neurotic man who lived separately and, for years, basically ignored her children? Why Woody Allen? "Because I thought he was so morally superior, and just superior in general," she said in earnest. "He was brilliant, although he was mean to me a lot. But he wasn't *always* mean. There were times when he was sweet and kind. But he was *not* a good father. And he was *not* a good mate. And he thought that marriage was just a piece of paper, that there was no reason to get married." I couldn't help thinking that women so often look to men as Mia did to Woody: worshipfully, as wise father figures, all-knowing centers of power. And I wondered, Do we inherit this deference from our own family dynamics, or from centuries of depending on men for shelter? To me, such blind worship seems totally prehistoric and old-fashioned. In my parents' household, my mom and dad are equal partners. As extraordinary as Mia is, she seemed to have had a need to be *less* intelligent, *less* moral, *less* powerful than Woody. And Woody had a need to make her feel that way. In the end these two extraordinary people were not immune to the same power plays that are common to so many ordinary couples.

It was difficult, too, for me to understand how Mia could consider the Woody who taunted her, did not sleep with her, and would not marry her to be "morally superior." I was puzzled, but when I continued to prod her, Mia threw up her hands and said sharply, as if someone had jabbed her with a knife, "That's my problem."

At other times, though, she seems more puzzled than I, certainly more puzzled than angry. It is then that she simply shakes her head and murmurs in disbelief, "He just didn't get it."

Yet on one recent occasion Mia wasn't so charitable. Looking at me, steely-eyed, and sounding more like the young wife in

Rosemary's Baby than like Mia, she observed: "Kristi, do you believe in the devil, or degrees of the devil? Because to some degree, that's what he is. He's evil. He wanted to destroy me and my family."

I would like to say that Mia and her children have come through their grief. Yet that remains to be seen. "I wish it were over, but it is far from over," Mia told me one winter afternoon as we sat in her kitchen drinking coffee from mugs imprinted with the words from *Footprints.* "Now we have to deal with visiting rights and legal fees that amount to more than 1.6 million dollars." She points out that although Woody had been ordered to pay court costs, he doesn't have to turn over a penny until such time as he can't appeal anymore. This could take years. No wonder Mia reluctantly accepted $500,000 from Britain's *Hello!* magazine for an interview and at-home layout.

Resigned to live in limbo for now, Mia sighed. "I wish it were over, but it is far from over." She shrugged. "Until it is, and until my children are out of danger, the truth is that I don't have any peace."

And she took one last sip of coffee before slipping on her schoolgirl blazer and rushing off. First stop, the pediatrician with Isaiah. Then a parents' conference at Dylan's school. A voice-over audition. And finally, back home. Here, later on, she would gather up the kids and herd them into Big Red for the drive up to Frog Hollow and the green countryside she loved so dearly.

Here, she hoped, she would eventually recapture the rhythms and pleasures of her life

Appendix

On September 24, 1993, Litchfield, Connecticut, County Prosecutor Frank Maco halfheartedly dismissed child-abuse charges against Woody while remarking that he had "probable cause" to believe Dylan. In reply, a furious Woody called a press conference and gave the following speech:

While one might think that I would be happy or grateful with the decision to drop the investigation by the Connecticut authorities, I am merely disgusted that my children have been made to suffer unbearably by the unwholesome alliance between a vindictive mother and a cowardly, dishonest, irresponsible state's attorney and its police. Even today as they squirm, lie, sweat, and tap-dance, pathetically trying to save face and justify their moral squalor by declaring that the investigation is being terminated because he and the mother suddenly do not want to put my daughter through any more, their cheap scheming reeks of sleaze and deception. Indeed, we were not even informed that there would be a decision today, but had to learn of it in the newspapers, although Miss Farrow was informed, consulted with them this week, and given information to leak in advance to the press.

The reason the authorities are dropping this case is purely

and simply because they know there is no chance they could possibly win it. If they felt they had even a prayer, the state's attorney would, with full maternal consent, proceed nonstop, even if it meant putting my little girl through a meat grinder. Suddenly, after fourteen months of brutalizing an innocent seven-year-old, using and manipulating her, subjecting her to endless indignities in a wheezing, salivating, desperate but unsuccessful attempt to fabricate a case, they now must wriggle like live bait to extricate themselves with some shred of credibility from the humiliating corner they are painted into. Yet they still tried to hide behind my child in trumping up their repulsive and transparent alibis. There was, of course, no case *ever*, not from the first day that my daughter's mother brought her to the doctor and was told he saw no evidence of molestation through the nauseating episode of the now-totally-discredited videotape that poor seven-year-old was forced to make over several painful days, and which somehow magically managed to find its way to various TV shows.

They knew it from an incriminating note written by the mother in advance of the allegations, from a phone call she made to a third party on the eve of the allegations, saying about me, "He must be stopped. I have to find a way." They knew it from the testimony of the children's therapists, from the testimony of my own therapist of twenty years, from the results of a lie-detector test I took which the mother refused to take, and, of course, they knew it conclusively over six months ago when the prestigious Yale team, a team that they themselves hired and who have done 1600 child-abuse investigations—a conservative group who overwhelmingly most often validate the charges, but who in this case, after an unusually exhaustive investigation in which they spoke to all parties, including my daughter, a number of times, wrote unequivocally in their findings that the molestation had never taken place and viewed the mother with suspicion.

Yet armed with this report, the authorities still kept the case open in a deliberate attempt to influence the ongoing custody trial I was involved in, realizing that dropping the case *before* a verdict would be helpful to me, and keeping it open, helpful to Miss Farrow. They were right; it cast a dark cloud over me, and the results of that trial have been catastrophic for the children. Not that they did not attempt to meddle in the trial, they *did* secretly turn over restricted evidence to Miss Farrow's lawyer, but this was discovered through a slip of her attorney's tongue during the trial, and it was appropriately dealt with. They also attempted to come to New York and be witnesses for Miss Farrow. Of course, their job was to be neutral truth-seekers. When we heard this, we subpoenaed them and all their alleged evidence, and they grew frightened, and this time the state's attorney was embarrassed and called them off.

There was no evidence against me. There is none now. I promise you, smear as they may, they will always claim to have evidence; but notice that somehow they will manage to find reasons why they can't quite show it to you. But why would they act so irrationally? Many times I have tried to understand the reason for Connecticut's illogical, *self-destructive* obsession with making a case against me. I say "self-destructive" because Connecticut is a state in shockingly poor fiscal condition, and here is a presumedly responsible official squandering large amounts of money on the frantic hope of a prosecution, when all reason and everything discovered or reported to him clearly demonstrated the folly of this quest.

You would have thought it was a scene from a movie of mine if you could have seen me cooperating with the Connecticut police. Numerous detectives from the major crime division hovered over me while hairs were pulled from my head, placed in glassine envelopes, and then fingerprints taken. Our sessions were sometimes punctuated by incoming murder reports. *Haven't these guys got anything better to do than devote all this time and manpower to me,* I thought as they flushed their taxpayers' money down the toilet month after month while actual crimes were still ongoing.

Once, early on, I worked to meet with the state's attorney, and he seemed quite interested, but then I asked that a Connecticut stenographer be present so we each have an honest record of what we both said, and he instantly backed out. And all the while they had no case to make. After all, did they not think it suspicious that a man of 57 with *no* history of sex crime would decide one day at the height of an acrimonious child settlement dispute—and while a guest visiting his children in the enemy camp in broad daylight and with adults around—pick that moment to suddenly embark on a career as a child molester? And when they received the testimony of the child's therapist of over a year who was abruptly fired when she told the mother she did not believe the abuse story, did they not suspect anything? And when they were privy to my lifetime psychological records—and when America's chief lie-detector expert flew in from the nation's capital, where he taught the FBI the skill of lie detection, and in testing me found me to be telling the truth while the child's mother *still* refused to take the test—did they not have any inkling that the child-molestation allegations were being used as a ploy?

And did not all of Miss Farrow's close friends and employees who testified contradict themselves in ways so preposterous that they provoked laughter in the courtroom? And even then, what they had to say was so pathetically innocuous. And when the authorities viewed the tape of my daughter, didn't they think something was amiss when she said she was frightened and ran into her sister Lark's arms— but indeed everyone, the mother, the police, knew that Lark wasn't in the state of Connecticut that day? Of course, they all knew I hadn't done anything to my daughter.

And yet knowing all this, the authorities chose to keep the investigation going anyway. Why? Many theories have been suggested, one that me being a celebrity, there was personal mileage to be gained, another theory was that they were against me because they disagreed with my publicized romantic relationship. But if so, should they allow their own personal lifestyle choices to supersede the duty to uphold the law? If that relationship is unconventional, it certainly is not illegal. Is it possible they were prejudiced against me because I am a diehard New Yorker and all that that implies, and Miss Farrow a Connecticut local? Did State's Attorney Maco choose to overlook the truth and become a stooge for Miss Farrow because he didn't like my films, my politics? What? Maybe it was a little of everything. Another real tragedy here is that because of the way the police handled the situation, it has become clear to other unstable and unscrupulous spouses that the scheme of choice in custody disputes is to fabricate child molestation. It works like a charm. I never did anything, nor was I ever charged with anything. And yet I've not been allowed to see or speak to my daughter now for fourteen months. And so because this is being taped, I want to send this message to my little girl:

I'm sorry that I missed your eighth birthday, but they just wouldn't let me do it. I love you and I miss you, and don't worry, the dark forces will not prevail. Not second-rate police or publicity-hungry prosecutors, not judicial setbacks, not tabloid press nor those who perjure themselves nor all who rush to judgment, not the pious or hypocritic or the bigoted. I'm too tough for all of them put together, and I will never abandon you to the Frank Macos of the world.

Finally, to Mia. Having just said all I said, I now reverse myself and beg for peace. If the Arabs and Israel can do it, we can. I publicly apologize for hurting you. I know you can be forgiving and quite terrific at times. You're a first-rate actress and a beautiful woman. As I said in front of the Yale–New Haven experts, Judge Wilk, Judge Roth, and now, for the sake of the little children, let's end all hostilities instantly and settle our situation. Not next month or next week, but today. I promise to do my best to be accommodating, and would hope you would also be generous. Please, let's now put this behind us. The only prerequisite I have is that you stop sending me bills from Alan Dershowitz.

Thank you.

SUPREME COURT: NEW YORK COUNTY   SU24A
INDIVIDUAL ASSIGNMENT PART 6

————————————————————————x
WOODY ALLEN,

Petitioner,   Index No.
-against-   68738/92
MARIA VILLIERS FARROW, also known as
MIA FARROW,

Respondent.

————————————————————————x
ELLIOTT WILK, J.°:

INTRODUCTION

On August 13, 1992, seven days after he learned that his seven-year-old daughter Dylan had accused him of sexual abuse, Woody Allen began this action against Mia Farrow to obtain custody of Dylan, their five-year-old son Satchel, and their fifteen-year-old son Moses.

As mandated by law, Dr. V. Kavirajan, the Connecticut pediatrician to whom Dylan repeated her accusation, reported the charge to the Connecticut State Police. In furtherance of their investigation to determine if a criminal prosecution should be pursued against Mr. Allen, the Connecticut State Police referred Dylan to the Child Sexual Abuse Clinic of Yale–New Haven Hospital. According to Yale–New Haven, the two major questions posed to them were: "Is Dylan telling the truth, and did we think that she was sexually abused?" On March 17, 1993, Yale–New Haven issued a report which concluded that Mr.Allen had not sexually abused Dylan.

This trial began on March 19, 1993. Among the witnesses called by petitioner were Mr. Allen; Ms. Farrow; Dr. Susan Coates, a clinical psychologist who treated Satchel; Dr. Nancy Schultz, a clinical psychologist who treated Dylan; and Dr. David Brodzinsky, a clinical psychologist who spoke with Dylan and

°I acknowledge the assistance of Analisa Torres in the preparation of this opinion.

Moses pursuant to his assignment in a related Surrogate's Court proceeding. Dr. John Leventhal, a pediatrician who was part of the three-member Yale–New Haven team, testified by deposition. Ms. Farrow called Dr. Stephen Herman, a clinical psychiatrist, who commented on the Yale-New Haven report.

What follows are my findings of fact. Where statements or observations are attributed to witnesses, they are adapted by me as findings of fact.

FINDINGS OF FACT

Mr. Allen is a fifty-seven-year-old filmmaker. He has been divorced twice. Both marriages were childless.

Ms. Farrow is forty-eight years old. She is an actress who has performed in many of Mr. Allen's movies. Her first marriage, at age twenty-one, ended in divorce two years later. Shortly thereafter, she married Andre Previn, with whom she had six children, three biological and three adopted.

Matthew and Sascha Previn, twenty-three years old, were born on February 26, 1970. The birth year of Soon-Yi Previn is believed to be 1970 or 1972. She was born in Korea and was adopted in 1977. Lark Previn, twenty years old, was born on February 15, 1973. Fletcher Previn, nineteen years old, was born on March 14, 1974. Daisy Previn, eighteen years old, was born on October 6, 1974.

After eight years of marriage, Ms. Farrow and Mr. Previn were divorced. Ms. Farrow retained custody of the children.

Mr. Allen and Mrs. Farrow met in 1980, a few months after Ms. Farrow had adopted Moses Farrow, who was born on January 27, 1978. Mr. Allen preferred that Ms. Farrow's children not be a part of their lives together. Until 1985, Mr. Allen had "virtually a single person's relationship" with Ms. Farrow and viewed her children as an encumbrance. He had no involvement with them and no interest in them. Throughout their relationship, Mr Allen has maintained his residence on the east side of Manhattan and Ms. Farrow has lived with her children on the west side of Manhattan.

In 1984, Ms. Farrow expressed a desire to have a child with

Mr. Allen. He resisted, fearing that a young child would reduce the time that they had available for each other. Only after Ms. Farrow promised that the child would live with her and that Mr. Allen need not be involved with the child's care or upbringing, did he agree.

After six months of unsuccessful attempts to become pregnant, and with Mr. Allen's lukewarm support, Ms. Farrow decided to adopt a child. Mr. Allen chose not to participate in the adoption and Ms. Farrow was the sole adoptive parent. On July 11, 1985, the newborn Dylan joined the Farrow household.

Mr. Allen's attitude toward Dylan changed a few months after the adoption. He began to spend some mornings and evenings at Ms. Farrow's apartment in order to be with Dylan. He visited at Ms. Farrow's country home in Connecticut and accompanied the Farrow-Previn family on extended vacations to Europe in 1987, 1988, and 1989. He remained aloof from Ms. Farrow's other children except for Moses, to whom he was cordial.

In 1986, Ms. Farrow suggested the adoption of another child. Mr. Allen, buoyed by his developing affection for Dylan, was enthusiastic. Before another adoption could be arranged, Ms. Farrow became pregnant with Satchel.

During Ms. Farrow's pregnancy, Mr. Allen did not touch her stomach, listen to the fetus, or try to feel it kick. Because Mr. Allen had shown no interest in her pregnancy and because Ms. Farrow believed him to be squeamish about the delivery process, her friend Casey Pascal acted as her Lamaze coach.

A few months into the pregnancy, Ms. Farrow began to withdraw from Mr. Allen. After Satchel's birth, which occurred on December 19, 1987, she grew more distant from Mr. Allen. Ms. Farrow's attention to Satchel also reduced the time she had available for Dylan. Mr. Allen began to spend more time with Dylan and to intensify his relationship with her.

By then, Ms. Farrow had become concerned with Mr. Allen's behavior toward Dylan. During a trip to Paris, when Dylan was between two and three years old, Ms. Farrow told Mr. Allen that "[y]ou look at her [Dylan] in a sexual way. You fondled her. It's not natural. You're all over her. You don't give her any breathing room. You look at her when she's naked." Her apprehension was fueled by the intensity of the attention Mr. Allen lavished on Dylan, and by his spending playtime in bed with her, by his reading to her in his bed while dressed in his undershorts, and by his permitting her to suck on his thumb.

Ms. Farrow testified that Mr. Allen was overly attentive and demanding of Dylan's time and attention. He was aggressively affectionate, providing her with little space of her own and with no respect for the integrity of her body. Ms. Farrow, Casey Pascal, Sophie Raven (Dylan's first French tutor), and Dr. Coates testified that Mr. Allen focused on Dylan to the exclusion of her siblings, even when Satchel and Moses were present.

In June 1990, the parties became concerned with Satchel's behavior and took him to see Dr. Coates, with whom he then began treatment. At Dr. Coates's request, both parents participated in Satchel's treatment.

In the fall of 1990, the parties asked Dr. Coates to evaluate Dylan to determine if she needed therapy. During the course of the evaluation, Ms. Farrow expressed her concern to Dr. Coates that Mr. Allen's behavior with Dylan was not appropriate. Dr. Coates observed:

> I understood why she was worried, because it [Mr. Allen's relationship with Dylan] was intense, . . . I did not see it as sexual, but I saw it as inappropriately intense because it excluded everybody else, and it placed a demand on a child for a kind of acknowledgment that I felt should not be placed on a child. . . .

She testified that she worked with Mr. Allen to help him to understand that his behavior with Dylan was inappropriate and that it had to be modified. Dr. Coates also recommended that Dylan enter therapy with Dr. Schultz, with whom Dylan began treatment in April 1991.

In 1991, Ms. Farrow expressed a desire to adopt another child. Mr. Allen, who had begun to believe that Ms. Farrow was growing more remote from him and that she might discontinue his access to Dylan, said that he would not take "a lousy attitude towards it" if, in return, Ms. Farrow would sponsor his adoption of Dylan and Moses. She said that she agreed after Mr. Allen assured her that "he would not take Dylan for sleepovers ... unless I was there. And that if, God forbid, anything should happen to our relationship, that he would never seek custody." The adoptions were concluded in December 1991.

Until 1990, although he had had little contact with any of the Previn children, Mr. Allen had the least to do with Soon-Yi. "She was someone who didn't like me. I had no interest in her, none whatsoever. She was a quiet person who did her work. I never spoke to her." In 1990, Mr. Allen, who had four season tickets to the New York Knicks basketball games, was asked by Soon-Yi if she could go to a game. Mr. Allen agreed.

During the following weeks, when Mr. Allen visited Ms. Farrow's home, he would say hello to Soon-Yi, "which is something I never did in the years prior, but no conversations with her or anything."

Soon-Yi attended more basketball games with Mr. Allen. He testified that "gradually, after the basketball association, we became more friendly. She opened up to me more." By 1991 they were discussing her interests in modeling, art, and psychology. She spoke of her hopes and other aspects of her life.

In September 1991, Soon-Yi entered Drew College in New Jersey. She was naive, socially inexperienced, and vulnerable. Mr. Allen testified that she was lonely and unhappy at school, and that she began to speak daily with him by telephone. She spent most weekends at home with Ms. Farrow. There is no evidence that Soon-Yi told Ms. Farrow either that she was lonely or that she had been in daily communication with Mr. Allen.

On January 13, 1992, while in Mr. Allen's apartment, Ms. Farrow discovered six nude photographs of Soon-Yi which had been left on a mantelpiece. She is posed reclining on a couch with her legs spread apart. Ms. Farrow telephoned Mr. Allen to confront him with her discovery of the photographs.

Ms. Farrow returned home, showed the photographs to Soon-Yi, and said, "What have you done?" She left the room before Soon-Yi answered. During the following weekend, Ms. Farrow hugged Soon-Yi and said that she loved her and did not blame her. Shortly thereafter, Ms. Farrow asked Soon-Yi how long she had been seeing Mr. Allen. When Soon-Yi referred to her sexual relationship with Mr. Allen, Ms. Farrow hit her on the side of the face and on the shoulders.[1] Mrs. Farrow also told her older children what she had learned.

After receiving Ms. Farrow's telephone call, Mr. Allen went to her apartment where, he said, he found her to be "ragingly angry." She begged him to leave. She testified that:

> [W]hen he finally left, he came back less than an hour later, and I was sitting at the table. By then, all of the children were there . . . and it was a rather silent meal. The little ones were chatting and he walked right in and he sat right down at the table as if nothing had happened and starts chatting with . . . the two little ones, said hi to everybody. And one by one the children [Lark, Daisy, Fletcher, Moses, and Sascha] took their plates and left. And I'd, I didn't know what to do. And then I went out.

Within the month, both parties retained counsel and attempted to negotiate a settlement of their differences. In an effort to pacify Ms. Farrow, Mr. Allen told her that he was no longer seeing Soon-Yi. This was untrue. A temporary arrangement enabled Mr. Allen to visit regularly with Dylan and Satchel but they were not permitted to visit at his residence. In addition, Ms. Farrow asked for his assurance that he would not seek custody of Moses, Dylan, or Satchel.

On February 3, 1992, both parties signed documents in which it was agreed that Mr. Allen would waive custodial rights to Moses, Dylan, and Satchel if Ms. Farrow predeceased him. On the same day, Mr. Allen signed a second document, which he did not reveal to Ms. Farrow, in which he disavowed the waiver, claiming that it was a product of duress and coercion and stating that "I have no intention of abiding by it and have been advised

1Ms. Farrow has commenced an action in the Surrogate's Court to vacate Mr. Allen's adoption of Dylan and Moses. In that proceeding, she contends that Mr. Allen began a secret affair with Soon-Yi prior to the date of the adoption. This issue has been reserved for consideration by the Surrogate and has not been addressed by me.

that it will not hold up legally and that at worst I can revoke it unilaterally at will."

In February 1992, Ms. Farrow gave Mr. Allen a family picture valentine with skewers through the hearts of the children and a knife through the heart of Ms. Farrow. She also defaced and destroyed several photographs of Mr. Allen and of Soon-Yi.

In July 1992, Ms. Farrow had a birthday party for Dylan at her Connecticut home. Mr. Allen came and monopolized Dylan's time and attention. After Mr. Allen retired to the guest room for the night, Ms. Farrow affixed to his bathroom door a note which called Mr. Allen a child molester. The reference was to his affair with Soon-Yi.

In the summer of 1992, Soon-Yi was employed as a camp counselor. During the third week of July, she telephoned Ms. Farrow to tell her that she had quit her job. She refused to tell Ms. Farrow where she was staying. A few days later, Ms. Farrow received a letter from the camp advising her that:

> [i]t is with sadness and regret that we had to ask Soon-Yi to leave camp midway through the first camp session. . . . Throughout the entire orientation period and continuing during camp, Soon-Yi was constantly involved with telephone calls. Phone calls from a gentleman whose name is Mr. Simon seemed to be her primary focus and this definitely detracted from her concentration on being a counselor.

Mr. Simon was Woody Allen.

On August 4, 1992, Mr. Allen traveled to Ms. Farrow's Connecticut vacation home to spend time with his children. Earlier in the day, Casey Pascal had come for a visit with her three young children and their baby-sitter, Alison Stickland. Ms. Farrow and Ms. Pascal were shopping when Mr. Allen arrived. Those present were Ms. Pascal's three children; Ms. Stickland; Kristi Groteke, a baby-sitter employed by Ms. Farrow; Sophie Bergé, a French tutor for the children; Dylan; and Satchel.

Ms. Farrow had previously instructed Ms. Groteke that Mr. Allen was not to be left alone with Dylan. For a period of fifteen

or twenty minutes during the afternoon, Ms. Groteke was unable
to locate Mr. Allen or Dylan. After looking for them in the
house, she assumed that they were outside with the others. But
neither Ms. Bergé nor Ms. Stickland was with Mr. Allen or
Dylan. Ms. Groteke made no mention of this to Ms. Farrow on
August 4.

During a different portion of the day, Ms. Stickland went to
the television room in search of one of Ms. Pascal's children.
She observed Mr. Allen kneeling in front of Dylan with his head
on her lap, facing her body. Dylan was sitting on the couch
staring vacantly in the direction of a television set.

After Ms. Farrow returned home, Ms. Bergé noticed that
Dylan was not wearing anything under her sundress. She told
Ms. Farrow, who asked Ms. Groteke to put underpants on Dylan.

Ms. Stickland testified that during the evening of August 4,
she told Ms. Pascal, "I had seen something at Mia's that day
that was bothering me." She revealed what she had seen in the
television room. On August 5, Ms. Pascal telephoned Ms. Farrow
to tell her what Ms. Stickland had observed.

Ms. Farrow testified that after she hung up the telephone, she
asked Dylan, who was sitting next to her, "whether it was true
that Daddy had his face in her lap yesterday." Ms. Farrow
testified:

> Dylan said yes. And then she said that she didn't like it one
> bit, no, he was breathing into her, into her legs, she said.
> And that he was holding her around the waist and I said,
> why didn't you get up and she said she tried to but that he
> put his hands underneath her and touched her. And she
> showed me where. . . . Her behind.

Because she was already uncomfortable with Mr. Allen's inappropriate behavior toward Dylan and because she believed that
her concerns were not being taken seriously enough by Dr.
Schultz and Dr. Coates, Ms. Farrow videotaped Dylan's statements. Over the next twenty-four hours, Dylan told Ms. Farrow
that she had been with Mr. Allen in the attic and that he had
touched her privates with his finger.

After Dylan's first comments, Ms. Farrow telephoned her attorney for guidance. She was advised to bring Dylan to her local pediatrician, which she did immediately. Dylan did not repeat the accusation of sexual abuse during this visit and Ms. Farrow was advised to return with Dylan on the following day. On the trip home, she explained to her mother that she did not like talking about her privates. On August 6, when Ms. Farrow went back to Dr. Kavirajan's office, Dylan repeated what she had told her mother on August 5. A medical examination conducted on August 9 showed no physical evidence of sexual abuse.

Although Dr. Schultz was vacationing in Europe, Ms. Farrow telephoned her daily for advice. Ms. Farrow also notified Dr. Coates, who was still treating Satchel. She said to Dr. Coates, "It sounds very convincing to me, doesn't it to you. It is so specific. Let's hope it is her fantasy." Dr. Coates immediately notified Mr. Allen of the child's accusation and then contacted the New York City Child Welfare Administration. Seven days later, during a meeting of the lawyers at which settlement discussions were taking place, Mr. Allen began this action for custody.

Dr. Schultz returned from vacation on August 16. She was transported to Connecticut in Mr. Allen's chauffered limousine on August 17, 18, and 21 for therapy sessions with Dylan. Dylan, who had become increasingly resistant to Dr. Schultz, did not want to see her. During the third session, Dylan and Satchel put glue in Dr. Schultz's hair, cut her dress, and told her to go away.

On August 24 and 27, Ms. Farrow expressed to Dr. Schultz her anxiety about Dr. Schultz continuing to see Mr. Allen, who had already brought suit for custody of Dylan. She asked if Dr. Schultz would

. . . please not come for a while until all of this is settled down because . . . I couldn't trust anybody. And she said she understood completely. . . . And soon after that . . . I learned that Dr. Schultz had told [New York] child welfare that Dylan had not reported anything to her. And then a week later, either her lawyer or Dr. Schultz called [New York] child welfare and said she just remembered that Dylan had told her that Mr. Allen had put a finger in her vagina. When I heard that, I certainly didn't trust Dr. Schultz.

Dr. Schultz testified that on August 19, Paul Williams of the New York City Child Welfare Administration asked about her experience with Dylan. She replied that on August 17, Dylan started to tell her what had happened with Mr. Allen but she needed more time to explore this with Dylan. On August 27, she spoke more fully to Mr. Williams about her August 17 session with Dylan and speculated about the significance of what Dylan reported. Mr. Williams testified that on August 19, Dr. Schultz told him that Dylan had not made any statements to her about sexual abuse.

Ms. Farrow did not immediately resume Dylan's therapy because the Connecticut State Police had requested that she not be in therapy during the investigation. Also, it was not clear if the negotiated settlement that the parties were continuing to pursue would include Mr. Allen's participation in the selection of Dylan's new therapist.

Dr. Coates continued to treat Satchel through the fall of 1992. Ms. Farrow expressed to Dr. Coates her unease with the doctor seeing Mr. Allen in conjunction with Satchel's therapy. On October 29, 1992, Ms. Farrow requested that Dr. Coates treat Satchel without the participation of Mr. Allen. Dr. Coates declined, explaining that she did not believe that she could treat Satchel effectively without the full participation of both parents. Satchel's therapy with Dr. Coates was discontinued on November 28, 1992. At Ms. Farrow's request, Dr. Coates recommended a therapist to continue Satchel's therapy. Because of a conflict, the therapist recommended by Dr. Coates was unable to treat Satchel. He did, however, provide the name of another therapist with whom Satchel is currently in treatment.

On December 30, 1992, Dylan was interviewed by a representative of the Connecticut State Police. She told them—at a time Ms. Farrow calculates to be the fall of 1991—that while at Mr. Allen's apartment, she saw him and Soon-Yi having sex. Her reporting was childlike but graphic. She also told the police that

Mr. Allen had pushed her face into a plate of hot spaghetti and had threatened to do it again.

Ten days before Yale–New Haven concluded its investigation, Dylan told Ms. Farrow, for the first time, that in Connecticut, while she was climbing up the ladder to a bunk bed, Mr. Allen put his hands under her shorts and touched her. Ms. Farrow testified that as Dylan said this, "she was illustrating graphically where in the genital area."

CONCLUSIONS

A) *Woody Allen*

Mr. Allen has demonstrated no parenting skills that would qualify him as an adequate custodian for Moses, Dylan, or Satchel. His financial contributions to the children's support, his willingness to read to them, to tell them stories, to buy them presents, and to oversee their breakfasts do not compensate for his absence as a meaningful source of guidance and caring in their lives. These contributions do not excuse his evident lack of familiarity with the most basic details of their day-to-day existences.

He did not bathe his children. He did not dress them, except from time to time, and then only to help them put on their socks and jackets. He knows little of Moses' history, except that he has cerebral palsy; he does not know if he has a doctor. He does not know the name of Dylan and Satchel's pediatrician. He does not know the names of Moses' teachers or about his academic performance. He does not know the name of the children's dentist. He does not know the names of his children's friends. He does not know the names of any of their many pets. He does not know which children shared bedrooms. He attended parent-teacher conferences only when asked to do so by Ms. Farrow.

Mr. Allen has even less knowledge about his children's siblings, with whom he seldom communicated. He apparently did not pay enough attention to his own children to learn from them about their brothers and sisters.

Mr. Allen characterized Ms. Farrow's home as a foster care

compound and drew distinctions between her biological and adopted children. When asked how he felt about sleeping with his children's sister, he responded that "[s]he [Soon-Yi] was an adopted child and Dylan was an adopted child." He showed no understanding that the bonds developed between adoptive brothers and sisters are no less worthy of respect and protection than those between biological siblings.

Mr. Allen's reliance on the affidavit which praises his parenting skills, submitted by Ms. Farrow in connection with his petition to adopt Moses and Dylan, is misplaced. Its ultimate probative value will be determined in the pending Surrogate's Court proceeding. In the context of the facts and circumstances of this action, I accord it little weight.

None of the witnesses who testified on Mr. Allen's behalf provided credible evidence that he is an appropriate custodian parent. Indeed, none would venture an opinion that he should be granted custody. When asked, even Mr. Allen could not provide an acceptable reason for a change in custody.

His counsel's last question of him on direct examination was "Can you tell the Court why you are seeking custody of your children?" Mr. Allen's response was a rambling *non sequitur* which consumed eleven pages of transcript. He said that he did not want to take the children away from Ms. Farrow; that Ms. Farrow maintained a non-traditional household with biological children and adopted children from all over the world; that Soon-Yi was fifteen years older than Dylan and seventeen years older than Satchel; that Ms. Farrow was too angry with Mr. Allen to resolve the problem; and that with him, the children "will be responsibly educated" and "their day-to-day behavior will be done in consultation with their therapist." The most relevant portions of the response—that he is a good father and that Ms. Farrow has intentionally turned the children against him—I do not credit. Even if he were correct, under the circumstances of this case, it would be insufficient to warrant a change of custody.

Mr. Allen's deficiencies as a custodian parent are magnified by his affair with Soon-Yi. As Ms. Farrow's companion, he was a frequent visitor at Soon-Yi's home. He accompanied the Farrow-Previns on extended family vacations and he is the father of

Soon-Yi's siblings, Moses, Dylan, and Satchel. The fact that Mr. Allen ignored Soon-Yi for ten years cannot change the nature of the family constellation and does not create a distance sufficient to convert their affair into a benign relationship between two consenting adults.

Mr. Allen admits that he never considered the consequences of his behavior with Soon-Yi. Dr. Coates and Dr. Brodzinsky testified that Mr. Allen still fails to understand that what he did was wrong. Having isolated Soon-Yi from her family, he left her with no visible support system. He had no consideration for the consequences to her, to Ms. Farrow, to the Previn children for whom he cared little, or to his own children for whom he professes love.

Mr. Allen's response to Dylan's claim of sexual abuse was an attack upon Ms. Farrow, whose parenting ability and emotional stability he impugned without the support of any significant credible evidence. His trial strategy has been to separate his children from their brothers and sisters; to turn the children against their mother; to divide adopted children from biological children; to incite the family against their household help; and to set household employees against each other. His self-absorption, his lack of judgment, and his commitment to the continuation of his divisive assault, thereby impeding the healing of the injuries that he has already caused, warrant a careful monitoring of his future contact with the children.

B) Mia Farrow

Few relationships and fewer families can easily bear the microscopic examination to which Ms. Farrow and her children have been subjected. It is evident that she loves children and has devoted a significant portion of her emotional and material wealth to their upbringing. When she is not working she attends to her children. Her weekends and summers are spent in Connecticut with her children. She does not take extended vacations unaccompanied by her children. She is sensitive to the needs of her children, respectful of their opinions, honest with them, and quick to address their problems.

Mr. Allen elicited trial testimony that Ms. Farrow favored her biological children over her adopted children; that she manipulated Dylan's sexual abuse complaint, in part through the use of leading questions and the videotape; that she discouraged Dylan and Satchel from maintaining a relationship with Mr. Allen; that she overreacted to Mr. Allen's affair with Soon-Yi; and that she inappropriately exposed Dylan and Satchel to the turmoil created by the discovery of the affair.

The evidence at trial established that Ms. Farrow is a caring and loving mother who has provided a home for both her biological and her adopted children. There is no credible evidence that she unfairly distinguished among her children or that she favored some at the expense of others.

I do not view the Valentine's Day card, the note affixed to the bathroom door in Connecticut, or the destruction of photographs as anything more than expressions of Ms. Farrow's understandable anger and her ability to communicate her distress by word and symbol rather than by action.

There is no credible evidence to support Mr. Allen's contention that Ms. Farrow coached Dylan or that Ms. Farrow acted upon a desire for revenge against him for seducing Soon-Yi. Mr. Allen's resort to the stereotypical "woman scorned" defense is an injudicious attempt to divert attention from his failure to act as a responsible parent and adult.

Ms. Farrow's statement to Dr. Coates that she hoped that Dylan's statements were a fantasy is inconsistent with the notion of brainwashing. In this regard, I also credit the testimony of Ms. Groteke, who was charged with supervising Mr. Allen's August 4 visit with Dylan. She testified that she did not tell Ms. Farrow, until after Dylan's statement of August 5, that Dylan and Mr. Allen were unaccounted for during fifteen or twenty minutes on August 4. It is highly unlikely that Ms. Farrow would have encouraged Dylan to accuse her father of having sexually molested her during a period in which Ms. Farrow believed they were in the presence of a baby-sitter. Moreover, I do not believe that Ms. Farrow would have exposed her daughter and her other children to the consequences of the Connecticut investigation and this litigation if she did not believe the possible truth of Dylan's accusation.

In a society where children are too often betrayed by adults who ignore or disbelieve their complaints of abuse, Ms. Farrow's determination to protect Dylan is commendable. Her decision to videotape Dylan's statements, although inadvertently compromising the sexual abuse investigation, was understandable.

Ms. Farrow is not faultless as a parent. It seems probable, although there is no credible testimony to this effect, that prior to the affair with Mr. Allen, Soon-Yi was experiencing problems for which Ms. Farrow was unable to provide adequate support. There is also evidence that there were problems with her relationships with Dylan and Satchel. We do not, however, demand perfection as a qualification for parenting. Ironically, Ms. Farrow's principal shortcoming with respect to responsible parenting appears to have been her continued relationship with Mr. Allen.

Ms. Farrow reacted to Mr. Allen's behavior with her children with a balance of appropriate caution and flexibility. She brought her early concern with Mr. Allen's relationship with Dylan to Dr. Coates and was comforted by the doctor's assurance that Mr. Allen was working to correct his behavior with the child. Even after January 13, 1992, Ms. Farrow continued to provide Mr. Allen with access to her home and to their children as long as the visits were supervised by a responsible adult. She did her best, although with limited success, to shield her younger children from the turmoil generated by Mr. Allen's affair with Soon-Yi.

Ms. Farrow's refusal to permit Mr. Allen to visit with Dylan after August 4, 1992, was prudent. Her willingness to allow Satchel to have regular supervised visitation with Mr. Allen reflects her understanding of the propriety of balancing Satchel's need for contact with his father against the danger of Mr. Allen's lack of parental judgment.

Ms. Farrow also recognizes that Mr. Allen and not Soon-Yi is the person responsible for their affair and its impact upon her family. She has communicated to Soon-Yi that she continues to be a welcome member in the Farrow-Previn home.

C) Dylan Farrow

Mr. Allen's relationship with Dylan remains unresolved. The evidence suggests that it is unlikely that he could be successfully prosecuted for sexual abuse. I am less certain, however, than is the Yale-New Haven team, that the evidence proves conclusively that there was no sexual abuse.

Both Dr. Coates and Dr. Schultz expressed their opinions that Mr. Allen did not sexually abuse Dylan. Neither Dr. Coates nor Dr. Schultz has expertise in the field of child sexual abuse. I believe that the opinions of Dr. Coates and Dr. Schultz may have been colored by their loyalty to Mr. Allen. I also believe that therapists would have a natural reluctance to accept the possibility that an act of sexual abuse occurred on their watch. I have considered their opinions, but do not find their testimony to be persuasive with respect to sexual abuse or visitation.

I have also considered the report of the Yale–New Haven team and the deposition testimony of Dr. John M. Leventhal. The Yale–New Haven investigation was conducted over a six-month period by Dr. Leventhal, a pediatrician; Dr. Julia Hamilton, who has a Ph.D. in social work; and Ms. Jennifer Sawyer, who has a master's degree in social work. Responsibility for different aspects of the investigation was divided among the team. The notes of the team members were destroyed prior to the issuance of the report, which, presumably, is an amalgamation of their independent impressions and observations. The unavailability of the notes, together with their unwillingness to testify at this trial except through the deposition of Dr. Leventhal, compromised my ability to scrutinize their findings and resulted in a report which was sanitized and, therefore, less credible.

Dr. Stephen Herman, a clinical psychiatrist who has extensive familiarity with child abuse cases, was called as a witness by Ms. Farrow to comment on the Yale–New Haven report. I share his reservations about the reliability of the report.

Dr. Herman faulted the Yale–New Haven team (1) for making visitation recommendations without seeing the parent interact with the child; (2) for failing to support adequately their conclusion that Dylan has a thought disorder; (3) for drawing any conclusions about Satchel, whom they never saw; (4) for finding that there was no abuse when the supporting data was inconclusive; and (5) for recommending that Ms. Farrow enter into therapy. In addition, I do not think that it was appropriate for Yale–New Haven, without notice to the parties for their counsel, to exceed its mandate and make observations and recommendations which might have an impact on existing litigation in another jurisdiction.

Unlike Yale–New Haven, I am not persuaded that the video-tape of Dylan is the product of leading questions or of the child's fantasy.

Richard Marcus, a retired New York City police officer called by Mr. Allen, testified that he worked with the police sex crimes unit for six years. He claimed to have an intuitive ability to know if a person is truthful or not. He concluded, "based on my experience," that Dylan lacked credibility. I did not find his testimony to be insightful.

I agree with Dr. Herman and Dr. Brodzinsky that we will probably never know what occurred on August 4, 1992. The credible testimony of Ms. Farrow, Dr. Coates, Dr. Leventhal, and Mr. Allen does, however, prove that Mr. Allen's behavior toward Dylan was grossly inappropriate and that measures must be taken to protect her.

D) Satchel Farrow

Mr. Allen had a strained and difficult relationship with Satchel during the earliest years of the child's life. Dr. Coates testified, "Satchel would push him away, would not acknowledge him. . . . If he would try to help Satchel getting out of bed or going into bed, he would kick him, at times had scratched his face. They were in trouble." Dr. Coates also testified that as an infant, Satchel would cry when held by Mr. Allen and stop when given to Ms. Farrow. Mr. Allen attributes this to Ms. Farrow's conscious effort to keep him apart from the child.

Although Ms. Farrow consumed much of Satchel's attention, and did not foster a relationship with his father, there is no credible evidence to suggest that she desired to exclude Mr.

Allen. Mr. Allen's attention to Dylan left him with less time and patience for Satchel. Dr. Coates attempted to teach Mr. Allen how to interact with Satchel. She encouraged him to be more understanding of his son when Satchel ignored him or acted bored with his gifts. Apparently, success in this area was limited.

In 1991, in the presence of Ms. Farrow and Dylan, Mr. Allen stood next to Satchel's bed, as he did every morning. Satchel screamed at him to go away. When Mr. Allen refused to leave, Satchel kicked him. Mr. Allen grabbed Satchel's leg, started to twist it. Ms. Farrow testified that Mr. Allen said, "I'm going to break your fucking leg." Ms. Farrow intervened and separated Mr. Allen from Satchel. Dylan told the Connecticut State Police about this incident.

That Mr. Allen now wants to spend more time with Satchel is commendable. If sincere, he should be encouraged to do so, but only under conditions that promote Satchel's well-being.

E) Moses Farrow

Mr. Allen's interactions with Moses appear to have been superficial and more a response to Moses's desire for a father — in a family where Mr. Previn was the father of the other six children—than an authentic effort to develop a relationship with the child. When Moses asked, in 1984, if Mr. Allen would be his father, he said "sure" but for years did nothing to make that a reality.

They spent time playing baseball, chess, and fishing. Mr. Allen encouraged Moses to play the clarinet. There is no evidence, however, that Mr. Allen used any of their shared areas of interest as a foundation upon which to develop a deeper relationship with his son. What little he offered—a baseball catch, some games of chess, adoption papers—was enough to encourage Moses to dream of more, but insufficient to justify a claim for custody.

After learning of his father's affair with his sister, Moses handed to Mr. Allen a letter that he had written. It states:

> . . . you can't force me to live with you. . . . You have done a horrible, unforgivable, needy, ugly, stupid thing . . . about

seeing me for lunch, you can just forget about that . . . we didn't do anything wrong. . . . All you did is spoil the little ones, Dylan and Satchel. . . . Everyone knows not to have an affair with your son's sister . . . I don't consider you my father anymore. It was a great feeling having a father, but you smashed that feeling and dream with a single act. *I HOPE YOU ARE PROUD TO CRUSH YOUR SON'S DREAM*.

Mr. Allen responded to this letter by attempting to wrest custody of Moses from his mother. His rationale is that the letter was generated by Ms. Farrow. Moses told Dr. Brodzinsky that he wrote the letter and that he did not intend for it to be seen by his mother.

CUSTODY

Section 240(1) of the Domestic Relations Law states that in a custody dispute, the court must "give such direction . . . as . . . justice requires, having regard to the circumstances of the case and of the respective parties and to the best interests of the child."

The case law of this state has made clear that the governing consideration is the best interests of the child. *Eschbach v. Eschbach,* 56 NY2d 167 (1982); *Friederwitzer v. Friederwitzer,* 55 NY2d (1982).

The initial custodial arrangement is critically important. "Priority, not as an absolute but as a weighty factor, should, in the absence of extraordinary circumstances, be accorded to the first custody awarded in litigation or by voluntary agreement." *Nehra v. Uhlar,* 43 NY2d 242, 251 (1977).

"[W]hen children have been living with one parent for a long period of time and the parties have previously agreed that custody shall remain in that parent, their agreement should prevail and custody should be continued unless it is demonstrated that the custodial parent is unfit or perhaps less fit (citations omitted)." *Martin v. Martin,* 74 AD2d 419, 426 (4th Dept 1980).

After considering Ms. Farrow's position as the sole caretaker of the children, the satisfactory fashion in which she has fulfilled that function, the parties' prelitigation acceptance that she continue in that capacity, and Mr. Allen's serious parental inadequacies, it is clear that the best interests of the children will be served by their continued custody with Ms. Farrow.

VISITATION

Visitation, like custody, is governed by a consideration of the best interests of the child. *Miriam R. v. Arthur D.R.*, 85 AD2d 624 (2d Dept 1981). Absent proof to the contrary, the law presumes that visitation is in the child's best interests. *Wise v. Del Toro*, 122 AD2d 714 (1st Dept 1986). The denial of visitation to a noncustodial parent must be accompanied by compelling reasons and substantial evidence that visitation is detrimental to the child's welfare. *Matter of Farrugia Children*, 106 AD2d 293 (1st Dept 1984); *Gowan v. Menga*, 178 AD2d 1021 (4th Dept 1991). If the noncustodial parent is a fit person and there are no extraordinary circumstances, there should be reasonable visitation. *Hotze v. Hotze*, 57 AD2d 85 (4th Dept 1977), *appeal denied* 42 NY2d 805.

The overriding consideration is the child's welfare rather than any supposed right of the parent. *Weiss v. Weiss*, 52 NY2d 170, 174–5 (1981); *Hotze v. Hotze, supra* at 87. Visitation should be denied where it may be inimical to the child's welfare by producing serious emotional strain or disturbance. *Hotze v. Hotze, supra* at 88; *see also, Miriam R. v. Arthur D.R., supra; cf., State ex rel. H.K. v. M.S.*, 187 AD2d 50 (1st Dept 1993).

This trial included the observations and opinions of more mental health workers than is common to most custody litigation. The parties apparently agreed with Dr. Herman's conclusion that another battery of forensic psychological evaluations would not have been in the children's best interests and would have added little to the available information. Accordingly, none was ordered.

The common theme of the testimony by the mental health witness is that Mr. Allen has inflicted serious damage on the children and that healing is necessary. Because, as Dr. Brodzinsky and Dr. Herman observed, this family is in an uncharted therapeutic area, where the course is uncertain and the benefits unknown, the visitation structure that will best promote the healing process and safeguard the children is elusive. What is clear is that Mr. Allen's lack of judgment, insight, and impulse control make normal noncustodial visitation with Dylan and Satchel too risky to the children's well-being to be permitted at this time.

A) Dylan

Mr. Allen's request for immediate visitation with Dylan is denied. It is unclear whether Mr. Allen will ever develop the insight and judgment necessary for him to relate to Dylan appropriately. According to Dr. Brodzinsky, even if Dylan was not sexually abused, she feels victimized by her father's relationship with her sister. Dylan has recently begun treatment with a new therapist. Now that this trial is concluded, she is entitled to the time and space necessary to create a protective environment that will promote the therapeutic process. A significant goal of that therapy is to encourage her to fulfill her individual potential, including the resilience to deal with Mr. Allen in a manner which is not injurious to her.

The therapist witnesses agree that Mr. Allen may be able to serve a positive role in Dylan's therapy. Dr. Brodzinsky emphasized that because Dylan is quite fragile and more negatively affected by stress than the average child, she should visit with Mr. Allen only within a therapeutic context. This function, he said, should be undertaken by someone other than Dylan's treating therapist. Unless it interferes with Dylan's individual treatment or is inconsistent with her welfare, this process is to be initiated within six months. A further review of visitation will be considered only after we are able to evaluate the progress of Dylan's therapy.

B) Satchel

Mr. Allen's request for extended and unsupervised visitation with Satchel is denied. He has been visiting regularly with Satchel, under supervised conditions, with the consent of Ms.

Farrow. I do not believe that Ms. Farrow has discouraged Satchel's visitation with Mr. Allen or that she has, except for restricting visitation, interfered with Satchel's relationship with his father.

Although, absent exceptional circumstances, a noncustodial parent should not be denied meaningful access to a child, "supervised visitation is not a deprivation to meaningful access." *Lightbourne v. Lightbourne*, 179 AD2d 562 (1st Dept 1992).

I do not condition visitation out of concern for Satchel's physical safety. My caution is the product of Mr. Allen's demonstrated inability to understand the impact that his words and deeds have upon the emotional well-being of his children.

I believe that Mr. Allen will use Satchel in an attempt to gain information about Dylan and to insinuate himself into her good graces. I believe that Mr. Allen will, if unsupervised, attempt to turn Satchel against the other members of his family. I believe Mr. Allen to be desirous of introducing Soon-Yi into the visitation arrangement without concern for the effect on Satchel, Soon-Yi, or the other members of the Farrow family. In short, I believe Mr. Allen to be so self-absorbed, untrustworthy, and insensitive, that he should not be permitted to see Satchel without appropriate professional supervision until Mr. Allen demonstrates that supervision is no longer necessary. The supervisor should be someone who is acceptable to both parents, who will be familiarized with the history of this family, and who is willing to remain in that capacity for a reasonable period of time. Visitation shall be of two hours' duration, three times weekly, and modifiable by agreement of the parties.

C) Moses

Under the circumstances of this case, giving respect and credence to Ms. Farrow's appreciation of her son's sensitivity and intelligence, as confirmed by Dr. Brodzinsky, I will not require this fifteen-year-old child to visit with his father if he does not wish to do so.

If Moses can be helped by seeing Mr. Allen under conditions in which Moses will be not be overwhelmed, then I believe that Ms. Farrow should and will promote such interaction. I hope that Moses will come to understand that the fear of demons often cannot be dispelled without first confronting them.

COUNSEL FEES

Ms. Farrow's application for counsel fees is granted. Mr. Allen compounded the pain that he inflicted upon the Farrow family by bringing this frivolous petition for custody of Dylan, Satchel, and Moses.

Domestic Relations Law §237(b) provides that upon an application for custody or visitation, the court may direct a parent to pay the counsel fees of the other parent "as, in the court's discretion, justice requires, having regard to the circumstances of the case and of the respective parties."

Ms. Farrow admits to a substantial net worth, although she is not nearly as wealthy as Mr. Allen. Clearly, she is able to absorb the cost of this litigation, although it has been extraordinarily expensive. However, "[i]ndigency is not a prerequisite to an award of counsel fees (citation omitted). Rather, in exercising its discretionary power to award counsel fees, a court should review the financial circumstances of both parties together with all the other circumstances of the case, which may include the relative merit of the parties' positions." *DeCabrera v. Cabrera-Rosete*, 70 NY2d 879, 881 (1987). Because Mr. Allen's position had no merit, he will bear the entire financial burden of this litigation. If the parties are unable to agree on Ms. Farrow's reasonable counsel fees, a hearing will be conducted for that purpose.

Settle judgment.
DATED: June 7, 1993.

J.S.C.